Jane Austen's

Guide to Dating

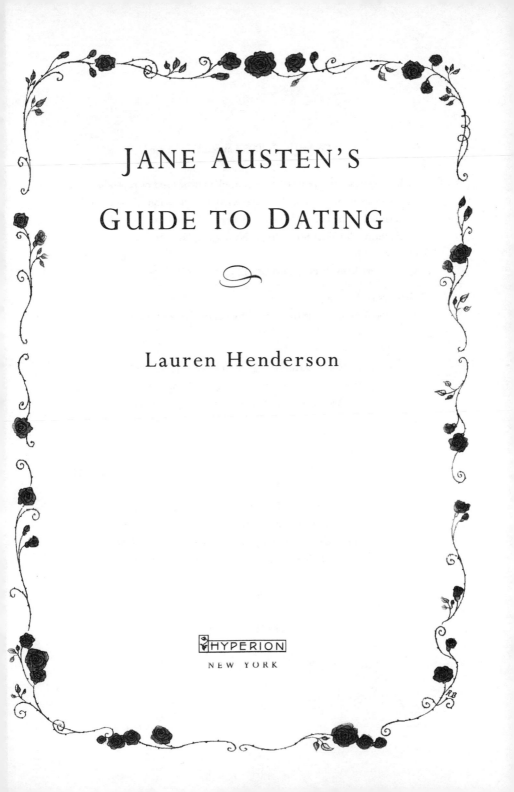

Jane Austen's
Guide to Dating

Lauren Henderson

HYPERION

NEW YORK

LIBRARY OF CONGRESS CATALOGING-IN-PUBLICATION DATA

Henderson, Lauren
  Jane Austen's guide to dating / by Lauren Henderson.—1st ed.
    p.   cm.
  ISBN 1-4013-0117-7
  1. Dating (Social customs)   2. Man-woman relationships.
3. Man-woman relationships in literature.   4. Austen, Jane,
1775-1817—Views on man-woman relationships.   I. Title.

HQ801.H454   2005
646.7'7—dc22

                                                    2004054009

Hyperion books are available for special promotions and premiums.
For details contact Michael Rentas, Manager, Inventory and
Premium Sales, Hyperion, 77 West 66th Street, 11th floor,
New York, New York 10023, or call 212-456-0133.

Book design by Richard Oriolo

FIRST EDITION

10   9   8   7   6   5   4   3   2   1

For my darling Greg, who brings out the Elizabeth Bennet
rather than the Mary Crawford in me . . .

CONTENTS

Jane Austen's
Guide to Dating

Introduction

DATING NOWADAYS CAN BE like walking through a mine-field, and every single woman I know is confused about how to navigate it. But, as an English girl who moved to America four years ago, I find it even harder over here. American dating is much more complicated than the European version. The market is full of books that give bizarre advice—like keeping an egg timer next to your phone so you don't talk to a man for too long, or treating men as if they come from a completely different planet from women. It seems to me that we have completely lost touch with first principles. That's what *Jane Austen's Guide to Dating* is for—to bring us back to common sense and good judgment. No wonder Jane Austen is still one of the most-read, and best-loved, authors in the world today—let alone one of the most frequently adapted for television and film. Her rules are as relevant today as they always were—maybe even more so. More than ever, we need a good injection of common sense, and Jane Austen is exactly the person who will give it to us.

I moved to America with an American boyfriend already in place, but when we broke up I felt utterly bewildered by the strange rules that women—and men—seemed to feel the need to follow. "Don't call men back for at least three days! Five is ideal!" yodeled a male friend, when I started dating again. "Don't call them back at all—that way they have to keep calling you and are insecure about whether you like them," suggested a female one. "You have to KEEP the POWER!" said the male friend very loudly. "It's all about KEEPING THE POWER!"

The particularly odd thing about this advice was that my male friend wasn't actually following it—he had met a girl, fallen head over heels for her, spent every minute he could with her, and asked her to move in three months later. (They're now happily married.) How did his girlfriend handle their fast-moving love affair? She treated him the way she wanted to be treated. She called him back when he rang, sounded happy to hear from him when he called her, and let herself get close to him relatively quickly, because she was getting the green light from him about his feelings for her and the kind of man he was. And yet, despite his not following his own advice in his successful relationship, this advice was so hard-wired into his brain that he was actually telling me to treat men like adversaries. He even lent me a book called *Intimate Terrorism,* which is all about the terrible games people in love can play with each other, ardently suggesting that I read it.

I'm not the kind of person who likes to play games, keep men insecure and scared, or think of them as being another species. Yes, men are different from us in many ways, whether it's because of biology or social conditioning. Yes, they like the chase. Yet they're people, too, with wants and dreams and insecurities, and a need to be in love and happy that's just as strong as ours.

After several bad experiences in the New York dating scene, I realized that I needed to figure out for my own benefit how I wanted to deal with the situation. And I did what I often do in a crisis: I turned to Jane Austen, whose books I've been reading since I was twelve years old. I have always loved her wit, her cleverness, her wisdom—and the occasional bitchy asides that remind us that she is all too human. Though I studied English literature at Cambridge, and actually wrote my second-year dissertation on courtship rituals in Jane Austen, I was pretty immature then—much too young, by modern standards, to have the faintest ability to understand the usefulness of the lessons in her books, what she has to teach us about finding the right mate. Or maybe I just wasn't ready to put them into practice! I spent my twenties living abroad, dating a lot of unsuitable—but very fun—young men, and partying hard while building my career as a writer. But in my thirties, wanting a more mature and successful relationship, I came back to her books. And I discovered that besides being wonderful stories in themselves, they are also manuals for anyone who wants to learn about finding someone to spend the rest of your life with, someone with whom you share values and similar qualities, someone trustworthy and true.

Of course, times were very different when Austen was writing. Ideally, you were supposed to be married by your mid-twenties at the very latest, and once you'd accepted someone, that was it. You were stuck with them for the rest of your lives—divorce was practically never an option, because if you did leave your husband, the scandal was so great that you could never enter society again. Remarriage was out of the question. One can see why choosing so carefully was of paramount importance. No traveling the world alone, having holiday romances, or snogging strangers in taxis for even the most spirited of Jane Austen's heroines. But in the freedom that comes with being able to stay "younger" longer, we've lost track of some of the most important things: knowing how to assess the people we meet as prospective life partners; taking a step back and looking at their characters and our own; and working out whether we will truly be compatible in the long run. The ever-increasing divorce rate indicates all too clearly our failure to consider our relationships properly before we embark upon them.

Naturally, times have changed tremendously since the early nineteenth century. And yet the principles for successful dating laid down in Jane Austen's six near-perfect novels apply just as much to us in the twenty-first century as to the infinitely more constricted society about which she was writing. It's almost miraculous how universal her clear-sighted perspective is.

Our experience of sex and romance is the polar opposite of Jane Austen's; women can now take for granted freedoms that in her time would have banned even the mention of one's name from polite society. But with our new liberty, we've forgotten the sensible aspects of her world, the seriousness with which she took compatibility and mutuality. I know I've thrown myself into a lot of relationships that I never would have embarked upon if I'd taken the time to apply the Austen Rules. And when I wasn't looking for a serious partner, that was fine. But when you are, it's a very different matter.

Just as I was finishing writing this book, I met an amazing guy and started dating him. I did my best to follow the ten Jane Austen Rules, which of course were running through my head the entire time. And things went wonderfully at first—until I let myself be swayed against my own feelings by the advice of my friends (completely ignoring Rule 4—Have Faith in Your Own Instincts). He and I had had a wonderful third date on a Friday, and we were so swept away by our growing attraction for each other that, though we had already planned to see each other the next Tuesday evening, we decided to meet up on Sunday instead—we didn't want to wait for four days till we saw each other again. He kissed me good night, I staggered upstairs to my apartment in a haze of bliss, and went to sleep. The next morning I rang some friends to tell them how brilliantly the date had gone. The English ones said: "Great! Wonderful! Have a lovely time on Sunday!"

And the Americans? *Every single one* told me I had made a mistake to push forward our next date. They said I would seem too keen. They said a man likes anticipation. They said I was giving him power by allowing my emotions to persuade me to see him too frequently. What did I do? I panicked. As an English girl abroad, I thought the Americans, on their home turf, *must* be right. I was dating an American man, after all, and we'd only had a few dates—maybe I didn't know him well enough, maybe they were reading the situation better than I was . . .

So I rang the poor guy and told him that I was busy on Sunday after all. We saw each other on Tuesday for lunch, but he said he had realized he had plans for that evening. We e-mailed each other for the next few days, but by the weekend I was sobbing into my pillow, a nervous wreck. We hadn't managed to arrange our next date, and I was getting the feeling that he was going off me—and I liked him so much, I'd thought he could be the one . . .

It was time for Jane Austen. I threw aside everything my American friends were telling me ("It's great that you haven't gotten together for five days! It makes you seem busy and in demand! It'll make him jealous and he will pursue you!"), because their advice was overcomplicating matters and encouraging me to treat him badly. More, it wasn't working! Instead of chasing me, he was pulling away. I followed Rule 1—If You Like Someone, Make It Clear That You Do—instead. We finally fixed a time to meet, and I suggested that he come round to my place for a drink; he'd never been in my apartment before. When he did, I kissed the hell out of him as soon as he came through the door. He was over the moon. He confided that he had thought I didn't like him romantically, that I only wanted to be friends, because of my canceling our date on Sunday night. That was why he had said he was busy for dinner on Tuesday, and why we hadn't managed to set a date for a whole week: he was scared of getting hurt by me. We fell into each other's arms, we've been ecstatic ever since, and never, ever again have I listened to a word of romantic advice from those American friends, much as I love them . . .

It seems to me that in America, we tend to overthink things and deal with the people we're attracted to in a highly complicated way that can often ruin a budding relationship. We've lost touch with our own instincts, and behave instead counterintuitively—treating someone mean to keep him keen, for instance, rather than being frank, open, and caring. It took a nineteenth-century British author to teach me to strip aside the American dating rules, and instead treat a man as I would myself like to be treated. After reading *Jane Austen's Guide to Dating,* you will be able to throw out a lot of the superficial, game-playing advice you've read in other books and concentrate on the fundamentals: How to find someone you really like. How to assess him and work out whether he's right for you. How to have confidence in yourself and nurture your own sense of self-worth. How to deal with your partner's bad behavior. And you will feel a sense of self-reliance and balance, rather than the constant sense of insecurity that comes from wondering all the time whether you're doing the right thing in a relationship.

Let Jane Austen be your guide, ladies. It worked for me! I really hope you have fun with this book, and fun putting its advice into practice. Remember, falling in love should be easy. If things are consistently difficult, if wires are getting crossed, if you feel that a man is playing games with you, then you're in the wrong relationship. And *Jane Austen's Guide to Dating* will help you find the right one.

ABOUT THE STRUCTURE OF THE BOOK—
AND HOW TO USE IT

IN *JANE AUSTEN'S GUIDE TO DATING*, I have distilled ten principles that Jane Austen lays out in her novels and given examples of how they work with her characters—what they get right, what they get wrong, and how, sometimes, they learn from their mistakes. After each example from Austen, there are modern-day examples: first a "What Not to Do," of people who didn't follow that rule, and then a "What to Do Instead," showing people who managed to put the rule into practice. There are three examples from Jane Austen in each chapter, giving a wide range of ways that the rule can operate successfully, so that you will be able to see throughout the course of the chapter how the rule can apply to your own behavior, and how to learn from it.

At the end of each chapter is a summary of the most important points about that principle. After that, I have added extra tips of my own. Naturally, Jane Austen didn't cover issues relating to the extra freedom that twenty-first-century women have—we have so many ways to communicate in the modern world, and so much more independence. In her society, it was very clear what you should and shouldn't do—no clandestine correspondence with your lover, for instance. When Marianne writes pleading letters to Willoughby, it's made clear that unless they are secretly engaged, it's a big no-no—and even then, they shouldn't be secretly engaged in the first place! But nowadays the possibilities we have make things much more confusing, and the rules are much less clear. So I have given tips that bring Jane Austen's expertise directly into the modern world, as an extra point of reference and help.

I have also written two quizzes, one that you can take to find out which of six archetypal Jane Austen characters you most closely resemble, and one to find out which male character represents the man you're interested in. Following the quizzes is a compatibility chart, which will help you work out whether you have any chance of having a successful relationship with your love interest. Having worked out which character you are, just follow along till that name intersects with the name of the character you like, and see from the symbol whether you are compatible or not.

Do note that many possible matches have a symbol saying that you will be able to have a successful relationship only under certain circumstances, and this is explained in the notes following the quizzes. If you are a Mary Crawford who can manage not to be too bitchy or game-playing . . . if you are a Lydia who's decided to try to curb her naughty ways and settle down . . . if the man you like is a Frank Churchill who is treating you like the One and not making you feel insecure . . . then you can go for it. But you have to assess your own strengths and weaknesses and take a good honest look at yourself for any good relationship to work—and *Jane Austen's Guide to Dating* will help this process along!

ONE

IF YOU LIKE SOMEONE, MAKE
IT CLEAR THAT YOU DO

Though Henry was now sincerely attached to
[Catherine] . . . his affection originated in nothing better
than gratitude; or, in other words, that a persuasion of
her partiality for him had been the only cause of his
giving her a serious thought.

—*NORTHANGER ABBEY*

THIS RULE IS SO fundamental to Jane Austen's view of dating and relationships that it had to be the first one I dealt with in this book. Austen repeatedly emphasizes the opinion that a woman who likes a man should make her preference for him clear —without, naturally, going overboard. She would have no truck with modern dating books that make a science out of playing hard to get. Of course, some tactics come into play once a man is interested in you, and even Austen would acknowledge that; men like the chase. Any man will respond better to a woman who shows she values herself and isn't just throwing herself at him blindly, so desperate to get a boyfriend that she doesn't take the time to get to know him as a person. She needs instead to gradually make a decision about his eligibility as a mate for her based on the information she gains about his character over a series of dates. But when Catherine Morland makes it obvious to Henry Tilney how much she likes him, Austen demonstrates that she is doing exactly the right thing—because the target of her affection is clearly showing himself to be a man worthy of her love. Contrary to most current dating advice, it is actually a great idea to show a man that you're interested in him—if, of course, your enthusiasm is in equal proportion to his. Look at these examples from Jane Austen's books, and then from real life, if you don't believe me . . .

HENRY AND CATHERINE

In finding [Henry] irresistible, [Catherine]
became so herself.
—*NORTHANGER ABBEY*

Henry Tilney, the hero of *Northanger Abbey*, is good-looking, charming, and, as both Jane Austen and Louisa May Alcott would put it, "heart-whole." He's not actively searching for a wife. But when he meets Catherine Morland, he's charmed by the fact that she is so obviously keen on him. Catherine is too young and naïve to think she needs to make any secret of how attractive she finds Henry. She doesn't throw herself at him, but she shows with unaffected pleasure how much she enjoys his company. And there's plenty in Henry to like. He has a great sense of humor and he makes a big effort to be agreeable. Catherine is modest. She can't quite believe, at the beginning of their acquaintance, that Henry would prefer her to the many other girls he's met. Catherine is "simplicity and truth, and without personal conceit." Every time Henry asks her to dance, she accepts immediately, showing a great deal of pleasure in his company, and he, being more sophisticated than she is, can see exactly how much she likes him.

The more they get to know each other, the more Henry falls for the fact that Catherine has fallen for him. He has a good healthy ego, and values himself highly—the fact that a girl likes him raises her in his estimation, rather than making him think that something must be wrong with her. And Catherine has pretty good judgment in affairs of the heart. She doesn't like Henry just because he asks her to dance and is good-looking, but for his intelligence, his sense of humor, his values, and the way he makes her feel. She realizes immediately how awful and full of himself her other admirer, John Thorpe, is, and does her best to get rid of him. She isn't flattered simply because John is interested in her; his compliments don't stop her from seeing what a bumptious idiot he is.

Henry comments approvingly on Catherine's "fresh feelings," and he's right. She doesn't pretend to be jaded or cynical, she's open and direct. When she misses going out for a walk with Henry and his sister because she's tricked into going with John Thorpe instead, she doesn't try to make Henry jealous or play John Thorpe off against him. Instead, she tells Henry immediately, the first chance she gets, how much she likes him, and apologizes for her inadvertent rudeness. "I had ten thousand times rather have been with you . . . ," she says; "if Mr Thorpe would only have stopped [his carriage], I would have jumped out and run after you."

Henry loves it. He likes her better than ever for telling him how much she likes him. "Is there a Henry in the world," Jane Austen asks, "who could be insensible to such a declaration?"

Note that Jane Austen says "Henry," rather than "man." Jane Austen is not saying that all men respond well to this. But a man with a good sense of self, a man who doesn't have the kind of low self-esteem that makes him think that if someone likes him there must be something wrong with her, will love it. You must assess whether a man is a hardened player, who counts girls who like him as tallies on his scorecard. Avoid these types! Luckily, there are plenty of Henrys out there who will respond very well to a nice girl who, without being pushy or clingy, clearly finds them attractive and wants to get to know them better.

LESSONS TO BE LEARNED

ENJOY THE MOMENT

What Not to Do: Don't Obsess Over Him

Catherine doesn't make the mistake of obsessing about Henry Tilney, much as she likes him, and eager though she is to see him again. She keeps her balance and distracts herself when he's not around—going out with her friends, reading her favorite book, *The Mysteries of Udolpho*, doing all the things she did before she met him and taking the same amount of pleasure in them, rather than feeling that everything she does is somehow diminished by the fact that Henry isn't there to share it with her. This is crucial. She doesn't seem desperate when she meets up with Henry again; she seems what she is, a nice healthy girl with a bit of a crush on him—not some crazed stalker who, on the basis of a few meetings, has already started to plan their wedding and doodle "Catherine Tilney" on every scrap of paper she can get her hands on. Nor does she drop her own interests to pretend instead that she likes his: she knows Henry doesn't think much of her favorite book, but she doesn't stop reading it on his account. Catherine keeps herself grounded and doesn't lose herself and her own pleasures just because a man is interested in her.

Catherine knows how to enjoy the moment without grabbing at hypothetical future possibilities. "I do not pretend to say that I was not very much pleased with [Henry]," she says to her friend Isabella, "but while I have 'Udolpho' to read, I feel as if nobody could make me miserable." She's not building castles in the air. Catherine is pacing herself very well. She isn't entertaining the kind of fantasies about marrying Henry that he would sense, and that would scare him off. "Once or twice . . . she had got so far as to indulge in a secret 'perhaps', but in general the felicity of being with him for the present bounded her views; . . . and her happiness being certain for that period, the rest of her life was at such a distance as to excite but little interest."

Not being able to enjoy the moment: let's look at this point in detail, because it tends to be such a problem for women. We tend to obsess about things much too early—sitting by the phone, trying to decode all sorts of hidden meanings in what men say when they do ring, initiating talks after three dates about where the relationship is going. This kind of behavior makes it near-impossible to relax into the pleasure you find in his company. Because—and I can't stress this point enough—to obsess about the relationship in this way means that you are worrying about whether *you* are pleasing him. For women, particularly in the early stages of dating, it should be the other way around.

What to Do Instead: Let Him Please You

A man needs to feel that he is courting you. Let him worry about where to take you on the next date, and whether it will be somewhere you will like. And let him pay for at least the first few dinners. If he's a nice guy, he'll like it. It makes him feel manly, chivalrous, and protective, all of which are qualities you want to encourage. You can split the drinks, if you're at a bar, but any nice man who likes you will protest this; he will want to pay for those, too. On my first five dates with my boyfriend, I tried to buy coffee after dinner, or an occasional drink. He wouldn't let me—he even went so far once as to secretly put his credit card behind the bar so the bar staff wouldn't take my money. Once I realized how much he wanted to pay for me, I stopped pushing him on it and thanked him instead, which made him much happier. In his mind, he was showing me how much he valued my company by insisting on paying. But he very much appreciated my offers—as long as I let him overrule me. So the best way to handle this is to make the offer, and then let him insist on paying. That way he sees that you aren't just after his money, but still gets to feel manly as he pulls out his wallet and picks up the tab. Once you're going out more regularly, he will probably be happy to let you pick up the check occasionally, or to split it with him. But at the beginning of a relationship, put aside any feminist pride you may have and let him pay. If you don't, he may very well take it as a sign that you are not romantically interested in him, and why risk that?

We probably all know this already, but let me just stress another point: if you go out on a first date with a man and he suggests you split the cost of dinner or drinks—well, either you've misunderstood things, and it isn't a date, or he's a cheapskate, and you shouldn't go out with him again. If a man doesn't offer to pay, he's not that into you. It's such an accepted convention by now that men pay—and they want to, if they like a girl and want to show it—that if a man doesn't follow that convention, he looks terrible. And if a man invites a woman on a date, he'll find the money to take her out. It doesn't have to be an expensive dinner, of course. But if a man asks a woman out and then expects her to split the check, it sends the wrong signals. The woman will be very surprised when he tries to kiss her at the end of the evening. And she will also be offended. The social residue that remains from Jane Austen's time is a sense that the woman needs to be courted.

We're talking about relationships here, not quick meaningless rolls in the hay. When a man takes the time to find out what kind of food you like to eat, what kind of movies you like to see, whether you prefer the theater or a ball game, and plans dates that chime with your tastes, he's showing you that he doesn't just want to have sex with you, but that he likes you as a person and wants to please you. He considers you valuable enough to want to treat you well— to court you. It's one of the last remnants of old-fashioned chivalry. So for goodness' sake, let him! Don't make too many upfront suggestions about where you should go on your dates—instead, let him ask you about your preferences and spend time working out what he thinks you will enjoy. By pleasing you, he will please himself, because he will get the satisfaction of seeing how happy he's making you.

If he's doing all the right things, you should continue to show him how much you like him. Make it clear that you are happy to hear from him when he calls. Don't play games like pretending you don't recognize his voice on the phone, to make him think that he's just one of many men calling you—my friend Melinda always does this. It just makes the poor saps anxious and insecure, and who wants a man who's in that state of mind? When you are on a date, show him how much you are enjoying yourself—don't play things too cool. Compliment his choice of restaurant, thank him for picking somewhere that he thought you would like. And enjoy the date for what it is—an opportunity to get to know him better. Maybe this will turn into a relationship, and the date will be one of the anecdotes you will talk over with each other, remembering the early stages when you were dating and you were nervous but excited and each evening was magical. But it's far too early to know that yet. Right now, you are having a lovely evening in the company of someone whom, so far, you like. Don't keep flashing ahead to the moment when he will kneel down in front of you and produce an enormous diamond.

MARIANNE AND WILLOUGHBY

> *"To have resisted such attractions, to have*
> *withstood such tenderness!—Is there a*
> *man on earth who could have done it!"*
> —SENSE AND SENSIBILITY

In *Sense and Sensibility*, Marianne Dashwood is just as good as Catherine Morland at showing a young man she likes him. Just watch her go. On the Dashwoods' first visit from Willoughby, "she gave him such a look of approbation as secured the largest share of his discourse to herself for the rest of his stay . . . She had neither shyness nor reserve in their discussion. They speedily discovered that their enjoyment of dancing and music was mutual . . . He acquiesced in all her decisions, caught all her enthusiasm . . ."

And Willoughby doesn't just respond to Marianne's enthusiasm, but charms everyone around him, taking an interest in them, paying them attention. Remember, showing people you like them is as good a way to make new friends as it is to find a mate. Willoughby is the guy in the room everyone wants to be friends with, because he seems so open and likable, with "quick imagination, lively spirits, and open, affectionate manners . . . a captivating person but a natural ardour of mind . . ." Marianne's whole family adores him.

Willoughby and Marianne's interest in each other seems completely mutual. "When he was present, she had no eyes for anyone else. Everything he did, was right. Everything he said, was clever." And Willoughby is equally smitten: "If their evenings at the park were concluded with cards, he cheated himself and the rest of the party to get her a good hand. If dancing formed the amusement of the night, they were partners for half the time; and when obliged to separate for a couple of dances, were careful to stand together and scarcely spoke a word to any body else."

Sadly, Marianne and Willoughby's romance doesn't end well: he marries another girl for her money, despite the fact that he's in love with Marianne. We'll look at more of Willoughby's and Marianne's behavior in the following chapters. Right now, however, what we're learning from Marianne is that her warm, open manner captured Willoughby's heart and made him fall deeply in love, despite the fact that he was planning only on having a light flirtation with her. As he later says to Elinor: "Your sister's lovely person and interesting manners could not but please me; and her behaviour to me, almost of the first, was of a kind . . . At first, I must confess, my vanity only was elevated by it . . . To have resisted such attractions, to have withstood such tenderness!—Is there a man on earth who could have done it!—Yes, I found myself, by insensible degrees, sincerely fond of her . . ."

Like Catherine, Marianne gets her man by showing how much she likes him—even though she doesn't get to keep him.

LESSON TO BE LEARNED

BE OPEN AND EASYGOING

What Not to Do: Don't Make Things Difficult

It's incredibly confusing to be single and dating today. We are bombarded with dating books that tell us to make ourselves mysterious and unavailable—or, confusingly, that we're not being forward enough. There's a book that tells you to keep an egg timer next to the phone so you don't talk to someone too long and come across as overavailable. It also tells you never to accept a date for the weekend if someone's asking you after Wednesday. Meanwhile, there are plenty of books and courses to teach people how to flirt properly. You can spend a hundred dollars signing up for a day spent learning how to raise and lower your eyes sexily, flick your hair, or give the right come-hither signals. What no one's telling you to do is the obvious—behave naturally, for God's sake! No wonder we are all so unsure of ourselves. How can you possibly be natural if you're worrying about talking to someone you like too long on the phone, or feeling that you ought to turn down a spontaneous invitation? How can you be yourself if you want to accept a Friday night invitation for a first date, but have been told by dating books that you should only go out on weeknights for the first month of dating?

Susanna had read so many dating books that she was completely blocked. She had no idea what the right dating procedure was anymore. Like Bridget Jones in the film *Bridget Jones's Diary*, she had a stack of those books next to her sofa and would consult them any time someone asked for her phone number. She had learned to think that a man was insulting her if he rang her up on a Thursday and asked her if she wanted to go to a party with him on Saturday, which is completely ridiculous. Men often don't plan that far ahead. It makes them nervous. Women like the anticipation, the having-four-days-to-plan-what-you're-going-to-wear-and-get-your-hair-and-nails-done. Men don't. They like to feel spontaneous. Susanna was actually turning down invitations from guys she liked because the dating books told her that they were asking her in the wrong way. Guess what? After a couple of rejections, the men rarely called back. Why should they? They'd been turned down. How were they supposed to know not to ask a girl for a date with only two days' notice? To them it seemed like a lot. And besides, they were asking Susanna out because they liked her and wanted to see her soon. They didn't want to have to wait.

And Susanna felt horribly frustrated. She liked these men! She wanted to go out on dates with them! And here she was, sitting at home all alone instead of out seeing a movie with a man she found attractive. Yet she was following exactly the rules recommended by the dating books. What was she doing wrong?

It's so obvious, of course. Susanna wasn't being herself. Her natural instinct, when asked out by a nice-looking man she'd recently met, would have been to say "Yes, thank you, I'd love to go to a party with you on Saturday night. What time are you picking me up?" Most dating books have a lot to answer for. They make the dating process seem like a minefield that you can pick your way through only when armed with a copy of one of these books. Instead what they are doing is planting mines that no one suspected were there. Whoever told you, before these books came on the market, that you shouldn't go out with someone you like? Whoever said that there are right and wrong days to invite a girl out? Whoever said that having a long conversation on the phone with someone is a bad thing, for goodness' sake?

It's supposed to be easy. That's what my sister's friend Alex told her, when my sister was struggling through a series of complicated, abortive relationships, and it's probably the single most important piece of advice I can give. A certain degree of anxiety is natural for both sexes in the dating process. But, if the other person is equally keen on you, the anxiety will be kept to a minimum. When my sister started dating her current boyfriend, he showed her so clearly that he liked her that her anxiety was at a very low level. Though they didn't make plans to meet up again at the end of every date, Lisa was sure that he would ring her in a few days, and he always did. Lisa learned from him the pleasure of being made to feel secure, and she did everything she could to make him feel equally secure—calling him, too, showing him how glad she was to see him. It was the smoothest and happiest dating process she had ever been through. They're now living together and have a lovely baby. And it was easy—the way it's *supposed to be*.

Modern dating advice is all about game-playing, manipulation, and treating the person you like as if he were an adversary. Why would you want to do that? Why would you adopt a hostile attitude toward someone you like and find attractive? Why would you assume he has the worst possible motives toward you? If you take that attitude, you may well turn a potentially nice person into an insecure paranoid who ends up treating you badly because he's so confused by the mixed signals you're sending him. Throw all those books away and rely on the good commonsense advice of Jane Austen instead. It will tally much better with your *own* instincts and common sense.

What to Do Instead: Trust Your Instincts

In Jane Austen's world it was difficult to meet new people, but nowadays we have a much wider range and many more social opportunities. Make the most of these encounters by being warm and friendly to people you like, whether or not you feel a romantic attraction to them. The more you try, the easier it will be. Practice! Look at Catherine in *Northanger Abbey*, who is always open, sincere, and ready to enjoy herself. "Catherine was all eager delight . . . She was come [to Bath] to be happy, and she felt happy already." People respond to that better than anything else. Be happy. Show people you like them. Be open to new opportunities and make the most of them.

When you meet a man you like, talk to him and show an interest. Give him your attention and show him that you're taking pleasure in his company. If you're at a bar or a party, your conversation may well be interrupted, and your tête-à-tête may get broken up. If he comes back to talk to you again, don't be afraid of showing him that you like him. Be brave. Don't throw yourself into flirting with other men to make him jealous; he may think that one of them is your boyfriend, and not come back to find you. Let him ask for your number and suggest going out sometime. Men love to do the chasing, and if you initiate the exchange of phone numbers, not only are you denying the man that opportunity, but you may be chasing someone who really isn't interested enough. If he wants to ask you out . . . he will. Let him. But show him that you're happy when he does.

If you give your number to someone and he rings you, respond appropriately. If you're happy to hear from him, show it. Be warm and friendly. If the conversation is going well, don't cut it short. If he asks to meet you soon, and you like him, why not go? My ex-boyfriend in Italy took me to meet his family the day after we met at a party! He knew he liked me, he was going to visit his mother the next afternoon, and he asked me if I wanted to come along and see San Gimignano, where she lived. I was a little taken aback, but he was so open and easygoing that I decided to agree. His mother was lovely to me, and it was clear from the way she greeted me that he didn't make a habit of bringing girls home so swiftly. We moved in together after a couple of months and he proposed at the same time. I felt I was too young to get married, and told him I just wasn't ready. But his enthusiastic interest in me, which he showed as soon as we met, made me feel very confident and secure, and we had three and a half very happy years together.

By all means, show a man you find him attractive physically. But again, pace yourself. Don't jump into bed with him straight-away; take some time to get to know him first. Take his arm when you're out, touch him to emphasize points you're making, let him kiss you good night at the end of the evening, allow the sexual attraction to build. Try not to find yourself alone with him in either one of your apartments late at night on the first few dates, to avoid irresistible temptation. The sex you eventually have will be all the better for a few weeks of anticipation. If you have sex with him too soon, you run the risk that this is the only way he'll ever think of you . . . sexually. And after all, you're looking for a relationship. If you just wanted to get laid, you would scarcely be reading *Jane Austen's Guide to Dating*. Let him demonstrate to you over the course of several dates that he is a trustworthy person who is interested in all aspects of your personality, not just out for a quick hookup.

Look at Henry and Catherine: they show in the early stages of their relationship that they are sexually interested in each other, as much as they could within the confines of the society they lived in.

They flirt, they banter, they dance together, they spend as much time as they can alone together. But at the same time they are also getting to know each other and deepening the attraction between them by strengthening all the other aspects of their relationship.

ELIZABETH AND DARCY; JANE AND BINGLEY

*"In nine cases out of ten, a woman had better show
more affection than she feels. Bingley likes your sister,
undoubtedly; but he may never do more than like her,
if she does not help him on."*
—PRIDE AND PREJUDICE

Two major characters in *Pride and Prejudice* almost lose the people they love: Jane, because she's not very good at showing Bingley how much she likes him, and Darcy, because he's absolutely atrocious at showing Elizabeth he likes her. Let's look at Jane first. Bingley makes it clear how much he admires her from the moment he meets her, at a dance, where she is the only girl he asks to dance twice. Not only that, he says that Jane is "beyond a doubt" the prettiest girl in the room. Every single time after that when Bingley is with Jane, he leaves her in no doubt of how much he likes her. "He was full of joy and attention . . . He . . . sat down by her, and talked scarcely to anyone else." As Elizabeth says to Jane: "No one who has ever seen you [and Mr. Bingley] together can doubt his affection."

Jane soon falls for Bingley, too, but, near fatally, she doesn't let him see the full extent of her feelings for him. Elizabeth's friend Charlotte sees the dangers in Jane's hiding her feelings so well. Charlotte warns Elizabeth: "It is sometimes a disadvantage to be so guarded. If a woman conceals her affection with the same skill from the object of it, she may lose the opportunity of fixing him; and it will then be but poor consolation to believe the world equally in the dark . . . There are very few of us who have heart enough to be really in love without encouragement. In nine cases out of ten, a woman had better show *more* affection than she feels."

Elizabeth points out that Jane doesn't know Bingley that well yet, and is holding back until she does. Charlotte disagrees, and Charlotte turns out to be right. The more Jane shows she likes Bingley, since it's clearly mutual, the more time he will spend with her, and the more she'll get to learn about his character! But Jane isn't forthcoming enough and, as a result, Bingley isn't completely sure that his feelings are returned. He leaves himself vulnerable to the snobbish persuasion of his sisters and Mr. Darcy, who don't want him to marry Jane because of her vulgar relations and convince him that Jane isn't in love with him. If she had shown him how much she liked him, that wouldn't have happened.

As soon as Jane does show him that she likes him, Bingley proposes in two seconds flat. All he needed was to know that his love was reciprocated.

Darcy, on the other hand, is a much more complicated piece of work than the open, straightforward Bingley. The first time he sees Jane, his reaction is this: "Miss Bennet he acknowledged to be pretty, but she smiled too much." Darcy—buttoned-up, proud, and snobbish—has a lot to learn. His dismissal of Elizabeth, when he first sees her at a dance, is famously horrible: "She is tolerable," he says, "but not handsome enough to tempt *me*."

And Elizabeth overhears. She manages to laugh it off, which is more than most of us would be able to do. But a few weeks later, when Darcy begins to realize how attracted he is to her, she snubs him firmly. Darcy spends the rest of the book trying to get into her good graces and only, finally, succeeds when he has broken down his snobbishness enough to be open and honest with her. Elizabeth makes a snap judgment of Darcy, too, thinking that he's proud, prejudiced, and haughty, and she's not wrong; but she doesn't see all the good qualities concealed by his unpleasant façade.

When Darcy proposes to Elizabeth, it comes as a complete surprise to her. She hasn't seen it coming, because he has done such a terrible job of showing her he likes her. Often he's come to visit and barely said a word to her: "Why Mr Darcy came so often to the Parsonage, it was difficult to understand. It could not be for society, as he frequently sat there ten minutes together, without opening his lips; and when he did speak, it seemed the effect of necessity rather than of choice—a sacrifice to propriety, not a pleasure to himself."

We can see from this that Darcy isn't even trying to attract Elizabeth. He's so confident she will accept him, so puffed up in his own self-esteem, that all he's doing is trying to make up his own mind. He's completely sure of her, so sure that he even proposes by telling her how much he's "struggled" against being in love with her because of her awful, vulgar family! Of course Elizabeth slaps him down, insulted. Though she can't help being flattered that she has brought him to his knees.

When they meet again, Darcy starts to court her once more, but does it properly this time. He makes a point of treating her with respect and attention, and makes it clear that he has been talking about her to his sister, telling Elizabeth that Miss Darcy "particularly wishes to be known to [her]." Elizabeth "immediately [feels] that whatever desire Miss Darcy might have of being acquainted with her must be the work of her brother, and without looking farther, it was satisfactory . . . His wish of introducing his sister to her was a compliment of the highest kind." She takes this, rightly, as a sign that he is still interested in her, and is trying to correct all the faults he showed before. Now he is "desirous to please . . . free from self-consequence or unbending reserve . . ." He was "most eager to preserve the acquaintance . . . was soliciting the good opinion of her friends, and bent on making her known to his sister. Such a change in a man of so much pride excited not only astonishment but gratitude . . . and as such its impression on her was of a sort to be encouraged . . ."

And Elizabeth does exactly the right thing. Shyly now, she indicates to him that she does like him, and would be interested in receiving another proposal from him, a better one. When Darcy again asks her to marry him, he's pretty sure that she will say yes—because now she's shown him that she likes him in return.

> LESSON TO BE LEARNED
>
> DON'T MAKE SNAP JUDGMENTS

What Not to Do: Don't Narrow Your Options

Amy had a very clear idea of the kind of man she wanted to date. He had to be well-off and have the kind of job that she did—a high-powered career in finance. So when she met Harry, who worked in her local bookstore, she never thought of him as a romantic prospect, despite the fact that he was attractive, interesting, and they had many good conversations about books. When Harry finally asked Amy out, she turned him down without thinking twice about it. Harry wasn't remotely on her prospective-boyfriend radar.

A month later Amy was hanging out with some friends in a local bar and she bumped into Harry. It turned out that Harry was a partner in that bar and a couple of others. He explained that while he loved managing the bookstore— Amy hadn't even been aware that Harry was the manager, because of his quiet, unassuming manner—he realized that it would never make him any money, and so he had invested in the bars, all of which were doing pretty well. Amy immediately readjusted her perspective on Harry. It transpired that Harry had a good inheritance from his wealthy family and had decided not to go into the corporate world, preferring instead to lead an alternative lifestyle; but his desire to make a good life for himself meant that he was making wise investments and earning well.

Amy regretted turning down Harry. She flirted with him that evening, and went back to the bookstore on a number of occasions, hoping that he would ask her out again. He never did. Finally she plucked up the courage to ask him out, but Harry said no, explaining that he was now seeing someone else. Amy did bump into Harry at the bar he co-owned a few times, but never saw him with a woman. She was never sure whether he really did have a girlfriend, or whether he had seen through her and realized that she was interested in him romantically only after she had found out he wasn't just a bookstore employee but a successful entrepreneur.

If Amy had accepted Harry's offer and gone on a date with him, she would probably have learned that evening about Harry's partnership in the bars and not blown her chances of going out with a good prospect. Of course, this would have been bad for poor Harry, who was the lucky one in the situation; he avoided dating a woman who was primarily interested in his bank account. But it goes to show how important it is not to rely on appearances or on your own assumptions. Even if you meet some shock-haired young man carrying a guitar in a downtown bar, why not talk to him for a few minutes if he seems nice? You may have a prejudice against unemployed musicians, but for all you know he may be a TV producer helping out a friend by looking after his guitar while the latter goes to the bathroom. Remember, be open and easygoing. What do fifteen minutes of conversation cost you, after all?

What to Do Instead: Be Open-Minded

Jeff was a downtown bartender who dated up a storm and rarely had relationships that lasted longer than a couple of weeks. So when he met an attractive woman at his bar one evening, he chatted her up, as he was very used to doing. He asked her out to the movies and she accepted. They got on like a house on fire. Lisa, his date, was gorgeous, smart, and successful. She didn't fall into his arms the first evening, as Jeff was used to girls doing, and would never stay out past eleven. After a few dates, Lisa explained why: she had a three-year-old daughter at home. She was divorced from the father and had primary custody.

Jeff was unnerved by this revelation. He didn't think he was looking for a serious relationship and he had never had any wish to date a woman who already had a child. Lisa said he could have some time to think about the situation and decide whether he wanted to go on seeing her. Jeff took a week, and found that he couldn't stop thinking about Lisa. He rang her up, went round and met her daughter, and was surprised to find that he really enjoyed hanging out with her and Lisa. Before he knew it, he was spending cozy family evenings at Lisa's. Jeff, who had never thought about having children, bonded quickly with Lisa's daughter, and, being free during the day, would often take her to the playground after school and make her supper before Lisa got home from work. He found himself respecting Lisa immensely for the way she was raising her daughter. Jeff and Lisa are now married and have a child of their own. Jeff does most of the school runs and the babysitting while Lisa does the bulk of providing financially for their family. Jeff still can't believe how happy he is in a situation that's the polar opposite of everything he thought he wanted. He followed his instincts and gave them a chance, rather than closing down his burgeoning relationship with Lisa because it wasn't his usual pattern.

When Sophie met Matt at a party, she wasn't initially interested in him. Sophie was a very attractive fashion plate, whose interests were primarily artistic; Matt was a jock who loved baseball and football and ran two fantasy sports leagues. But they ended up having a great conversation, and when Matt bumped into Sophie at another party given by mutual friends, he found himself seeking her out. Matt wasn't Sophie's type at all; she usually preferred more sophisticated, artsy men. But again, she was surprised to find how much she liked spending time with him. Over the course of time, they met repeatedly at their mutual friends' houses and finally Matt asked Sophie out.

To her surprise, she found herself agreeing to go, even though she really wasn't thinking of Matt as a long-term prospect. Matt made the mistake of taking Sophie to a sports bar, which she hated—but she made the best of it, and again, they found themselves having a great conversation. Matt asked her out again, and this time he made sure to take her to the kind of place she preferred. Gradually, Matt and Sophie found their common ground: movies, good food, and mountain biking. They agreed to let each other pursue his or her own interests without being threatened by them. Sophie had her own group of friends with whom she could go to the theater and the symphony. Matt went to games with the guys. They supported each other and enjoyed their times together while giving each other space. Sophie will never like team sports, and Matt will never enjoy classical music, but they have enough in common to keep them together, and they actually find that having time apart is good for their relationship. Matt and Sophie would never have made a match of it on Internet dating; their profiles would have been completely different. But they've been together for four years, just got engaged, and are planning to go mountain biking in Tuscany for their honeymoon. Their friends call them Beauty and the Beast, which both Matt and Sophie find very amusing. Because they didn't make snap judgments, they could take the time to realize how much they liked each other.

SUMMARY

Do

- *Be open and easygoing.* If you like a man, show him that you do. Show him that you're happy to hear from him, return his calls within at least a couple of days, and if you like the sound of an invitation, accept it, without holding out for what you've heard is the "right" first-date invitation or being sulky because you expected an expensive dinner and you've been asked to the movies instead.

- *Enjoy the moment.* Take pleasure in what you're doing at the time. Let the attraction grow naturally. Keep your feet firmly on the ground—don't lose yourself in someone new.

- *Take time to get to know new people.* Make allowances for ones who may be shy, and who may not reveal their personalities the first time you talk to them. Though there may not be an instant attraction it may come with time; keep your options open by waiting to see if someone grows on you.

Don't

- *Rush.* Don't put pressure on a new relationship to be the love of your life when it's only been going on for a couple of weeks. Don't force anything along.

- *Chase a man.* Let him come after you. Don't call him more than he calls you. Don't make excuses for his tardiness or lack of enthusiasm. If he seemed keen but then pulled back, let him go.

- *Make snap judgments.* Don't be blinded by your own preset ideas of what you are looking for. The right person for you may not be the same as the ideal image you've constructed in your head. Don't make a template of who you want and reject people instantly because they don't fit into it.

❖   ❖   ❖   ❖

Tips for Telling If a Man Really Likes You

❖ He will ask you for dates in advance—though he may spontaneously call and ask you out for the same night, he will also plan ahead to schedule time you can spend together.

❖ When he kisses you, he will take your hand and kiss it, or give you an extra good-night kiss on the forehead— he'll kiss you on the mouth, too, but his attentions to you will be romantic as well as sexual.

❖ He will remember things you told him about what you've been doing at work or socially, and ask you how they went.

❖ He won't make you feel insecure; he will call when he says he will and turn up on time for your dates.

❖ He will make an effort with his appearance—on your dates he will be well dressed and groomed.

❖ He may well call or e-mail you after a date to say what a great time he had. This is one of the best signs of all that he likes you seriously!

❖ He will make you feel included in his life by telling you about his day, his friends, and his interests.

Don't Put Your Feelings on Public Display, Unless They're Fully Reciprocated

WE'VE ALREADY SEEN THAT showing some-
one you like him is a good thing. But *only as long
as you're getting from him at least as much as you're giving.* In
this chapter, we will look at examples of women who
went overboard with the men they liked, even when the
men were clearly indicating that they were no longer in-

terested. Remember, there are plenty of game-players and toxic flirts out there, and you have to make sure you protect yourself. You need to stay alert and keep watching for the signals he gives you. Just because a man once liked you, that's no reason to let down your guard if you feel that you can no longer trust him. You may have a cell phone filled with lovely text messages he sent you last month, but if he isn't in touch this month, or only phones you late at night for a booty call, the situation has changed, and you have to respond to that and pull back to keep yourself from being hurt. There are no guarantees in life. A sensible woman will always look after her own interests and make sure, as best she can, that she isn't being used by a man who is taking her for granted. And remember, cases of a woman's making the first move with a man and things turning out well are comparatively rare. This isn't sexist: it's related to the very different ways that male and female sexuality work. You have to be aware that men have anxieties we don't have—anxieties to do with their sexual performance and their insecurities about whether they'll be able to satisfy a woman. If they don't have the courage to commit to making a pass at you, they will probably not be able to commit to continuing the relationship and keeping you satisfied in bed.

MARIANNE AND ELINOR

Elinor could not be surprised at [the] attachment
[between Marianne and Willoughby]. She only wished
that it were less openly shown: and once or twice did
venture to suggest the propriety of some self-command to
Marianne. But Marianne abhorred all concealment . . .
—*SENSE AND SENSIBILITY*

As we've already seen from *Sense and Sensibility*, Marianne Dash wood's romance with Willoughby starts wonderfully; she shows him how much she likes him and captures his heart as a result. But Willoughby, under threat of losing his inheritance, dumps Marianne abruptly for an unpleasant heiress whom he eventually marries. Marianne, unable to understand what's happening, pesters him with letters and finally makes a fool of herself in public, running up to him at a dance only to be horribly snubbed. "Oh! why does he not look at me?" she asks Elinor. And then, still not understanding: "Good God! Willoughby, what is the meaning of this? Have you not received my letters? Will you not shake hands with me?" She can't bring herself to understand that Willoughby is dropping her. And because she's been so indiscreet, showing her love to the world before an official announcement of an engagement, she becomes the laughingstock of half of London. "Upon my word," says their friend Mrs. Jennings, a terrible gossip, "I never saw a young woman so desperately in love in my life! . . . I hope . . . he won't keep her waiting much longer, for it is quite grievous to see her look so ill and forlorn."

No matter how interested in you someone once seemed, if he appears to be losing that interest, you must be aware of it. There must always be mutuality. If someone is going, you must let him go.

Like Catherine Morland, Marianne gets her man by showing him how much she likes him. Sadly for her, she doesn't get to keep him: Willoughby chooses to marry for money rather than love. Marianne is absolutely right to make it clear to Willoughby in the beginning that she has a strong preference for him. But she's wrong to *keep* showing him how much she likes him when it's clear that he's pulling away. She could have spared herself a lot of extra pain if she'd looked more clearly at the truth of the situation. That's what Marianne has to teach us. You should show someone you like him only as long as you feel that the attraction is, or can be, mutual.

Marianne's sister Elinor, on the other hand, knows not to show her feelings so openly. Although she is in love with the sweet, shy Edward Ferrars, she is careful to be discreet about it. Her family is aware of her feelings, and so is Edward, but there are obstacles that must be surmounted before they can be together, and for a large part of the book it looks as if Edward will be trapped into an unhappy marriage with the awful Lucy Steele, a nasty little schemer. So Elinor must, for her own self-respect, keep quiet about her love for Edward. She won't show her emotions until there is some hope for her. Elinor and Marianne represent two opposite poles: Marianne, by constantly spilling out her feelings, turns them into an obsession and finally drives herself into such a state of nervous collapse that she nearly dies. Elinor, who has self-control, restrains her emotions and preserves her pride and her health. We can sympathize with poor Marianne's love, and then her anger at being betrayed, but we don't want to be her. She needs to learn a lesson from her sister and find some self-discipline, painful though it may be.

> LESSON TO BE LEARNED
> ─────────────
> ## MUTUALITY

What Not to Do: Don't Ignore the Evidence

Jane Austen is the reigning queen of good common sense; at every opportunity she advises against overromanticizing. Even if someone has shown in the past that he likes you, that's no guarantee that his feelings will remain the same.

Lori had known John for a year or so through mutual friends. She could tell he was interested in her, and a couple of times he called her on the spur of the moment when he had theater tickets for that evening, to ask her if she would like to come along. Lori accepted these invitations, and they had a nice time, but John never made a pass at her at the end of the evening, so she came to the conclusion that he didn't want to get romantically involved with her. After the third of these dates, however, John rang her up two days later and asked her to a movie that week. They went, and Lori invited John in for coffee. Again, he didn't make a move, but he did ask her out later that week. He came in for coffee again at the end of the evening, and they watched a movie, during which Lori, now sure that John liked her and frustrated that he wasn't initiating anything, kissed him as they sat on the sofa. John responded with great enthusiasm and they made out for a while. When they kissed good night, he asked her out again, and over the next couple of dates the pattern was that John would end up on Lori's sofa, making out with her. The sexual attraction grew and grew, and when they made a date for that Saturday night, Lori was sure that she and John would finally have sex.

That evening at six, John rang Lori to cancel, saying he was working all weekend and couldn't make it. He said he would call her on Sunday, but he didn't. At this point, Lori should have seen what was going on; John was pulling away. Whether this was performance anxiety, fear of getting too involved, or any other reason in the world was immaterial. He had made two promises he hadn't kept, and that should have been enough to tell her that things had changed. But what did Lori do? She behaved like Marianne and chased John down like a dog. She rang him on Monday and left a message on his voice mail. She sent him a cute, very flirtatious e-mail two days later, hoping to stir up his attraction to her. John finally got in touch, but only by e-mail, and he didn't ask her for a date or apologize for his disappearing act. They exchanged e-mails and phone messages for a few weeks before Lori finally realized that she had to let it go. John just wasn't going to step up to the plate.

In this case, Lori should never have made the first move. If John wasn't going to do it, that was a clear indication from the beginning that he had ambivalent feelings about her, or even about getting sexually involved with a woman in general. She had given him enough encouragement already by accepting his last-minute invitations and inviting him in for coffee. If he couldn't nerve up the courage to kiss her first, he probably wasn't going to have enough courage to follow through with their burgeoning relationship. And then, when he canceled on Saturday night and didn't ring her the next day, she should have wiped his number from her cell phone and moved on.

I know it's hard when a man creates feelings in you and gets you attached to him. It's very difficult to cut those feelings off cold. But if Lori had been able to say to herself, "He doesn't want to be involved with me anymore and there's nothing I can do about it," she would have recovered much faster. The mutuality was gone, but by thinking about John all the time and sending seductive e-mails to try to win him back, Lori was fooling herself. She needed to open her eyes and see the situation clearly. She was trying to breathe life into a corpse—and even if you manage to do that, all you get is a zombie.

The wish to be in love, to find your life partner, is completely natural and understandable. But you won't find the right person by clinging to a situation that is obviously not going anywhere just because you want to be in love. If someone isn't there for you anymore, you have to let him go. And that goes, too, for someone you are with who isn't necessarily breaking up with you, but whose feelings for you may have changed. By all means, try to work out any problems you are having. But if you feel that person is just staying with you out of habit or convenience, rather than because he loves you, the mutuality is gone and you need to leave. Don't keep yourself tied down to something that's over. Marianne managed to move on and marry Colonel Brandon, but before that she made herself so ill with her feelings for Willoughby that she nearly killed herself in the process. Don't follow her example!

What to Do Instead: Respect His Signals

Liza met Alex at a Christmas office party and they got on brilliantly. He took her number and said he'd ring her the next day. Well, he did, and after ten days they managed to get together—neither of them was being coy or making excuses, but the Christmas holidays had intervened. They had a lovely night out. They were very happy to see each other and made it clear. The conversation flowed like the champagne they were drinking. They stayed out very late, really enjoying getting to know each other. They discovered lots of things they had in common—books, music, movies. On finally saying good night, they had a great and very promising kiss. Alex said he'd call Liza the next day, and he did. But he sounded odd and made an excuse about why he couldn't see her for a while. He said he'd try to call her in a week or so. And then, guess what? He never called her again.

Liza was mightily aggrieved and disappointed. She rang a friend for commiseration, and the friend provided it by reminding her of the several times the same thing had happened to her—perfect first date, lovely kiss good night, followed by . . . nothing. It seemed inexplicable. Liza and Alex obviously liked each other: all the right energy and enthusiasm were present. And then Alex just vanished. But no matter how much Liza wanted to know why, she couldn't ask for an explanation. It was just a first date; Alex didn't owe her anything. There are many possible reasons for Alex's sudden disappearing act. An ex-girlfriend might have unexpectedly come back into his life. He might have been made nervous precisely by the fact that the first date went so well. He might have decided that he wasn't ready for a relationship after all. But whatever it was, Liza would never know. She couldn't beat herself up about it—she had done everything as well as she could—and she just had to let it go. Because, although there was mutuality on the date, it had vanished, along with Alex.

Liza could have called Alex; she could have pestered him with phone calls and e-mails and text messages. But he wouldn't have responded, and it would only have made Liza feel humiliated. He had already called her, sounding weird, and then had never called again, even though he had said he would. Clearly something was wrong. Liza wouldn't have gained anything by chasing after him. All she could do was let it go and hope that perhaps she would hear from him again if he changed his mind. Annoyed and frustrated though she was, she needed to focus on a healthy sense of self-protection. In the later stages of dating, when you've got to know someone over a course of time, you can certainly call him and see if anything's wrong, or ask him why he sounds odd when he calls you. Even so, you may not get an answer you like. The person may be slipping away from you and not want to admit it. But when you've just met, things are very tentative, and all you can do is keep checking with your own instincts and common sense to see if there's a good mutual give and take. Make sure you feel you're getting what you're giving.

JULIA AND MARIA BERTRAM

Maria felt her triumph [with Henry], and pursued her
purpose careless of Julia; and Julia could never see Maria
distinguished by Henry Crawford, without trusting
that it would create jealousy, and bring a
public disturbance at last.
—*MANSFIELD PARK*

Both Julia and Maria Bertram, the spoiled sisters of *Mansfield Park*, are in love with the devilishly charming and flirtatious Henry Crawford, who plays them against each other for his own amusement. This behavior is obvious to Fanny, the heroine of the book, who worries about both of the sisters. Maria is engaged to the boring but rich Mr. Rushworth, and Julia is single, but the sisters are in equal danger of being seduced by Henry. Both Fanny and Mary, Henry's sister, are perfectly aware of what is going on. Mary thinks Henry is merely amusing himself, but Fanny is worried about the consequences, and she's absolutely right to be concerned. Maria is ready to chuck her fiancé at the slightest encouragement from Henry, and Julia is furious that Henry prefers Maria—though he only favors Maria because she's already engaged and thus he's safer from entanglements. In the end, Maria marries poor tedious Mr. Rushworth because Henry disappears from the scene; but when they meet up again in London, she and Henry recommence their flirtation and end up running away together, causing an enormous scandal. And Julia, angry and jealous, elopes to Gretna Green with a young man as stupid and silly as Mr. Rushworth. Maria is abandoned by Henry, divorced by her husband, and condemned to live isolated in the countryside; Julia is stuck with a husband she doesn't even like. It's a huge disaster for everyone.

LESSON TO BE LEARNED

DON'T LET A MAN PLAY YOU
OFF AGAINST OTHER WOMEN

What Not to Do: Don't Throw Yourself at a Player

Julia and Maria fight continually over Henry. They don't ever pause to think that if he were really serious about one of them, he would show that clearly, rather than play them off against each other for his own amusement. This happened to Daisy and Karen, friends in college, who both had a huge crush on a guy in their social group named Seth. Seth, like Henry, loved to flirt and have girls in love with him. He had a whole string of girls he dated, without serious intentions toward any of them. Instead of stepping back and assessing the situation, Daisy and Karen fell into the trap of competing for Seth's attentions. They ignored the fact that if a man really likes you, he will show it clearly and exclusively. Seth was doing exactly the opposite: he'd ask Daisy out one day, and Karen a few days later, sleeping with both of them—and a lot of other girls, too—without ever taking either of them seriously as potential girlfriends. Daisy and Karen grew more and more desperate in their courtship of Seth, and it became very obvious to everyone around them. The winner in the situation, of course, was Seth; girls were after him constantly, from whom he could pick and choose at will, without ever committing to one of them. It ruined Daisy and Karen's friendship and, naturally, neither of them ever succeeded in getting Seth, who is still playing the same games, years later. Not only that—Daisy and Karen felt completely humiliated. The more they chased Seth, the more blatant their behavior was, and they became public laughingstocks.

What to Do Instead: Protect Your Feelings

Naomi, another girl in Daisy, Karen, and Seth's social circle at college, was initially very attracted to Seth, like the majority of girls with whom he came into contact. But Naomi was totally turned off by Seth's behavior. She didn't think he showed much discrimination, and she thought the way he was behaving with Daisy and Karen was cruel. So when Seth started pursuing her, Naomi cut him off dead, even though she couldn't help finding him very charming and seductive. However, she was able to take a step back and assess Seth for what he was—a player who had no serious intentions toward any girl he courted.

Naomi managed to keep her attraction to Seth secret, instead of sighing over him the way that Daisy and Karen did. This way, she protected herself. She wasn't the butt of jokes when her friends saw Seth out with another girl; she didn't have to defend herself from the sly comments that women make to other women when they think that they have been disappointed in love. It was hard for Naomi, because she genuinely was very keen on Seth, and when he flirted with her it was difficult for her not to respond. But she managed to keep her feelings hidden from everyone else, and she had her reward when she saw how tough it was on Daisy and Karen, who allowed themselves repeatedly to be picked up and dropped by Seth according to his whims. By restraining herself and concealing her attraction to Seth, Naomi kept herself protected, and she recovered much faster than Daisy and Karen, who were deeply damaged by Seth's games.

KITTY AND LYDIA BENNET

*"From all I can collect by your manner of talking, you
must be two of the silliest girls in the country."*
—PRIDE AND PREJUDICE

Kitty and Lydia Bennet, the two youngest sisters from *Pride and
Prejudice*, are the wildest, craziest flirts that Jane Austen ever created. They're mad for any man in uniform—"they could talk of
nothing but officers," Austen writes—and spend all their free time
in the village where the local militia is stationed, trying to meet as
many soldiers as possible. Their behavior is so obvious and embarrassing that Mr. Darcy cites it, along with Mrs. Bennet's awful
pushy manners, as a reason for his dissuading Bingley from proposing to Jane: "a total want of propriety," he calls it. And he has a
point. When Lydia is invited to Brighton, a seaside resort, by the
wife of a colonel in the regiment, she imagines herself "seated beneath a tent, tenderly flirting with at least six officers at once."

Elizabeth is all too aware of how badly Kitty and Lydia behave.
She even warns her father that if he doesn't rein them in now, Lydia will "be the most determined flirt that ever made herself and her
family ridiculous. A flirt too, in the worst and meanest degree of
flirtation; without any attraction beyond youth and a tolerable person; and from the ignorance and emptiness of her mind, wholly
unable to ward off any portion of that universal contempt which
her rage for admiration will excite. In this danger Kitty is also com-
prehended. She will follow wherever Lydia leads. Vain, ignorant,
idle and absolutely uncontrolled!"

Elizabeth, as so often, is quite right. Lydia's complete inability
to control her desperate need for attention leads her to run away

with Wickham, a charming, unprincipled rake who has no inten-
tion of marrying her. Lydia would have been ruined for life if Mr.
Darcy, out of love for Elizabeth, hadn't stepped in and bribed
Wickham to make an honest woman of Lydia.

LESSON TO BE LEARNED
SELF-CONTROL

What Not to Do: Don't Throw Yourself at Men

Lydia and Kitty make idiots of themselves because they throw
themselves at any vaguely good-looking officer in a red coat. They
are indiscriminate; they have no self-control, no ability to pause
and sum up the character of the latest man they have a crush on.
Like them, Jennifer has a new crush every few weeks. She's barely
met a man at a party before she's ringing up all her friends, telling
them how wonderful he is and how right they are for each other.
Jennifer—much to the envy of some of her friends—has no trouble meeting men. She's very attractive and seems a little vulnerable, and this combination means that men are initially very
interested in her. But the romances always fizzle. Jennifer is so
desperate to be in a relationship that she ignores all the warning
signs. Her friends try to warn her, but to no avail. One man was
rude to her and treated her badly; one insisted that she always
come over to his place, and would never visit her apartment; one
was so close to his ex-girlfriend that he would often suggest that
he, Jennifer, and the ex all go out together in the evenings. Jennifer's friends pointed all these flaws out to her, but she wouldn't
listen, and she still won't. It's never Jennifer who breaks up with

the men, no matter how badly things are going; she's always the one to be dumped.

Jennifer simply throws herself at any available and eligible man, and, because she's so attractive, the men will catch her for a while, before chucking her away again. She has no self-control whatsoever when it comes to relationships. Although she complains about relationships going badly, she won't pause for the few minutes it would take to do the math and come to the conclusion that a man who's not treating her well isn't right for her. It's got to the point that her friends roll their eyes whenever Jennifer calls them to recount how she's met a new man. In the last year, she's dated at least ten men, and it hasn't worked out with any of them. It's as if Jennifer just doesn't factor herself into the equation—her own likes and dislikes, her own need to be treated well. Her obsessive need to be in a relationship makes her ignore a more important, basic need—to be treated well. It really seems as if Jennifer is incapable of saying no to a man: No, I don't want to go out with you and your ex-girlfriend. No, I don't want to come round to your place again tonight, when you never come round to mine. No, I don't want to see you anymore.

Not all of Jennifer's boyfriends treat her badly; some are nice guys, looking for something serious, who nevertheless are quickly put off by the overeagerness with which she rushes into a relationship. Remember the "Do" from Chapter One, Enjoy the moment? It's the perfect principle for Jennifer, but she doesn't have enough self-control to follow it. Though very successful in her career, romantically she's like a little child grabbing at candy, unable to wait for gratification. Jennifer never learned that delayed gratification is usually more satisfying and more profound than a quick greedy grab at what you want. If she doesn't develop some self-control, she is doomed to keep repeating her pattern, and she'll never find what she's looking for.

Just because you met a gorgeous prospect in a bar last night and gave him your phone number doesn't mean that you have to start getting stressed at lunchtime the next day because he hasn't called you yet. If you start building castles in the air too soon, a man will pick up on that and be put off by it. We all know how unattractive a desperate-seeming person is. Also, it's not really flattering to the man you are interested in. Because if you're that desperate, like Jennifer, you will just latch on to the next vaguely eligible man you meet, without taking the time to get to know him as a person. You're not seeing him for who he really is. A man naturally likes to feel that you want him for himself, not just as any old buffer against the loneliness of being single.

What to Do Instead: Let Him Breathe

When Matthew met Sally, he had recently finished a fling with another girl, and though he liked Sally, he wasn't sure yet about his true feelings: was she a rebound? He knew that he was still a little confused and shaken up by the fling, which hadn't ended well, and he didn't want to rush into anything until he felt that he had his emotions more under control. So he took things much more slowly than he usually would have. They went out a couple of nights a week, to the movies or to dinner, but Matthew didn't make a move on Sally for a month. He wanted to get to know her and to give himself time to figure out what was going on. It was the longest Matthew had ever waited before kissing a girl, but he wanted to be sure that he really liked Sally before he rushed into something with her, and then panicked because he wasn't ready.

Sally knew that Matthew had just broken up with someone, and she sensed that he wasn't ready yet. She also managed to keep her feelings under control and not push Matthew to make a move before he was ready—though, of course, she was very much hoping that this would happen sooner rather than later! She had the harder task—Matthew, due to his confusion about his attraction to Sally and the feelings he still had for his ex, was naturally able to go slower. Sally's job was to discipline herself, keep her growing feelings for him under wraps, and not pressure him.

She knew she had to leave it to Matthew to make the move, because if she were the one to take the first step, one way or another it would go wrong. Either Matthew would respond, they would end up in bed together, and it would be too early, causing him to get nervous and need some time out; or he would reject her. Sally naturally found this very difficult. Still, she had a couple of good friends to confide in, and she vented to them. Meanwhile, Matthew kept ringing her and they kept going out on lovely dates. Sally let Matthew do most of the work. And finally, when Matthew did make a pass at her, it went wonderfully. They were both more than ready and they acknowledged right away how much they liked each other. Sally and Matthew have been together ever since.

SUMMARY

Do

- *Avoid giving more than you get.* Don't let yourself get into a situation where the person you're dating is taking you for a ride and not really interested in a serious relationship with you. Don't throw yourself blindly at someone—you'll lose yourself and forget what *you* really want and need.

- *Keep your self-control.* You might fall head over heels for a man you meet at a party, but you know very little about someone you've only talked to for a couple of hours. Even if you fall into bed with him that very night, you still hardly know him! Which is why it's a good idea to take things slowly and maintain self-control so you can work out what kind of person he really is, and whether he can be trusted with your love.

- *Be discriminating*. There are plenty of attractive people out there with whom you will be compatible. Just because someone is flirting with you and you are attracted to him doesn't mean that you shouldn't give yourself time to see how strong the compatibility is.

Don't

- *Overconfide in your friends*. People—even ones with the best intentions—gossip terribly. In the early stages, play your cards close to your chest. Overconfiding can also make you obsessive about a man—don't talk about someone new constantly. Remind yourself that you have a life!

- *Overindulge your feelings*. The more Marianne dwells on her love for Willoughby, the sicker she makes herself. If your love is clearly hopeless, try not to think about it every hour of the day and night. Distract yourself as much as possible and put it from your mind. It will make your recovery much faster.

- *Get into a competition*. Remember, you should be letting him chase you, not chasing him! And that means not putting your feelings more on display than his are. If a man is making you feel that you need to war against other potential prospects for his attentions, it's a big warning sign. Instead, he should make you feel that you are the only person he really wants to get to know. If he doesn't, you should cross him off your list immediately. Any relationship you have with him will always make you feel insecure.

❖   ❖   ❖   ❖

Tips for Showing a Man You Like Him Without Going Overboard

❖ When he tells you that you look gorgeous, don't respond by paying him a compliment in return. Instead, say, "You make me *feel* gorgeous." Trust me—he will love this much more than hearing that he's handsome, because his main concern should be pleasing you.

❖ Spontaneously comment on something he's wearing and tell him how much you like it—not to return a compliment he's paid you, but just because you want to.

❖ Always thank him for taking you out and choosing a movie/restaurant/concert you enjoyed—but don't thank him more than once—once is enough.

❖ Comment on things he talked about on previous dates; if you saw an article about something he's interested in, you can mention it. But *don't* cut that article out and bring it along, or e-mail it to him—that's too much.

* If he e-mails or texts you after your date to say what a nice time he had, respond in kind. But keep it short, and if he sends you another message, don't answer the second one.

* Try not to contact him spontaneously with news of yours in the first month of dating, even if you think you have something to tell him that he'll really enjoy. He's not your boyfriend yet—save that for later, when you've been going out for a while. But if he contacts you spontaneously, by all means don't keep him waiting too long for an answer.

* Don't dump problems on him in the early stages of dating that he can't really help with (like a fight with your mother). But by all means ask him for practical help—men adore showing you how to program your VCR or helping you plan a route for a trip you're taking. Helping a woman to fix a concrete, solvable problem always makes a man feel wonderful!

THREE

DON'T PLAY GAMES OR
LEAD PEOPLE ON

*Vanity, while seeking its own guilty triumph at the
expense of another, had involved [Willoughby] in a real
attachment, which extravagance . . . had required to be
sacrificed. Each faulty propensity, in leading him to evil,
had led him likewise to punishment.*

—*SENSE AND SENSIBILITY*

WHAT GOES AROUND COMES around—and
I'm not just talking about the negative karma you
create when you treat people badly. If you make a practice of playing with men's feelings for your own amusement, or because you're insecure and need the
reassurance, you will get into bad patterns of behavior

that will cause you to sabotage any possibility you have to form a good relationship. We often criticize men who behave badly, and goodness knows, there are plenty of them. But we also need to look at our own behavior and make sure that we are treating people as we want to be treated in order to make the kind of open, loving, trusting connection that we really want to form with one special man. And you don't make that kind of connection by playing games with him, keeping him insecure and off balance, or being mean to keep him keen.

WILLOUGHBY

*"Careless of [Marianne's] happiness, thinking only of
my own amusement, giving way to feelings which I had
always been too much in the habit of indulging, I
endeavoured, by every means in my power, to make
myself pleasing to her, without any design of
returning her affection."*
—SENSE AND SENSIBILITY

In his own words, Willoughby shows us how callous and hardened he was when he met Marianne in *Sense and Sensibility*. He admits that he only flirted with Marianne as a way to amuse himself during a few weeks' stay in the countryside. And what happens? He gets caught in his own trap. Meaning simply to emotionally seduce Marianne, he falls genuinely in love himself, and gets into terrible trouble. He can't ask Marianne to marry him, because he doesn't have enough money to provide for a wife. So he returns to London and proposes instead to a rich girl he doesn't love. This breaks Marianne's heart, and she goes into a decline that nearly kills her; while

Willoughby has trapped himself in a disastrous marriage with a woman he neither cares about nor respects. Worst of all, he finds out, when it's too late, that if he'd held true to his love for Marianne, he might well have had enough to support them after all—his rich aunt would have approved of his being in love with a respectable girl and provided them with a sufficient income for their needs.

Willoughby never had any intention of taking Marianne seriously. He was just doing what he usually did to pass the time—play his usual game with her of working up a light flirtation for his own amusement. He knew he couldn't afford to fall in love with a poor girl and was looking out for one with a decent income instead. Falling in love with Marianne took him completely by surprise— and it was entirely his own fault. Because if he hadn't started flirting with Marianne practically the moment that he met her, responding enthusiastically to the obvious interest she had in him, he would never have come to know her well enough to fall in love with her. Their initial attraction would never have deepened into something more serious. Willoughby could have held back and kept both himself and Marianne safe, but he thought he wasn't in any danger—and he was much too selfish to think for a moment (knowing how badly he was capable of behaving) that he ought to protect her from himself. Willoughby leads Marianne on, and ends up worse off than her; he's stuck in a loveless marriage to an (understandably) jealous bitch, whereas Marianne has Colonel Brandon, a good man who loves and takes care of her.

LESSON TO BE LEARNED

LEADING PEOPLE ON CAN REBOUND ON YOU

What Not to Do: Don't Treat Men Like the Enemy

Emily is a hardened game-player who loves to string men along. She always seems to have a series of men running after her, and she maintains their interest by giving them half promises to go out and then canceling at the last minute, flirting with them crazily and then not quite following through, and continually throwing them off balance so they're never sure of her.

Emily lives her life in a whirl of excitement and complications; she often has to juggle men, make up stories as to why she can't see them, and switch her phone off when she's on a date with one of them so that another one doesn't ring and catch her out. To some of her friends, jealous because Emily always has men calling her, and to Emily herself, it seems like she has it all. But Emily doesn't in fact have what she really wants—a good relationship. Emily acts this way because, deep down, she doesn't trust men, and she won't let anyone get close enough to her for them to see the "real" Emily; she's frightened that, if they do, they will reject her.

This is behavior that Emily has learned from her mother, a very attractive but insecure woman who has four divorces behind her already, and who has passed on to Emily her own distrust of men. Her mother is always lining up the next husband almost as soon as she marries the current one; convinced that men will betray her eventually, she wants to do it first. With a background like this, it's very hard for Emily to imagine that a man might actually want to stay with her forever, and as a result she is incapable of commitment. Emily is actually right not to settle down with any of the men who are chasing her—because what they are attracted to is her unavailability. They're hung up on the perpetual chase. None of them are long-term prospects, because if they were, they would soon see through the way Emily is leading them on and dump her, to search instead for a woman who doesn't treat them like toys. You can snag some men by playing games with them—keeping them insecure, not returning their calls, pretending when they ring you that you don't recognize their voices on the phone—but any decent man will quickly be put off by this. All you will get, acting that way, is the kind of player who will never be any good in a steady long-term relationship.

Emily is caught up in a cycle that will never change as long as she keeps behaving in the same way. What she actually needs to do is to stop dating, take a deep breath, and do some work on figuring out exactly why she treats men the way she does—and work on the self-esteem issues that stop her from getting too close to any one man. Leading men on as Emily constantly does, glamorous though it seems from the outside, is actually hampering her from getting what she really wants. But so far, she hasn't been brave enough to break the pattern and build a new one. And the dating books she's grown up reading haven't helped—they've just encouraged her to use their techniques as a way of improving her skills: keeping men perpetually off balance, giving them encouragement one minute but pulling back the next.

What to Do Instead: Be Genuine

There's nothing wrong with flirting and having a good time, nothing wrong with getting out there and putting your energy into being extroverted and attracting people. There *is*, however, a problem when flirting becomes a drug, and you use your power indiscriminately. You run the risk, like Emily, of being so into the game of seduction and manipulation that you can't rein yourself in and get in touch with your own feelings.

Leading people on is never a good way to behave. Exploiting other people will always rebound on you as soon as you want to connect with someone in a serious and honest way. Your reputation will precede you, and you won't even trust yourself when you're being direct and open; it won't seem real to you anymore, because you'll be so used to skating over surfaces lightly that this will be the technique you'll use any time you try to win someone over.

Valerie lived to flirt. She was every girl's nightmare and every boy's dream. She always had plenty of men after her, and she enjoyed the attention and the flattery. But as she got to know Bob, a new coworker, she realized she had serious feelings for him. Valerie knew that she could get Bob interested in her by using her usual wiles, but that wasn't what she wanted. She wanted Bob to get to know her as a person. If he was going to ask her out, she didn't want it to be just because he was hoping to go to bed with her.

Valerie certainly did flirt with Bob. She was wise enough to know that it was an essential part of her personality; she would always have a flirty side, and there was no point to her suddenly dressing like a nun and pretending to be somebody she wasn't. It was hard for her at first, because she was so used to winning men over by joking with them, fluttering her eyelashes, and generally coming across as a woman who wasn't looking for a serious relationship. But she made sure that she also talked to Bob about things that were important to her: her family, her hobbies, all the other sides to her character that she generally didn't access around men because she wasn't looking to make a deep connection with them. She felt that if Bob did ask her out, she wanted it to be because he liked all of her, not just her sexy, flirtatious side. She was worried that she was taking a risk, but she knew that if she wanted a proper relationship with him, he would have to see her as a human being, not simply a woman he wanted to have sex with.

It took much longer for Bob to ask Valerie out than it usually did with men, and she found it very hard to wait. She was tempted to slip back into her normal tactics with him, but she held on womanfully, making it clear that she was not playing games. She didn't flirt with other men in the office to make him jealous, because she didn't want to give Bob the wrong impression.

And the wait paid off. After about a month of getting to know each other, Bob suggested that they go to a movie together. Valerie was excited. She felt that Bob was asking out the "real" Valerie, not just the superficial, happy-go-lucky Valerie that was usually all she allowed the world to see. Gradually, she relaxed with Bob, letting her joking, flirtatious side fully emerge once more, but tempering it with conversations about things that mattered to her, so that she would be sure that Bob wasn't just attracted to her as a sex object, but as a woman he might want to have a serious relationship with. Bob and Valerie got married after a year of dating, and Bob had got to know Valerie so well by that time that he wasn't threatened if she let her hair down a little at parties and flirted with other men. He realized that it was part of her character, a part of her that he found very attractive, and it shouldn't make him feel insecure. He felt that he knew the real Valerie, the part of her that the other men didn't see, and that his connection with her was so strong that he could trust her even when she was having a good time and joking with other men.

FRANK CHURCHILL

"How could he tell what mischief he might be doing?—
How could he tell that he might not be making me in
love with him?—very wrong, very wrong indeed."
—EMMA

Frank Churchill is the naughty boy who, through pure luck and charm, manages to make his behavior come right by the end of

Emma. He's engaged to Jane Fairfax, a beautiful and virtuous girl who's much too good for him, but the engagement has to be kept secret so that he doesn't anger his aunt, who holds the purse strings. When he comes to visit his father, who lives close to Emma, Jane Fairfax is also visiting in the village; to conceal his attraction to her, he flirts with Emma instead, covering up his true feelings and drawing attention away from the amount of time he spends with Jane. Jane, of course, gets jealous, and for a while Emma herself is at risk of falling for Frank.

It's a very dangerous game he's playing, and not really necessary. Frank could just have kept his feelings under control and not flirted with Emma in the first place. But Frank is a game-player. He likes risk and danger and excitement; he likes seeming to do one thing and secretly carrying out another plan. In the course of the book, he hurts Jane so badly that she breaks off with him, and he has to use all his charm to convince her to marry him; and he risks Emma's falling in love with him and getting her heart broken. He even amuses himself by criticizing Jane to Emma—terrible behavior. Emma is very lucky indeed that she doesn't get badly hurt by the thoughtless way Frank leads her on.

> LESSON TO BE LEARNED
>
> DON'T GET ADDICTED TO FLIRTING

What Not to Do: Don't Get Too Caught Up in the Game

Dating books aren't only for the victims of love, you know. They don't exist solely to help you chart your way through the maze of other people's good—or bad—intentions toward you. No, like Jane Austen's novels, they are also supposed to help you take a good hard look at your own behavior and work out what you're doing wrong. And in this case, what we're looking at is your potential bad behavior toward other people. Have you ever flirted with someone to make somebody else jealous? And has it ever backfired in ways you couldn't have imagined?

Darla and John met through mutual friends and often hung out in a large group. They were definitely attracted to each other, and would flirt when they found themselves sitting next to each other, but John never asked Darla out. This was because Darla loved to flirt; to John, it seemed that she behaved the same way with every man she talked to. John never felt that Darla considered him at all "special"—he thought she treated him exactly the same as she did everyone else.

And Darla felt the same way about John. She liked him a lot, but he was so easygoing and flirty with all the girls that she never thought of taking things to a more serious level with him. She thought he wasn't any more attracted to her than he was to the rest of the girls in the group.

One evening, John ended up giving a few people a lift home, and Darla was the last person he dropped off. She invited him in for coffee, and, rather to their surprise, they ended up making out. They were due to meet at a party at a mutual friend's house the next day, so they left things awkwardly, saying that they would see each other there.

The problem here was the front they both put up. Darla and John considered themselves, and presented themselves to the world, as cool, fun-loving party animals: flirty, sexy, never showing their more serious feelings. Despite their having made a really nice connection that evening, both of them were stuck in their roles and their images of themselves. Neither of them wanted to break down their pride enough to admit that they actually liked the other and might have more serious emotions. They didn't know what to expect the evening of the party, so they both fell back into their flirty, devil-may-care personas. Darla got there first, and flirted heavily with a lot of guys, wanting to seem attractive and pursued by men when John arrived. John gave a ride to a friend of his, so Darla saw him arriving at the party with another woman. He wasn't at all sexually interested in her, but it gave completely the wrong signal to Darla. He did come over and try to talk to Darla, but she gathered her posse of men around her and treated him as lightly as she did the rest of them. John was put off by this and retreated. Both of them had so much pride that they didn't make an effort to reach out to each other. John decided to leave the party, but he went up to Darla and told her he was going, in a final attempt to engage with her. Darla wrapped her arm around another man and said good-bye to John in the most casual voice she could muster. They were both unhappy and dissatisfied with how things had turned out, but they never managed to get together, despite the fact that they were very attracted to each other and could potentially have been a very good match. Like Frank Churchill, they played games with the opposite sex so much that they were unable to stop, even when it wasn't appropriate or necessary. Flirting had become a vice, instead of a pleasant social activity. And this was not the only potential relationship that John's and Darla's flirting nipped in the bud.

What to Do Instead: Take a Good Look at Your Own Behavior

When you flirt and lead people on, what you are really doing is trying to get everyone to like you. You feel insecure, and you need to have everyone around you interested and hanging on what you may say next as a way of reassuring yourself about your own attractiveness. You may even feel that you will disappear, become invisible, if you're not constantly the center of attention. This is exactly how Frank Churchill behaves; he always needs to be the one that people are looking at, the one who organizes the action, the one who's essential to making any party go with a swing. If you act like Frank, you seem very confident, and people are often jealous of your social security. If they only knew that it was exactly the opposite, that you need to pump yourself up to generate enough energy to continually put out this flirty, super-energetic behavior, and you secretly feel that people won't like or want to be around you if you're not in full form that evening.

If you recognize yourself in this description, you need to pull back. Because if you are really looking for a serious relationship, flirting and trying to mentally seduce most people you meet is not the way to do it. You will attract a lot of casual hookups, but you won't meet the serious, more emotionally honest person with whom you could really build a relationship.

Georgie always had lots of wild stories to relate to her more settled friends. She'd meet a gorgeous guy ten years younger than her at a party, take him home, and have a crazy night of animal sex with him. She always had men chasing after her in bars and at parties. On holiday she even hooked up with the masseur at the spa she was staying at, and had a passionate weekend affair with him. Her friends got a real buzz out of Georgie's stories. But they gradually realized that she never seemed to meet anyone with whom she could have a serious relationship—which is really what she was looking for. If all Georgie wanted was to go on that way—having a wonderful, sexually free time with a series of young studs—she'd be in heaven. But any time she met someone more serious, she didn't connect with him—she didn't think he was fun or wild enough for her.

Georgie was addicted to the conquest and the buzz she got seducing men with her wit and her charm. It was a high-octane
charge. But, like most addictions, it was hard to give up. Georgie
was living on a constant fizz of flirtation and seduction, and it was
difficult for her to slow down and appreciate the more steady and
long-term attraction of a man who wasn't just going for a quick
pickup. It was like being addicted to fast food, with its instant
availability and all the chemicals it's pumped with, rather than
slowing down and eating food that's better for you, cooked more
slowly, and that takes more time to prepare. Georgie needed to
deliberately ignore all the men like her—the ones who loved to
flirt, who turned their seduction abilities on like flicking a switch,
who were looking for a quick fix to prove to themselves that they
were attractive.

The key word here is "prove." Georgie wanted to impress her
married friends with her constant ability to pull men. But her
friends, and the men she met, *already knew* that she was attractive.
She needed to believe in herself and take the time to trust herself—
and deliberately resist the temptation to flirt with men who, like
herself, were after a quick fling. One of Georgie's friends once told
her to look for the quiet guy at the back of the room, rather than
the flashy type sitting up front at the bar. At the time, Georgie
laughed it off, but it was very good advice. And a month later, on
one of her bar crawls, she started talking to a sexy guy. It turned
out, however, that he had a steady girlfriend, and had struck up a
conversation with her because his friend thought she was gorgeous
but was too shy to approach her. He introduced his friend, Mike,
and the three of them hung out at the bar. After an hour or so,
Georgie realized that she had been talking to Mike for almost the
entire time; his sexy friend had been withdrawing from the conversation to give Mike a chance, and when he said he was leaving,
Georgie barely noticed. Mike, though initially shy, was so much

fun and asked Georgie so many questions about herself that she had really opened up to him. Georgie was amazed by what a good time she was having with Mike, who though nice-looking and friendly, wasn't by any means the kind of stud she usually dated.

Mike ended up walking Georgie home and asking for her number. He didn't try to kiss her good night, let alone jump on her, and that made Georgie surprisingly insecure. She was so used to quick hookups and seeing her value in sexual terms that Mike's making it clear that he wasn't pushing for an instant night of passion made her feel vulnerable. Mike called her two days later, and they arranged to meet. Georgie told herself that it didn't mean anything that she was going on a date with Mike; she'd liked his company, but that was all. She was scared of getting involved with someone on a more serious basis; deep down, she felt that men were interested in her only because they wanted to have sex with her, not because they wanted to get to know her as a person.

Mike and Georgie's date went really well, and again, Mike walked her home. This time he gave her a kiss on the cheek and said he would call her soon. It took three dates before Mike kissed her properly, and Georgie was incredibly relieved. She immediately invited him to come into her apartment. But Mike said no—he told her he wanted to take things slowly.

This was so unusual for Georgie that she didn't know how to react. And yet, despite the insecurity Mike's behavior provoked in her—because if a man didn't want to have sex with her straightaway, that must mean he was interested in a more serious relationship, and Georgie wasn't sure she knew how to do that—something kept making her agree to go on successive dates with him. By the time they did have sex, the buildup had been great, and Georgie realized she had serious feelings for Mike, something she had always avoided. This made her panic, which bewildered Mike. He told her he was serious about her, too, and what they were doing was his normal behavior—he wanted to get to know a girl first, and then have sex with her when they were ready. Gently and decisively, he reassured Georgie without scaring her by rushing her too much. He showed her that having a relationship wasn't as frightening as she had always thought—that the more he got to know her, the more he liked her. Gradually Georgie conquered her anxiety and began to relax into the reality of having a relationship. She realized that she didn't want to see other men; she appreciated the stability and security that Mike gave her. Mike was like a stealth missile who had sneaked up on Georgie's blind side. She managed not to talk about her feelings of panic to him, letting off steam instead to her friends, who were very happy to see her dealing with a relationship and offered her a lot of support. Georgie and Mike have been seeing each other exclusively for more than six months, and to her great surprise, she's never been so happy. Mike has managed to convert a party girl into a serious girlfriend.

HENRY CRAWFORD

Mr Crawford did not mean to be in any danger; the Miss
Bertrams were worth pleasing, and were ready to be pleased;
and he began with no object but of making them like him.
He did not want them to die of love; but with sense and
temper which ought to have made him judge and feel
better, he allowed himself great latitude on such points.
—MANSFIELD PARK

Naughty, naughty Henry Crawford. Like Willoughby, he comes down into the country to visit his aunt, finds two pretty girls, Julia and Maria Bertram, at the house next door, and decides to while away the time by flirting desperately with them—and, yes, making them fall in love with him if he can manage it. He has absolutely no serious intentions toward either of them and he doesn't care that Maria is engaged to be married; in fact, he flirts harder with her, because he feels himself to be safer. "I like her the better [for being engaged]," he says of Maria. "An engaged woman is always more agreeable than a disengaged . . . All is safe with a lady engaged; no harm can be done."

Henry tells Maria repeatedly how sad he is that she is getting married, and hints heavily at his regret that he didn't meet her before her engagement. He does everything he can to convince her that he has serious feelings for her. Maria is ready to break off her engagement for Henry, if he would only give her a sign that that's what he wants. But Henry, very accomplished at playing the game, manages to stay just the right side of the line, enjoying himself without ever quite going so far as to encourage Maria to break her engagement, while messing with her head as much as he possibly can. She is better prey for him; as he says, she's "safer." He can push the game further with her, because she is already committed to someone else.

Henry's behavior is so appalling that we are very happy when he gets his just deserts. After Maria has reluctantly married her boring fiancé, and Julia has left with her for the wedding trip, Henry realizes that he is actually in love with Maria and Julia's quiet little cousin Fanny Price. Henry's attraction to Fanny begins when he sees that she seems immune to his easy charm; he is titillated by the prospect of making a new, more difficult conquest.

"I will not do [Fanny] any harm, dear little soul!" he tells his sister. "I only want her to look kindly on me, to give me smiles as well as blushes . . . to think as I think, be interested in all my possessions and pleasures, try to keep me longer at Mansfield, and feel when I go away that she shall never be happy again. I want nothing more."

If we needed any further proof of Henry's character, here it is. This is the moment we realize what a nasty piece of work Henry truly is. Toying with Julia and Maria was bad enough, but they were at least more equal adversaries. They are rich, confident, and secure. Fanny, on the other hand, is a poor relation, ignored by most of her family, with no confidants but Edmund. Unlike Julia and Maria, she is quiet, shy, and capable of deep feeling. Leading her on and then dumping her would do her really serious damage. But, to Henry's great surprise, in the process of trying to win Fanny over, he becomes sincerely attached to her, and for the first time in his life, proposes marriage.

Of course, Henry is very keen on the chase; what better challenge than to convince a woman who doesn't like you much that she actually wants to marry you? And he loves, too, the idea of playing King Cophetua to her penniless beggar maid.

Fanny might possibly have agreed to marry Henry under other circumstances, particularly because she thinks that the man she really loves, Edmund, is about to propose to Henry's sister. But she is completely put off by Henry's previous bad behavior with the Bertram sisters, which she has witnessed. She just won't believe that Henry is sincere about her. And her instincts are right. While courting her, Henry is continuing his flirtation with the now-married Maria, and ends up by running off with her, frustrated by Fanny's repeated rejection of him. Henry loses Fanny, the woman who might have actually settled him down and reformed him. He ruins Maria for life and does great damage to his own reputation in the process. In leading Maria on, he gets much more than he bargained for—and it's all bad.

```
LESSON TO BE LEARNED

DON'T BE FLATTERED BY TOXIC FLIRTS
```

What Not to Do: Don't Be Taken In by Hype

Henry brings his fate on himself. No wonder a sensible, sincere woman like Fanny won't go anywhere near him—because he just can't stop trying to seduce every woman he meets. Henry takes up with Maria again, once she's married, precisely because she snubs him: "He was received by [Maria] with a coldness which ought to have been repulsive, and have established apparent indifference between them for ever; but he was mortified, he could not bear to be thrown off by the woman whose smiles had been so wholly at his command; he must exert himself to subdue so proud a display of resentment . . . He was entangled by his own vanity, with as little excuse of love as possible."

"Vanity" is the key word in all of this. Henry, like Georgie in the second example, is absolutely addicted to feeding his self-image. Everyone has to be in love with him, even the women he doesn't really want. As a result, he gets everyone *but* the woman he really wants.

It's like being a compulsive eater. They continually stuff food down their throats without really enjoying any of it; compulsive eaters, even while gorging on one kind of food, are always looking anxiously toward their next fix. They can never stop long enough to enjoy the moment, because they are in the grip of their compulsion. If Henry were a modern character, he would be diagnosed with sexual addiction. He seems to be in control, but actually he is driven by forces over which he has no power.

Jane Austen gives us a clear psychological explanation of

why Henry is like this: his parents died young, and he was brought up, together with his sister, by a widowed uncle whose morals were bad, whose vices were legion, and who was obviously unable to express love to either of his wards, who were damaged by their upbringing. Henry looks for love everywhere, voraciously tearing through his victims, but can't stop to enjoy it once he has it. He only values the women who don't love him, because he throws all his energy into winning them over. And once he has, he discards them the way compulsive eaters throw away the fast-food wrappings or the empty box that contained their latest binge food, disgusted with themselves and with the food they've just eaten.

It's really not difficult to spot a Henry, or a Georgie, or a Willoughby, or even a Frank Churchill. They will be the people who seem interested in you way beyond anything they actually know about you. They will pay you elaborate compliments, laugh at all your jokes, and seem to focus all their attention on you before they even know what you're like as a person—and they will never bother to find out what you're like as a person, because they don't care. They will concentrate all of their considerable talents on praising your superficial qualities. If they do have a deep conversation with you, they will probably have forgotten most of the details by the next morning. They don't really want to know about you; all they want is to seduce you into liking them.

Look at that last quote about Henry. Jane Austen really nailed him. He had once had Maria's "smiles . . . wholly at his command," and he couldn't bear that she had slipped away from his control; he had to win her back. That's not treating Maria as a person, but as a toy, a doll, whose buttons only he knows how to press. There's a degree of the sociopath in Henry, as there is with all the Henrys of this world. We have probably all been victims of people like this, people who have made us feel as if they just rolled over us with a tank, people about whom we have said to our friends, amazed: "But he seemed so into me two days ago! And now he behaves like I don't even exist!"

This is the single best way to spot a Henry Crawford: he will rush you. Henrys, like all addicts, need their quick fix of adulation, and they're in a hurry for it. If you feel swept off your feet, hurried into something before you can catch your breath, by someone who seems too good to be true—someone who, if you think about it honestly, you realize doesn't really know that much about you, certainly not enough to be sure that you're the one for him, despite the fact that he's saying that you are—you are in the grip of a Henry. And it's very easy to test this out. Tell him to slow right down. If he's not a Henry, he will. But if he is . . . you won't see him for dust. Don't be seduced by someone who's rushing you and overpowering you with his charm. It will always end in tears.

What to Do Instead: Value Your Own Feelings

Don't let your own vanity make you weak and vulnerable. That's what makes people prey to a Henry Crawford. They are so flattered by the attentions of a charming person who, for a few brief hours or days, is focusing all their concentration on them, that they fall like dominoes.

Don't even think about getting a Henry to take you seriously. Even if you are the woman he really does fall for, it won't last. Despite the fact that Henry really loved Fanny, he couldn't even concentrate exclusively on Fanny long enough to seal the deal and marry her; he had to have his quick fix of Maria at the same time. And if he had managed to control himself, and waited long enough to court Fanny successfully and marry her? Well, Henry's sister,

Mary, sums up his character very well, even if she's trying to reassure Fanny at the time: "[Henry's] fault," Mary says, "the liking to make girls a little in love with him, is not half so dangerous to a wife's happiness, as a tendency to fall in love himself, which he has never been addicted to."

Even if Henry doesn't fall in love with the girls he flirts with, what a prospect for a wife! If you manage to hold out and get a Henry to the altar, you'll be condemned to a lifetime of watching him flirt madly with women at parties, and watching his victims chase after him. I would hardly wish that future on my worst enemy.

So what should you do about a Henry? If you really think you could care about him, you have to avoid him like the plague, because he will be very dangerous to you. As we've seen, he's not that difficult to spot. But if you're just looking for a good time—and you honestly think you won't get emotionally involved—a Henry is also very good for a brief affair. He's a holiday romance, a quick fillip if you're having a boring time, a rocking one-night stand. If you truly think that you're not going to fall for a Henry, if you know yourself well enough to feel that you'll be safe, by all means have a fling with him. But for God's sake don't do it because you're trying to play his game—because you think that having a fling with a Henry and discarding him first will make him interested in you. The likelihood is that it won't work. And even if it does, you'll be trapped in an ever-increasing sequence of game-playing that will get you in deep and break your heart, because a Henry will always win. Only if you are perfectly sure that all you're looking for is a quick fling with him should you let yourself fall. And if that's the case, by all means go for it. You'll probably have a lot of fun! But remember—it won't lead anywhere but that quick good time, and if you're reading this book, that's not what you're looking for.

SUMMARY

Do

- *Have fun!* Flirt, get out there, meet new people, enjoy yourself. But also control yourself—use your flirting skills with tact and discretion. Remember, one of the previous rules was to be discriminating.

- *Be on your guard* for people who are trying to play you. Keep your eyes open and don't give away too much of yourself too soon.

- *Use your flirting skills* as a way to get to know people, not as an end in themselves.

Don't

- *Be a toxic flirt, addicted to leading people on.* Like all addictions, it will take you over. You'll end up messing up other people—and yourself.

- *Flirt to get attention and flattery.* You need to get your self-esteem from within yourself, not from other people who don't know the real you.

- *Assume that playing games is the way to a man's heart.* Don't try to make him jealous by flirting with other men, or pretending that you don't remember him when he calls, or telling him that you're busy for the next two weeks to make yourself seem busy and popular—in the end, a nice man will take these indicators as a snub and will be less encouraged to ring you again, which isn't what you want!

❖   ❖   ❖   ❖

Tips for Spotting a Toxic Flirt

- ❖ He is all over you from the first moment he meets you, even before you've exchanged two words.

- ❖ He asks you very little about yourself and your life, preferring to flirt wildly instead.

- ❖ His banter is sexually charged and he pays you lots of exaggerated compliments.

- ❖ He is often very physical with you, touching you almost immediately.

- ❖ If you're out with friends, he tries to separate you from the group instead of joining it and getting to know the people you're with.

- ❖ He asks for your number as soon as he can, and may suggest that the two of you go to a late-night bar that same evening, where he will try to make out with you.

- ❖ He puts pressure on you to have sex with him the first time you go out.

FOUR

HAVE FAITH IN YOUR
OWN INSTINCTS

Had Edward been intentionally deceiving her? Had he
feigned a regard for her which he did not feel? . . .
No . . . his affection was all her own. She could not be
deceived in that . . . It was not an illusion of her own
vanity. He certainly loved her.

—*SENSE AND SENSIBILITY*

YOU CAN READ ALL the dating books in the
world, ring your friends every half hour for in-depth
analyses of what's going on with the man you're seeing,
and spend the rest of the time reading the e-mails he's
sent you and trying to work out what kind of messages
he's conveying to you through his choice of words and

how he signs off. But in the end, there's one thing you have to rely on more than all of these indications, or you'll never manage to work out how you're really feeling. What are your own instincts telling you? When you put your own insecurities aside, is he making you feel secure and cherished, or keeping you off balance? Is he the kind of person you really want to be dating, or are you only seeing him because you're afraid of being alone? Are the two of you really compatible, and is he meeting your needs and making you feel that you are meeting his? If you don't learn to trust your own instincts, you will never be able to answer the most important questions of all.

ELINOR DASHWOOD AND EDWARD FERRARS

*Elinor remained . . . well assured within herself of being
really beloved by Edward. . . .*
—SENSE AND SENSIBILITY

Elinor Dashwood, one of the two heroines of *Sense and Sensibility*, is in love, almost from the beginning of the book, with Edward Ferrars, the brother of her awful sister-in-law, Fanny. Edward is a quiet, shy, unassuming, and inexperienced young man, who years before was enticed into a secret engagement with Lucy Steele, the niece of his tutor at a private school in Plymouth. Edward has known for some time that he isn't in love with Lucy, but out of a sense of duty feels honor-bound to maintain the engagement, despite the fact that he has fallen in love with Elinor, who in every way is much more suitable for him. When Elinor meets Lucy, she can see immediately that Lucy isn't remotely in love with Edward, but she understands instinctively that Edward's sense of honor will lead him to be true to his previous promise of marriage; he is incapable of being dishonorable enough to break the engagement, and he is also too noble to see that Lucy has no genuine feelings for him. Lucy's only wish is to marry a man—any man—whom she thinks will have a sufficient income to enable her to live in the style to which she wishes to become accustomed.

All Elinor can do, therefore, is sit still and wait, with no hopes for the future. She is tormented by Lucy, who senses that Elinor is her rival and does everything she can to blight Elinor's hopes by rubbing in the fact that she, Lucy, is secretly engaged to Edward. Lucy, in fact, is always scheming; she smarms up to Fanny and then reveals the engagement to her. Fanny reacts very badly and rushes off to tell her mother about the engagement. Shocked by the news that Edward is engaged to a penniless girl of poor family, their mother immediately settles a large sum of money on Robert, Edward's younger brother—money that should by rights have gone to Edward, as the elder son.

Ironically, this has the effect of freeing Edward from Lucy's clutches. Lucy elopes with the now-rich Robert, rather than tying herself to the penniless Edward. Edward, a clergyman, is given a small country living by Colonel Brandon, who will end up marrying Elinor's sister Marianne; and as soon as Edward is free from Lucy, and with an income, though not large, that will enable him to support a wife, he shoots off to propose to Elinor, and they shortly become "one of the happiest couples in the world."

Throughout all these vicissitudes, Elinor maintains a quiet self-control, seeming as tranquil and composed as Marianne, suffering from Willoughby's betrayal, is hysterical and undisciplined. And what enables Elinor to keep her calm? Her faith in herself and her own instincts. She knows that Edward loves her. Nothing can shake this belief, and she is right. Even though Edward is engaged to another woman, even though Elinor has no reason to believe that she and Edward will end up together, she keeps control of herself because she feels, rightly, that she knows the truth of the situation, and she takes strength from the fact that, even though her love may be hopeless, she knows herself to be loved. No one has succeeded in messing with or deceiving Elinor. She doesn't have anything to reproach herself with—and, even more important for her self-esteem, she never has to feel like a fool. Unlike Marianne, she has done nothing on impulse. She has waited and watched and regulated her behavior to that of the people around her; she's kept her calm and never let anyone throw her off balance. The only time Elinor breaks down is right at the end of the book, when Edward comes to tell her that Lucy has eloped with Robert, and he, Edward, is finally free: "[Elinor] almost ran out of the room, and as soon as the door was closed, burst into tears of joy, which at first she thought would never cease."

What relief we feel for Elinor, that she is at last free to express her feelings! She has done everything right through the entire book, and she completely deserves her reward: that, in the end, she can allow herself to give way to her deepest, truest emotions. No longer does she need to hold her feelings in and be careful.

LESSON TO BE LEARNED

TRUST YOURSELF

What Not to Do: Don't Let Your Insecurities Get the Better of You

Judy had always had a strand of insecurity to her personality. She never thought she was as pretty, as charming, as well-dressed, as smart as her older sister, Lynn. And neither did Lynn, who put Judy down every time she could, criticizing her looks, telling her she needed to lose weight, that her choice of clothes wasn't flattering, that her manner with men wasn't sufficiently alluring. When Judy went away to college, it was the first time in her life she was free from Lynn's put-downs, and she blossomed. She found a serious boyfriend, Rod, whom she adored. Rod loved Judy for who she was; they were extremely compatible and made each other very happy.

But then Judy brought Rod home for Thanksgiving, and everything started to fall apart. Lynn undermined Rod and Judy every chance she got. And Judy was very susceptible to Lynn's influence, as she had always been. Lynn made Judy feel that she wasn't good enough for Rod. She told Judy that she was worried that Judy might not have the personality or the looks to hold Rod for long. Lynn planted the seeds of concern, but it was Judy who took them back to college with her and watered them till they grew into flourishing plants.

Now, Judy was watching Rod with different eyes. She became very jealous of Rod's platonic girlfriends and of the time he spent apart from her. She took to calling him late and dropping in on him unexpectedly, to try to catch him out. She made him continually reassure her about her attractiveness, her intelligence, her charm—things for which Rod had always spontaneously praised her. But now that he was being forced to provide an endless stream of reassurances, he felt put on the spot, and no longer free to come out with the easy, instinctive compliments that he had always been more than happy to give her.

Rod and Judy's relationship swiftly went downhill. Judy turned into a nag who was incapable of being satisfied—the more support Rod gave her, the more she demanded. Nothing was ever enough. Lynn had made Judy feel so insecure that no amount of bolstering from Rod would fill the gaping hole in her ego. Which was exactly the reason Rod finally gave when, reluctantly, he broke up with her. He said that he still loved her, but that she had turned into a different girl from the one he had originally fallen in love with, and he just couldn't give her what she seemed to want and need.

Judy couldn't hear what Rod was saying. She blamed him for everything. But the saddest thing was that deep down, she knew he was right. Years later, when Judy had finally figured out how destructive Lynn was, Judy knew that everything Rod said had been true, and that some part of her had known it all along. She had allowed Lynn to mess with her and turn her into someone she wasn't. After the breakup with Rod, Judy dated a lot of other guys, but she has never met anyone she loves as much and is as good for her. If Judy had listened to her instincts, rather than her older sister, she would have seen clearly that Rod did love her, that he wasn't about to dump her for another girl, and that they had a good, strong relationship. Judy did eventually learn to trust herself, but it was too late for her and Rod—that well had been poisoned. Judy is still looking for a man who can give her what Rod did. And she wouldn't have lost that love if she had listened to the small voice of sense within her, rather than to someone she knew, instinctively, that she couldn't really trust.

What to Do Instead: Have Faith in Yourself

Like Lynn, Lucy Steele did her absolute best to mess with Elinor's head. And it was only Elinor's good sense and faith in her own instincts that kept her safe. But it's not just outsiders who can sabotage your relationship—sometimes it's your partner, too.

Sally and Derek had had a tempestuous five-year relationship. Almost as soon as they met, they fell passionately in love. They lived in different cities and had a long-distance relationship for the first year. Then Derek got a transfer to San Francisco, where Sally lived, and they moved in together. But neither of them was completely emotionally ready for a serious, committed relationship. Scared by the idea of commitment, Sally flirted with men and occasionally cheated on Derek. They would break up for a while, and Derek would try to date other women, but their feelings for each other were so strong that they always ended up getting back together.

Sally did a lot of hard thinking, and after several years, and a lot of therapy, she decided that she was no longer going to undermine their relationship. She told Derek that her cheating was in the past, and that she was totally committed to him. This provoked a lot of fear in Derek, who was used to their on-off relationship and couldn't deal with Sally giving up her wild ways. When away on an extended business trip, he started an affair with a work colleague and then moved out to be with her, announcing to Sally that their relationship was over; he was 100 percent in love with the new woman.

Derek was expecting Sally to cry, fight for him, pester him with phone calls, and try to make him jealous by embarking on an affair with another man. In short, he expected her to continue in their old pattern. But Sally, after the work she had done on herself, had learned to trust her instincts. She refused to fall into Derek's trap. Instead, she told him that she was setting him free: if what he wanted was this new woman, she wouldn't stand in his way.

Sally told all her friends that she was sure Derek would come back to her. She trusted in the deep love that was between them and that had always reunited them, no matter how badly they had treated each other. She wanted things to change, and she felt instinctively that Derek was having this affair as a way of punishing her for her own affairs in the past. This instinctive knowledge gave her the strength to hold firm, not to pester Derek, but to keep herself grounded. She went out with her friends, she kept herself busy, and she waited. Her friends were worried for her, but her strength and confidence never wavered.

Derek was incredibly impressed with Sally's maturity. He had been expecting her to throw scenes as she had in the past—threaten suicide, become hysterical, hang around his neck. But instead, she was behaving like a grown-up, and it made Derek want to be with her again. In the space of a mere month, he realized how much he missed Sally and how much he wanted to build a solid, adult relationship with her. Derek came back to Sally and within another month he proposed. They have been married for a year now, and they're happier than they've ever been. And it was all because Sally learned to have faith in herself, to reach for the strong, solid part of herself rather than the insecurity that had previously motivated her behavior, and to listen to her instincts.

FANNY PRICE

[Fanny] would not, could not believe that Mr Crawford's affection for her could distress him long; his mind was not of that sort. London would soon bring its cure . . . She could not . . . suppose that Mr Crawford's attachment would hold out for ever; she could not but imagine that steady, unceasing discouragement from herself would put an end to it in time.
—MANSFIELD PARK

As we have already seen in previous chapters, Henry Crawford leads on Fanny Price's cousins so badly that Fanny, a silent witness to his actions, forms such a bad opinion of him that when he turns his attentions to her, she rejects him out of hand.

"I cannot approve his character," she tells her cousin Edmund after Henry has proposed to her. "I have not thought well of him from the time of the play. I then saw him behaving, as it appeared to me, so very improperly and unfeelingly . . . so improperly by poor Mr Rushworth, not seeming to care how he exposed or hurt him, and paying attentions to my cousin Maria, which—in short, at the time of the play, I received an impression which will never be got over . . . I am persuaded that he does not think as he ought, on serious subjects."

Henry had been teasing Mr. Rushworth, Maria's fiancé, by flirting heavily with Maria before his eyes; and he had also been playing Maria's sister, Julia, off against her. Fanny is absolutely right to refuse to have anything to do with Henry after this, and it's extraordinary that Henry himself could not work out that his flirtations with Fanny's cousins might have anything to do with Fanny's rejection of him.

Despite the fact that Henry is attractive, charming, eligible, shares her interest in literature, and has actually proposed to her—something he never got close to doing with either of her cousins—Fanny is absolutely convinced that he is not the right man for her. She is already in love with Edmund, but even if she weren't, we don't believe for a moment that she would consider marrying Henry. She has observed his behavior over time and made a very negative judgment of him. Despite the encouragement from everyone around her—her uncle, Edmund, and Henry's sister, Mary—Fanny doesn't believe that a leopard can change its spots. She is sure that Henry is morally deficient, and she won't marry a man like that, no matter how keen he seems on her and how many material advantages he has. "If it were possible for me to do otherwise," she tells Edmund, "[I would accept Mr Crawford]; but I am so perfectly convinced that I could never make him happy, and that I should be miserable myself."

And Fanny, as always, is right. Henry can't and won't change. Under the "steady, unceasing discouragement" she duly gives him, he does indeed start looking around for diversions—because Henry, as Fanny has perceived, always needs to have somebody in love with him—and throws himself back into a flirtation with the now-married Maria, who runs away with him, destroying all his hopes of reforming himself by marrying Fanny. Fanny gets her Edmund in the end, the reward for holding true to her instincts and believing in them even when everyone around her is trying to get her to betray them.

LESSON TO BE LEARNED

KEEP YOUR BALANCE

What Not to Do: Don't Be Dependent on Your Boyfriends for Reassurance

Fanny Price is a quiet, shy girl, living in seclusion in a house in the country, who has never been out in society or met a man who treats her as an attractive woman. One would think, therefore, that she would be easy prey for a man like Henry Crawford, who is a world-class flirt and seducer.

But Fanny remains absolutely unaffected by Henry's attentions. She is grateful to him for a favor he does for her brother, but that's all. She has already decided that he's not the man for her, and she won't be swayed even when he directs the full beam of his charm and flattery onto her. (Ignore the recent movie of *Mansfield Park*, which has Henry kissing Fanny when he goes down to visit her in Portsmouth. This, and several other liberties it takes with the plot, makes it in many ways a complete travesty of the book.)

Unlike Fanny, Laura was a very pretty, clever girl with a lot of advantages. But, equally unlike Fanny, Laura didn't have a quiet confidence in herself and her own self-image. This is very common in women nowadays, when we are so bombarded with images of movie stars and pop singers with perfect, liposuctioned bodies. My grandmother could never understand the modern obsession with incessant dieting: "In my day," she would say firmly, "you were fat or thin or middling and that was just the way you were. And there was always a man who preferred women who looked like you, so there was absolutely no reason in the world to be silly about banting." (She came from Yorkshire, and "banting" was the local word for dieting.)

Laura, unfortunately, didn't have the benefit of my grandmother's sensible advice. It made her very susceptible to men who knew how to place a well-turned compliment. And these men are usually the ones of whom you have to be wary. Sadly, some things haven't changed since Jane Austen's time: the men who flatter women, the easy, charming, smooth ones, tend to be the Wickhams or Henry Crawfords or Willoughbys, the ones her heroines need at all costs to avoid. Real heroes are like Mr. Darcy, Mr. Knightley of *Emma,* or Captain Wentworth of *Persuasion,* who, when they court a woman, are often clumsy or overdirect, embarrassed by their own emotions and not practiced enough in courtship to control every word that comes out of their mouths. Honesty and truth often come in a less well-packaged guise than the smooth flatteries of the Henry Crawfords of this world.

This was something Laura had never learned. She was much too vulnerable to a good-looking man in a bar who would strike up a conversation by complimenting her eyes, her hair, or her skin. She blossomed under the flattery, not seeing it for what it was— a practiced maneuver designed to win her over with minimum effort. She would fall for one charmer after another whose only intention was to get her into bed as quickly as possible.

As every woman knows, it can be harder than pulling teeth to get a compliment out of your boyfriend. If you're lucky, he'll mumble that your dress looks nice or reassure you under duress that no, your bottom doesn't look too big in those trousers. It's a great disappointment for women, but it's one we have to learn to tolerate, and, hopefully, with time, you can train your boyfriend to realize that a spontaneous compliment from him every now and then will really make your day. If, like Laura, you are overdependent on reassurance from men, you are simply making yourself vulnerable to the worst kind of man—the kind who will spot this weakness and use it against you to get what he wants out of you.

What to Do Instead: Look to the Right Places for Positive Reinforcement

Who are the best people at giving you compliments about your looks and your clothes? Your best girlfriends and your gay male friends. These are the people you can really trust. We all love to hear how good we look, that people can tell that we've lost weight or toned up; it's the most natural human instinct, and not one we should be ashamed of. Even a mild dose of judicious flattery sometimes can do wonders for our egos. But sadly, straight men who try to sweep you off your feet with compliments are often only doing so because they know how vulnerable a woman is to that kind of attention.

Paula was attractive, well-dressed, and worked out regularly; she took a lot of care with her appearance. And when she met Dan in a bar, his opening line was to ask her about her exercise regime, complimenting her for being in such good shape. Paula was very flattered, and they started a conversation about the gyms they both went to. Dan went on to tell her how pretty she was, how sexy her shoes were, and various other things about her appearance that he really liked. Paula, naturally, lapped up the attention he was paying her, and though she tried to keep a level head, she couldn't help but be swayed by how intensely Dan was concentrating on her; he seemed to notice every detail about her—her hair, her eyes, the outfit she had carefully put together. Dan made Paula feel that she was the absolute center of his attention. He asked her out, and she was happy to give him her number.

Dan turned out to be very unreliable. He would cancel dates with her at the last minute—always with a very plausible excuse—and leave her hanging, waiting for a phone call he had promised that would come three days late. But whenever she met up with him, he was as intensely focused on her as he had been the first time they met, which made Paula think that he was really into her. Despite the stress and anxiety she went through waiting for him to call, when they did manage to get together on a date, Dan made her feel amazing: beautiful, desired, and very special. He had the knack of making every woman he went out with feel like this, and it was a very powerful force, because it was able to make Paula push to the back of her mind the fact that he was actually treating her badly.

If someone doesn't ring when he says he will, or makes excuses, or forgets plans you've made—not just once, but a few times—you should knock it on the head straightaway. Some people are insecure and nervous themselves, and provoke the same feeling in others—whether deliberately or unconsciously is immaterial. If you feel a degree of anxiety that seems excessive, you are probably dating someone like this, and the feeling will only get worse the longer you are together.

Dan had worked out a very successful strategy with women. He knew how insecure most of us are about our looks, and he played on that. The reassurance he gave Paula when he did go out with her was so strong and intense and seductive that every time she saw him, despite the fact that she meant to confront him about his unreliability, she was swept away again by the intensity of the compliments and the attention he was paying her.

Dan and Paula dated on and off for about three months. Paula knew in her heart that Dan wasn't going to be the man for her; his behavior never improved—there were regular last-minute rainchecks on their dates, and he rarely rang her when he said he would—but the way he treated her on the dates made her ignore this, believing instead that, because he was so extraordinarily attentive when he saw her, his actions would change when he eventually realized how much he liked her. Of course, it never happened that way. Dan stopped calling altogether, and Paula was devastated. She missed Dan terribly, but her real cause of upset was with herself. She knew that all along she had been deliberately blinding herself to Dan's bad qualities. If she had kept her balance, rather than allowing Dan to sweep her off her feet, she would have had the strength to decide that the way he treated her was unacceptable. Looking back, she could see that for three months she had been continually made unhappy by Dan's unreliability, living in a constant state of high anxiety and insecurity, desperate for him to call her and make her feel attractive. If Paula had trusted her instincts, rather than being motivated by her need for reassurance, she would have seen through Dan a lot sooner, and might even have summoned up the courage to dump him.

ANNE ELLIOT

"Mr Elliot is an exceedingly agreeable man,
and in many respects I think highly of him,"
said Anne; "but we should not suit."

—*PERSUASION*

Years before *Persuasion* starts, when Anne Elliot, its heroine, was only nineteen, she met Captain Wentworth and they fell very much in love. Captain Wentworth proposed, but Anne, much though she wanted to marry him, was persuaded against accepting him by her best friend and surrogate mother, Lady Russell, who felt that Anne could do better. Captain Wentworth, though ambitious and determined, was young and penniless, with no connections and no immediate prospects of making money. Lady Russell saw Anne either trapped in a long engagement, or married to a man who could not support her and the children they might have. Captain Wentworth went on to have a successful and prosperous career. After only a couple of years, he would have been amply able to support a wife. But, angered and discouraged by what he saw as Anne's lack of faith in him, he didn't come back to find her and renew his proposal of marriage.

As *Persuasion* begins, we meet Captain Wentworth again; by chance, he has come to visit his sister, who, with her husband, has rented Anne's family's house, Kellynch Hall. But Captain Wentworth is no longer interested in Anne, and she has to watch him courting and being courted by her two sisters-in-law, Henrietta and Louisa.

Anne, in turn, is courted by her cousin, Mr. Elliot. On paper, he seems the ideal man. Not only does he admire her greatly, he is good-looking, intelligent, and highly eligible—in fact, since he is the heir to her family home, marrying him would mean that on her father's death she would become Lady Elliot (since Mr. Elliot would inherit the family baronetcy), and return to the house where she grew up and which she loves, living next to Lady Russell and her sister Mary. Mr. Elliot seems ideal. Lady Russell (who always gives bad advice, despite having the best intentions) is determined that Anne should accept him when he proposes.

But Anne cannot bring herself to like Mr. Elliot enough to marry him. She finds him a little bit of a snob: "They did not always think alike. His value for rank and connexion she perceived to be greater than hers." Though she is tempted by the idea of becoming the mistress of her family home and following in her mother's footsteps, she rejects the idea of marrying Mr. Elliot to achieve this. She simply doesn't think well enough of his character. And Anne's judgment of Mr. Elliot is very subtle. He's not a drunk, or a loud-mouth, or a boor. "That he was a sensible man, an agreeable man,—that he talked well, professed good opinions, seemed to judge properly and as a man of principle,—this was all clear enough." And yet there is something about him that Anne doesn't trust. She follows her instincts: "She could not be satisfied that she really knew his character . . . She would have been afraid to an-swer for his conduct . . . He was not open . . . Mr Elliot was too generally agreeable."

On observing Mr. Elliot, Anne feels that he tries too hard to get along with everyone, even people she knows that he does not respect. He wants to be universally liked, and this is a quality that she finds unreliable. Anne's decision has been made: "She never could accept him." And Jane Austen is careful to add that this is be-cause Anne has judged Mr. Elliot on his own merits, and not just because she is still so in love with Captain Wentworth that she is blinded to the good qualities of any other suitor. "It was not only that [Anne's] feelings were still adverse to any man save one," Austen tells us. "Her judgement, on a serious consideration of the possibilities of such a case, was against Mr Elliot."

We will find out later what happens to Anne and Captain Wentworth. Suffice it to say for now that Anne's instincts with regard to Mr. Elliot are spot-on. He turns out to be a scheming manipulator, disloyal to old friends. Though genuinely interested in Anne, he was also playing a deep and complicated game to stop his uncle from marrying again and possibly breeding a male child who would supplant him in his right of succession to the baronetcy and inheritance of Kellynch Hall. If Anne had only trusted those good instincts of hers, rather than listening to her friend Lady Russell, and agreed to marry Captain Wentworth when he first proposed, she would have spared them both years of unhappiness and regret.

LESSON TO BE LEARNED

FRIENDS DON'T ALWAYS GIVE GOOD ADVICE

What Not to Do: Don't Keep Seeing Someone You Feel Is Wrong for You

When I was at college, I met Martin in my second year. He was handsome, funny, and really, really into me. He courted me very hard, asking me to dinner, leaving funny notes in my pigeonhole, making a real effort to get on with my friends and fit into my life. I was flattered by the attention, and I liked Martin a lot. But there was something about him, something I couldn't put my finger on, that made me think Martin wasn't the man for me.

On paper, he seemed perfect. He was serious and motivated; he shared a lot of my interests, he came from the same part of London as I did, and he was mad about me. I definitely felt attracted to him. But whenever he tried to kiss me at the end of the evening, for some reason I would move away. My friends couldn't see what the problem was. The girls told me I was lucky to have a guy like Martin so unequivocally serious about me, and the guys thought he was great company. When I was out with Martin and a group of my friends, I really enjoyed having him around. I could see that he would make a great boyfriend. But somehow, there wasn't that click in my head that I should have felt—that sensation that, yes, Martin was the One.

I thought that this was because Martin was rushing me, which he was. I asked him to slow down a bit and give me some breathing space. Martin didn't react very well to this, but he initially tried to do what I had asked. And yet, whenever we did go out, I realized that he was already treating me like his girlfriend, despite the fact that we hadn't even kissed properly yet. I didn't want to lead Martin on, but I was young and confused, and I probably strung him along longer than I should have. My friends were still telling me that Martin was the one for me, that I was just afraid of commitment. They said I needed to throw myself into the relationship and then I would realize how great it was. The friends who were coupled up wanted me to settle down with a nice guy; the single ones were jealous of how keen Martin was on me, and couldn't see why I would pass him up.

But I had doubts that I just couldn't get over. Finally, Martin came round to my room at about eleven one night. He said I was driving him crazy, that we needed to get past this, and he refused to leave, no matter how many times I asked him to go. And then, believe it or not, Martin got into my bed and wouldn't get out. I was too much of a wimp in those days to do what I should have done—go next door to the flat where three male friends of mine lived, and get them to throw him out. I was too embarrassed by the potential for gossip—I could see them telling the entire college that they'd had to throw a man out of my room at midnight.

So—and do remember I was only nineteen, fairly sheltered, and, obviously, a total idiot—what was my solution to this? I put on my longest nightie, tied it in a knot at the hem so his hands couldn't go wandering up my legs, and, in floods of tears, got into bed next to him and practically cried myself to sleep. When I woke up in the morning, Martin was gone, and I never saw him again. I knew that my instincts had been right. I had been correct to think that Martin wouldn't sexually assault me if he slept next to me, despite the fact that he didn't care how uncomfortable and upset his presence made me, and I also had been correct in thinking that Martin was definitely not the man for me. Under his pleasant and charming façade was a person who wouldn't take care of my needs or listen to me if what I wanted conflicted with what he wanted.

I've always remembered this story as a lesson to myself: if it doesn't feel right, it isn't right, not even if ten of your closest friends are telling you it is. Friends often tell you what they think you want to hear, not what they really believe.

What to Do Instead: Remember That You Know Your Relationship Better Than Your Friends Do

Let's go back to Sally and Derek, the couple we met earlier in this chapter. Every time Sally and Derek broke up—and in the course of their tumultuous five years of on-and-off cohabitation, they broke up a lot—they would immediately ring all their friends and cry on their shoulders. At first, their friends were sympathetic. They thought Sally and Derek were a great couple going through some teething problems, which they attributed to Sally and Derek's having got together so quickly. Their friends thought they had rushed each other too much at the beginning and were having natural difficulties settling into the relationship.

But after a year or so, their friends, understandably, became a lot less sympathetic. Sally and Derek's problems always seemed the same, and they weren't making any progress. After a while, their friends' advice changed, from "Hang on in there, you guys are a great couple, you just need to work at things" to "Are you sure you guys should actually be together? You seem to be hurting each other all the time. Maybe breaking up really is the right thing to do."

Frustratingly for their friends, Sally and Derek didn't listen to a word they said when the advice was to break up. Sally and Derek would cry on their shoulders when things were going badly, and then insist things were 100 percent fine when they were together again. Toward the end of their years of crises, many of Sally's and Derek's friends would just shout: "Jesus Christ, will you dump him (or her) already!" into the phone, and refuse to discuss their situation further.

But Sally and Derek paid no attention to this advice, sensible though it may have been. They knew instinctively that they were meant to be together, if only they could manage to find a way through the maze in which they had trapped themselves. Throughout all the pain, heartache, and betrayals, Sally and Derek never truly thought that they would ever be apart. They had a deep faith in their bond with each other—and, more important, a trust that it could be a healthy one, if they could only work through their issues.

Of course, this last point is crucial. If Sally and Derek had been hitting each other, using drugs, or engaging in really self-destructive behavior, they would have been in a death spiral, and their faith in their love would have been that of two people addicted not to a solid mutual love, but to the negative feelings they provoked in each other. Despite how much their infidelities hurt, Sally and Derek always felt instinctively that they were symptoms of a disease that could be cured, not a kind of behavior that fundamentally characterized their relationship. And in the end, they were right. They held on to their love and their instincts, and they are now, after all that suffering, a very solid, stable couple who are happily married, have bought a lovely house, and are planning to have a baby. They listened to themselves, not to their friends—who are now reconciled with them and very happy that Sally and Derek managed to work things out so successfully.

SUMMARY

Do

- *Listen to your own inner voice.* If a man looks great on paper, but there's simply something about him that doesn't work for you, don't force yourself against your instincts into dating him. It will never work out.

- *Learn to trust yourself.* If a man seems too good to be true, he probably is. Don't be so swayed by compliments or courtship that you deliberately blind yourself to faults of his that may mean the relationship has no future.

- *Keep yourself grounded.* What really happens when someone sweeps you off your feet? You lose your balance and he's still standing up. Is that what you want to happen at the start of a relationship?

Don't

- *Be overpersuaded by your friends.* You're the one who has to date him, not them. Of course, your friends will be right if they try to put you off an addict, cheater, or axe murderer. But don't be pushed into a relationship you don't feel is right for you just because your friends are keen on the person—and don't break up with someone you like and who treats you well because he doesn't immediately jell with your friends.

- *Be self-destructive.* Don't be so desperate for a relationship that you go against the healthy self-protective instincts that we all possess. Learn to listen to and be guided by them.

- *Be fooled by flattery.* Be wary of someone who tries to overwhelm you with compliments. How did he get to be so good at that? By doing the same thing with a lot of other people. You'll end up just another mark on his well-notched bedpost.

✧　✧　✧　✧

*Tips for Spotting a Man Who's Trying
to Reel You In and Then Dump You*

✦ He will keep you off balance by being unreliable—not calling when he says he will, canceling dates without much notice.

✦ He won't introduce you to his friends—he doesn't want you to feel the security of being part of his life.

✦ He will talk about things you can do together in the future that, however, somehow never materialize—if you bring them up, he will have an excuse as to why they're not possible right now.

✦ He will try to rush you into bed with him before you're ready—he may ask to come into your apartment every chance he gets, using an excuse like wanting a cup of coffee or to use your bathroom, hoping that he can seduce you once he gets you alone.

✦ He will try to make you feel that you have a special bond with him very quickly, when realistically you know that you haven't dated him long enough for one to have formed.

FIVE

DON'T FALL FOR
SUPERFICIAL QUALITIES

[Mr Bennet,] captivated by youth and beauty, and that
appearance of good humour, which youth and beauty
generally give, had married a woman whose weak
understanding and illiberal mind, had very early in their
marriage put an end to all real affection for her. Respect,
esteem, and confidence, had vanished for ever; and all his
views of domestic happiness were overthrown.

—*PRIDE AND PREJUDICE*

W E'VE ALL FALLEN FOR men because they're
drop-dead gorgeous, have tremendous athletic
talent, or have other standout qualities with which we
want to be associated. But when we do this, it's less about
being mad about them than it is about expressing our own
lack of self-esteem. Believing that we aren't beautiful, or

talented, or clever enough, we try to achieve these qualities by attaching ourselves to men who possess them, rather than working on improving ourselves. There aren't any shortcuts to making yourself feel better about your own worth. My first-ever boyfriend was incredibly handsome—he looked like the young Robert Mitchum—and being seen out with him made me feel like the most beautiful girl in the world. The only trouble was that he wasn't that bright, and I didn't actually have anything to say to him while we were out. We had nothing in common. Of course, you need to be physically attracted to the person you're dating! But it's just as important to have things in common, not just tastes but your aims and goals in life. And it's equally important that he makes you feel loved and reassured—and, in return, isn't treating you just like arm candy either.

JAMES MORLAND AND ISABELLA THORPE

[Isabella] saw herself . . . the envy of every valued old
friend . . . with a carriage at her command, a new name
on her tickets, and a brilliant exhibition of
hoop rings on her fingers.
—*NORTHANGER ABBEY*

James Morland, the brother of Catherine, the heroine of *Northanger Abbey*, proposes during the course of the book to pretty, flirty Isabella Thorpe. Isabella is the sister of his college friend John, and as the four young people spend time together in Bath, James falls in love with Isabella, who agrees to marry him. Catherine, who makes friends with Isabella in Bath, is too naïve at the beginning of their friendship to see the truth of Isabella's character: she's an awful,

self-absorbed man-chaser, incapable of feeling love and always on
the lookout for a rich husband. James, too, is utterly taken in by Isabella's flirtatious, teasing ways, completely failing to spot that she
has no concern for anyone but herself. If he had been a little older
and wiser (he's a college student when they meet), he would have
noticed, for instance, that Isabella, despite her professions of devo-
tion to Catherine, uses the latter like a prop in the games she plays.
One evening, for instance, Isabella leaves poor Catherine sitting hu-
miliatingly alone at a dance waiting for her partner, rather than
waiting with Catherine until the man scheduled to dance with her
turns up, as any good friend would do; the next day, she's trying to
bully Catherine into going out driving with her, James, and John, so
that she and James can be chaperoned by the other couple, even
though Isabella knows perfectly well that Catherine has a prior engagement to go out walking with Henry Tilney (the man Catherine
has a crush on) and his sister, Eleanor.

Isabella's wiles as she tries to persuade Catherine to dump
Henry and Eleanor should be manifestly obvious to James, who is
present the entire time. First she tries flattery: "She was sure her
dearest, sweetest Catherine would not seriously refuse such a tri-
fling request to a friend who loved her so dearly." When that
doesn't work, "Isabella then tried another method. She reproached
[Catherine] with having more affection for Miss Tilney, though she
had known her so little a while, than for her best and oldest friends;
with being grown cold and indifferent . . ."

Poor Catherine still manages to hold out under this pressure—
after all, she arranged to go out walking with the Tilneys before the
drive was even suggested—and Isabella brings out the big guns,
pretending to cry so that Catherine will give in: "Isabella . . . applied her handkerchief to her eyes; and [James] Morland, miserable
at such a sight, could not help saying, 'Nay, Catherine, I think you

cannot stand out any longer now. The sacrifice is not much; and to oblige such a friend—I shall think you quite unkind, if you still refuse.'" James is not only incapable of seeing what a bully Isabella is, he even ends up siding with her, putting extra pressure on Catherine. He is so swept away by Isabella's prettiness and charm that he cannot—or will not—perceive how selfish she is being in trying to convince Catherine to change her plans and do something she doesn't want to do. Throughout *Northanger Abbey*, Jane Austen contrasts his complete lack of perception with that of Henry Tilney, Catherine's lover, who is always clear-sighted and able to see through people's façades to their real selves.

Poor James pays dearly for his failure to take a step back and look at the behavior of the woman he loves. When Isabella finds out that his family is less rich than she thought, she reacts badly in Catherine's presence. She complains about how little James and Catherine's father can give them to live on, even though, as usual, she pretends that it's in James's interests rather than hers that she's upset: "It is not on my own account that I wish for more; but I cannot bear to be the means of injuring . . . [James], making him sit down upon an income hardly enough to find one in the common necessaries of life. For myself, it is nothing; I never think of myself."

If James and Catherine weren't so nice—and so naïve—they would see right through Isabella's hypocrisy; the truth is that all she ever thinks about is herself. Her true character becomes clear when Henry's older brother, Captain Tilney, a dashing army officer who is heir to the family estate, turns up in Bath. Isabella sets her sights on this rich and eligible prospect, and they immediately start a wild flirtation. Isabella, convinced that Captain Tilney will propose, dumps poor James, who finally realizes what has been going on.

"Her duplicity hurts me more than all," he writes to Catherine. "Till the very last, if I reasoned with her, she declared herself as much attached to me as ever, and laughed at my fears. I am ashamed to think how long I bore with it . . . "

Isabella gets her just deserts: Captain Tilney, who has just been amusing himself with her, never proposes, and though she does her best to get James back, he has finally seen through her and won't have anything to do with her. We can only hope that James has learned something from the experience, and that next time he meets a pretty, charming girl who pays him flattering attention, he will be able to observe how she treats the people around her and form his opinions about her real character, not the fake one she's showing him in order to win him over.

LESSON TO BE LEARNED

LOOK AT SOMEONE'S BEHAVIOR IN ITS ENTIRETY

What Not to Do: Don't Close Your Eyes to His Bad Behavior

Lesley had been dating Steven for several months. He seemed to be exactly what she had been looking for—funny, charming, with a great job. Steven was a workaholic, but made a real effort to shoehorn time for Lesley into his schedule, and though they couldn't see too much of each other during the week, he would take her away for romantic weekends and lavish attention on her.

Lesley was so happy that she had found a man like Steven that for some time she deliberately blinded herself to the fact that there were some parts of his behavior that she didn't like. Although Steven was always generous and open with her, he was rude and dismissive with many of the service staff with whom they came into contact. He openly and rudely criticized waiters, limo drivers, and the staff of the hotels they stayed in. It made Lesley increasingly uncomfortable and she tried to talk to Steven about it, but he dismissed her concerns. He said airily that he was paying these people a lot of money and he wanted good service in return—and he added that if he was hard on them, it was because he wanted everything to be perfect for Lesley.

Lesley found it hard to argue with this. She was flattered by the idea that Steven was so preoccupied with giving her the best time possible, and thus she was willing to ignore the fact that she found his attitude toward others—particularly people with less status than him—very unpleasant.

But after the honeymoon period was over, Lesley understood why she should have taken Steven's behavior to others more seriously. Gradually, once he felt more secure, Steven began to let his façade slip, and he started to criticize Lesley. It started with trivial things: Lesley didn't fold back the sections of the newspaper after she'd read them; she was wearing a perfume she knew he wasn't fond of; she was ten minutes late to dinner. At first Steven would point these things out in private, and Lesley would immediately apologize, saying that she hadn't realized they mattered to him. In the future, she would remember to fold the newspaper, wear a different perfume, and do her best to be on time. They seemed such tiny, unimportant things, and, after all, everyone had a few character flaws; she could handle Steven's being a little picky about minor details.

The situation, however, began to escalate. The things Steven was criticizing Lesley for remained fairly trivial, but now he was doing it in public. If she even ran five minutes late for dinner, despite her best efforts, he would bawl her out in front of the maitre d'. He would pick fights in the limo, walking past his doorman, in the street. At first, Lesley tried to calm him down, thinking that he was just feeling a little insecure about something she couldn't fathom. But the more she tried to pacify him, the worse it got. The final straw came when she and Steven were out with a group of her friends at an exhibition opening, and Steven loudly told her and one of her friends that their views on modern art were completely ill-informed. Lesley's friend was so offended that she walked away; Lesley was horrified that Steven had humiliated her and her friend like that. She took a look at the relationship and realized that the Steven she thought she was with was not the real person. She had only seen the mask and not the reality.

Lesley dumped Steven the same evening. She didn't want to be with someone who treated her that way. And she wanted children, and she could see what an appalling father Steven, with his hyper-critical behavior, would make.

Lesley could have spared herself months of distress—and that awful final scene—if she had taken a good hard look at Steven's behavior from the beginning of the relationship. Someone who is rude and dismissive to other people (particularly subordinates, or people whose jobs, being in the service industry, place them in a position of vulnerability) will always end up treating you the same way. If you find yourself making excuses for your partner along the lines of "I know he seems difficult in public, but he's always wonderful to me," you're in trouble. If James Morland had bothered to notice how Isabella was treating his sister, he would have seen the truth about her character. People can't sustain a façade for long, and they usually give you hints along the way about what's behind it.

What to Do Instead: Put His Flattery Aside When You're Sizing Him Up

Lucy knew she was a nice-looking girl, but nowhere near model status. Like practically all of us, she had some figure flaws she was insecure about, and she spent a lot of money on dermatologist-approved skin products, trying to clear up her occasional break-outs. So when she met Frank, a very good-looking man, she felt she was completely out of his league. Frank had been an athlete in college and as a result had not only a handsome face but a knockout body. She never thought for a moment that Frank would be attracted to her, so when she met him at a party and they got into a conversation in the kitchen, she just laughed and joked with him without trying to flirt or seduce him.

Lucy had a great sense of humor and a very sweet personality. Frank was very charmed by her, and also by the fact that she seemed so relaxed with him—he was used to women who were so smitten by his good looks that they couldn't just let go and have a nice relaxed conversation. Frank wasn't the best talker in the world—he was quite shy and reserved, and not particularly bright. But Lucy more than made up for it—she could chat to just about anyone, and she and Frank got on very well. She was very surprised when Frank asked for her number and rang her the next day to ask her out. And, obviously, she was hugely flattered.

Frank and Lucy started dating. Lucy found it hard to believe that a man as handsome as Frank was interested in her, and she was overwhelmed by her good luck. Going out with Frank made her feel incredibly attractive, and she loved the looks of jealousy other girls gave her—not to mention the reaction of her friends, who all congratulated her on having landed such a good-looking guy.

But after the initial amazement that Frank wanted to date her wore off, Lucy slowly began to see that she and Frank didn't have much in common. Frank wasn't the sharpest tool in the box, and he didn't have much to say for himself. Lucy continually had to bear the brunt of the conversation, and she felt that Frank was just sitting back a lot of the time and relying on her to do the work. Though she knew he liked her and wanted to go on seeing her, she felt that she had to "pay" for the privilege of dating Frank by being perpetually "up" and interesting. If she was tired one evening, and didn't have a lot to say, the date would sag; Frank wouldn't step up and be entertaining for her benefit. He had fallen for Lucy because she was so vivacious and funny, and he relied on that more and more, expecting Lucy to give him the liveliness he lacked.

Gradually the effect of Frank's good looks began to wane, and Lucy saw beyond them. Reluctantly, she had to accept that she and Frank weren't a good match, and she broke up with him. She found it hard—Frank was a nice, reliable man, and, of course, he was devastatingly handsome, which still had a big effect on her. But she knew that she couldn't ever love a man with whom she couldn't communicate properly.

ELIZABETH BENNET AND MR. WICKHAM

As to [Wickham's] real character, had information been
in her power, [Elizabeth] had never felt a wish of
enquiring. His countenance, voice, and manner, had
established him at once in the possession of every virtue.
She tried to recollect some instance of goodness, some
distinguished trait of integrity or benevolence . . . But
no such recollection befriended her. She could see him
instantly before her, in every charm of air and address;
but she could remember no more substantial good than
the general approbation of the neighbourhood . . .
—*PRIDE AND PREJUDICE*

Mr. Wickham is one of Jane Austen's great charmers. Arriving on the scene in *Pride and Prejudice*, he is introduced with the most flattering and lengthy description that Austen ever spends on a handsome young man: "[Wickham] wanted only regimentals to make him completely charming," she writes. "His appearance was greatly in his favour; he had all the best part of beauty, a fine countenance, a good figure, and very pleasing address . . . a happy readiness of conversation—a readiness at the same time perfectly correct and unassuming . . ."

Wickham wastes no time in choosing someone to flirt with, and his choice falls on Elizabeth, who can't help feeling gratified by his attention, and, naturally, even more likely to find him "completely charming," as Austen puts it. "Mr Wickham was the happy man towards whom almost every female eye was turned, and Elizabeth was the happy woman by whom he finally seated himself; and the agreeable manner in which he immediately fell into conversation, though it was only on its being a wet night . . . made her feel that the commonest, dullest, most threadbare topic might be rendered interesting by the skill of the speaker."

Wickham is implicitly being contrasted here with Mr. Darcy, who falls into silences, needs to be coaxed to talk, and is much harder work socially than the easygoing, chatty Wickham. As a result of his good looks and charm, everyone falls like a ton of bricks for Wickham—even Elizabeth's father, the sarcastic Mr. Bennet, can't help liking him. Wickham spins Elizabeth a hard-luck story the very first evening they talk. He tells her that he has been cruelly treated by Mr. Darcy—denied a legacy left him in Darcy's father's will—and Elizabeth is completely taken in. Wickham circulates the story around the neighborhood, which is all too ready to believe him; he is so handsome and plausible, after all, and Darcy is so haughty and tongue-tied. Austen makes it clear that one of the reasons everyone takes Wickham's side is precisely because he is so good-looking. Even Elizabeth's sister Jane, who isn't romantically interested in him, finds herself unable to "question the veracity of a young man of such amiable appearance as Wickham."

Elizabeth isn't completely swept away by Wickham's flirtatiousness. Her aunt is concerned that she may be falling for Wickham—which would be imprudent, as neither of them has any money to get married on—and Elizabeth reassures her that she isn't. "At present," she tells her aunt, "I am not in love with Mr Wickham; no, I certainly am not." She sees clearly that a marriage between them would be financially impossible, and does not blame Wickham when he starts courting another young woman, Miss King—who has a fortune of ten thousand pounds. "[Elizabeth's] heart had been but slightly touched, and her vanity was satisfied with believing that *she* would have been his only choice, had fortune permitted it."

Later in the book, of course, it turns out that Wickham is the villain of the story, and Mr. Darcy the hero. Wickham, far from being badly treated by Mr. Darcy, tried to elope with Darcy's sister when she was only fifteen—motivated rather by her thirty-thousand-pound fortune than by any attraction to underage girls, one hastens to add. The story of the legacy in the will is also false: Darcy's father left Wickham a living as a clergyman, but Wickham asked Darcy to give him a lump sum of cash instead, which Darcy did. In short, Wickham has not only behaved very badly, but added insult to injury by trying to cast Darcy as a selfish monster.

Elizabeth is shocked to hear this news. And yet, when she looks back, she is unable to think of any proof she has of Wickham's good character that will allow her to believe that he is incapable of such bad conduct (see the quotation that opens this section). Indeed, his behavior at the time absolutely belies his own stated intentions: "She remembered that he had boasted of having no fear of seeing Mr Darcy . . . yet he had avoided the Netherfield ball [where Darcy would be present] the very next week. She remembered also, that till [Darcy] had quitted the country, [Wickham] had told his story to no one but herself; but that after [Darcy's] re-

moval, it had been everywhere discussed; that he had then no re-
serves, no scruples, in sinking Mr Darcy's character, though he had
assured her that respect for [Darcy's] father, would always prevent
his exposing the son."

In short, Elizabeth instantly sees that all the clues to Wickham's
true character were always present, and that she—and everyone
else—was so blinded by his good looks and charm that she couldn't
read them correctly: "How differently did every thing now appear
in which he was concerned! His attentions to Miss King were now
the consequence of views solely and hatefully mercenary . . . His
behaviour to herself could now have no tolerable motive . . . [He]
had been gratifying his vanity by encouraging the preference which
she believed she had most incautiously shown."

And she realizes in retrospect that it was extraordinary of
Wickham to have confided such a personal story to her—a young
woman he barely knew—the very first time they met: "She was *now*
struck with the impropriety of such communications to a stranger,
and wondered it had escaped her before. She saw the indelicacy of
putting himself forward as he had done, and the inconsistency of his
professions with his conduct."

Wickham ends up showing his true colors by running off with
Elizabeth's sister Lydia, having no intention of marrying her. Mr.
Darcy has to save the day by bribing Wickham to do the right thing.
But if everyone who met Wickham could see beyond his charm and
handsome face, Wickham wouldn't be able to get away with half of
the bad things he does. It's as much the fault of the people he meets
that they are taken in as it is Wickham's.

> LESSON TO BE LEARNED
> _____
>
> DON'T FALL FOR FLASHY,
> CHARMING PEOPLE

What Not to Do: Don't Be Too Ready to Think You're Anything Special to a Player

The most important thing to remember about the Wickhams and Henry Crawfords of this world is that no matter how much they may be flattering and making a fuss about you, they are like that to *everyone:* the clerk in the grocery store, the bartender in their local hangout, even the teller at their bank. They can charm the birds out of the trees. It's their hobby, their raison d'être; it's meat and drink to them. Though they will make you feel special for the comparatively brief moment that you are enjoying the full beam of their attention, you *aren't* special to them except in that moment. You are just another target, another challenge to be won over.

So don't take it personally, one way or the other. By which I mean: don't be offended if, after devoting a lot of attention to you, they head off to charm someone else. It's just the way they're made.

Of course, there are some charmers who are actually capable of being serious. But you must take your time—a lot of time—to work out whether the one you've met is really, deep down, capable of a solid, monogamous relationship. He will have to pay you court consistently, for at least a month or two, for you to agree to date him. He must make you feel that you are the most important person in his life; even if he flirts with the waitstaff, or people at parties, you must be the one he comes back to and concentrates his attention on.

And, very important, you have to be the kind of person who isn't threatened by having a boyfriend whom everyone finds attractive. If you are at all lacking in confidence and need reassurance—and there's nothing wrong with that, unless you take it to an exaggerated level—this kind of man is never going to be the right person for you. His manner will trigger all your feelings of insecurity. You will keep demanding assurances from him, which in the beginning he will be willing to give but will quickly end up boring him. And, no matter how much he cares about you, he will start taking you at your own evaluation. If you keep insisting that you feel inferior compared to his outgoing personality, it will be hard for him, in the end, not to see you that way.

What to Do Instead: Learn from Your Mistakes

Even people as intelligent as Elizabeth are won over by Wickham's practiced charm. And Elizabeth, generally, has very good instincts: she turns down the proposal of marriage made by her cousin Mr. Collins, who, as the heir to her father's property, is certainly eligible. But Mr. Collins is a dead bore, and Elizabeth knows she won't be happy with him. More significant, she also rejects Darcy the first time he proposes, because his manner is so rude and insulting. Elizabeth consistently refuses to compromise her principles for the financial gain of a rich husband.

But with Wickham—even though she doesn't actually fall in love with him—she is much more vulnerable. Her head is turned by his handsomeness, his plausibility, and his attentions to her, and it takes her a long time to realize his true character.

If someone as sensible as Elizabeth can be swept away by a Wickham, we all can. And if it happens to us, we should just pick ourselves up, learn from our mistakes, and be wary of the warning signals when the next Wickham comes along. A Wickham wants to use his charm to get something from you that you would normally not be ready to give. In the case of their female targets, it's usually sex; with the male ones, it's usually money. There are of course exceptions to this rule—there are male Wickhams who exploit vulnerable women with an eye to their bank accounts, rather than their sexual favors—but in general it holds true. I could give many examples of Wickham-style behavior, but they're always so similar that they become generic: he's the man who charms the pants off women, literally, and then dumps them after he's got what he wanted. Basically, the bottom line is that if someone seems too good to be true . . . he probably is. If you must proceed with one, do it with extreme caution. But it's usually better not to get involved with him in the first place.

MR. AND MRS. BENNET; SIR WALTER AND LADY ELLIOT; MR. AND MRS. PALMER

[Sir Walter Elliot's] good looks and his rank had one fair
claim on his attachment; since to them he must have owed
a wife of very superior character to anything
deserved by his own.
—*PERSUASION*

During the time in which Jane Austen was writing, divorce was such a scandalous thing that it was to be undertaken only in the most extreme of circumstances—like Maria Rushworth's leaving her husband and running off with Henry Crawford, for instance. Once the ring was on your finger, you were in that marriage for life. And Austen's books are strewn with examples of couples who have married in haste and repented at leisure. Mr. and Mrs. Bennet, in *Pride and Prejudice,* are the prime example of this. She's too stupid and self-obsessed to understand her husband at all; decades of marriage have not helped her to work out his dry humor and know when he's joking. Mr. Bennet understands his wife all too well, and doesn't like what he sees—apart from when he's perversely entertained by her ridiculous behavior.

"To his wife he was very little otherwise indebted," Austen writes, "than as her ignorance and folly had contributed to his amusement. This is not the sort of happiness which a man would in general wish to owe to his wife; but where other powers of entertainment are wanting, the true philosopher will derive benefit from such as are given."

Austen demonstrates how much Mr. Bennet's disillusionment in his marriage—and his own bad judgment in picking a woman with whom he had so little in common—has damaged his character. Elizabeth, his most clear-sighted daughter, is all too aware of "the impropriety of her father's behaviour as a husband," the way he makes fun of his wife in front of their children. Elizabeth describes it as "that continual breach of conjugal obligation and decorum which, in exposing his wife to the contempt of her own children, was so highly reprehensible." In her opinion, her father's retreat into cynicism has made him unable to fulfill his parental responsibilities; he lets his sillier daughters run riot, amusing himself—just as with Mrs. Bennet—with their "ignorance and folly." Elizabeth feels his lack of fatherly duty very deeply, because the poor behavior of her sisters has damaged her and Jane's chances of making good marriages. "She had never felt so strongly . . . the disadvantages which must attend the children of so unsuitable a marriage, nor ever been so fully aware of the evils arising from so ill-judged a direction of [her father's] talents; talents which rightly used, might at least have preserved the respectability of his daughters, even if incapable of enlarging the mind of his wife."

In the following chapter we will look at a related rule—one that tells you to marry someone who will bring out your best qualities. Mr. Bennet, sadly, has married a woman who brings out his worst—his sarcasm, his cynicism, his withdrawal from the paternal duty of making sure his children are well brought up. And the reason for his mistake? He married a pretty young thing without bothering to notice first whether she had any character at all, and found out too late that, as Austen puts it, "she was a woman of mean understanding, little information, and uncertain temper."

Then there's Lady Elliot, Anne's deceased mother in *Persuasion*. "An excellent woman, sensible and amiable," Lady Elliot married her husband, Sir Walter, swept away by what Jane Austen describes as a "youthful infatuation." Why? Because of his good looks. "He had been remarkably handsome in his youth; and, at fifty-four, was still a very fine man." But that handsomeness is all he has to offer. Poor Lady Elliot saddled herself with a stupid, snobbish man of whom Austen writes: "Vanity was the beginning and end of [his] character."

Lady Elliot made the best of a bad situation, once she realized her mistake: "though not the very happiest being in the world herself, [she] found enough in her duties, her friends, and her children, to attach her to life . . ." While being impressed with her ability to look on the bright side and take pleasure in what life has to offer, her fate is definitely not one we would wish for ourselves.

And nor is that of Mr. Palmer, in *Sense and Sensibility*. He, too, has found after his marriage "that through some unaccountable bias in favour of beauty, he was the husband of a very silly woman." Mr. Palmer is grumpy and unsympathetic, but his wife's constant mindless prattling would be enough to make anyone curmudgeonly. Jane

Austen is constantly warning us that if we allow ourselves to be dazzled by the beauty of the person with whom we're infatuated, our judgment may be fatally impaired. Every one of her books contains an example of this rule—and an example, too, of the consequences of ignoring it.

LESSON TO BE LEARNED

BEAUTY FADES; CHARACTER DOESN'T

What Not to Do: Don't Date People Who Just Want You Because You Look Good

It's perfectly normal to be dazzled by someone's beauty. We all have this tendency: we fantasize about movie stars and pop singers, we gawp when we see someone on the street who looks like a model. And, as many studies have shown, attractive people get better treatment in life—higher-paid jobs and faster promotions, for instance. It's a universal prejudice, but a juvenile one, because beauty, of course, is only skin deep. And people who are attracted on a regular basis to those more beautiful than themselves tend to do so because they are filling a gap in their own insecurities—look, I'm dating someone gorgeous! My value is going up as a result! The TV show *Sex and the City* identified a type of man called the modelizer—a guy who hangs around fashion shows in the hopes of dating one model after another. And naturally, these are always men who are less attractive than the women they're chasing. They want to have a series of beautiful trophy girlfriends to impress others; they're not interested in the women's personalities, just in their outward appearances.

If you are regularly attracted to people who are more beautiful than you, you need to work on your own self-esteem rather than trying to find it through others. Remember, beautiful people have feelings, too! No one—except the most shallow, money-grubbing people, whom you wouldn't want to be involved with anyway—likes to think that people want them only because of the way they look.

I was at school with a girl who, at sixteen, was already a famous model. She was spectacularly beautiful—tall, blond, blue eyes, lissome figure, the works—and spectacularly shy. She was so nervous that people would want to be friends with her just because of her lifestyle and the way she looked that she hardly had any friends at all. I was in various classes with her for two years and she hardly said a word in all that time. She was actually, hard as it may seem to believe, quite embarrassed by her own beauty and the effect it had on others, and tried to downplay it as much as possible. Because of the way she looked, people would assume that she was stupid, which she hated, but her shyness prevented her from contradicting this. At parties I would watch guys hit on her—and of course every single guy in the room would try—and she turned them all down cold, because she was perfectly aware that all they were interested in was the way she looked, not what she was like as a person.

She ended up, to my great surprise, going out with someone who treated her pretty badly; he was rude and dismissive to her and would often neglect her at parties. But I gradually realized that, in her mind, the fact that he was rude to her meant that he wasn't dazzled by her beauty. She felt, God help her, that he was treating her like a "real person" because he wasn't following her around with his tongue hanging out, like all the other boys she knew. In her mind, the fact that he seemed relatively unaffected by how gorgeous she was—unaffected enough to ignore her or to talk to her curtly—meant that his affection for her was in some way more genuine. I don't know what happened to her after we left school, but I hope she learned that the two things were by no means connected.

I thought of her years later, when I met Camilla. Camilla's an absolute knockout, but she doesn't believe that she is. As a result, she's vulnerable to unscrupulous men. Her latest guy, Philip, picked her up in a bar by telling her that her hairstyle didn't suit her. Camilla, who doesn't have an ounce of excess fat, is continually at the gym, trying to lose nonexistent extra pounds, because Philip told her that he was worried she was getting plump. Philip is deliberately undermining her, because he's figured out that beautiful women are often very insecure, feeling that their whole attraction hangs on their looks rather than their other qualities. Camilla is so used to men paying her compliments—which she doesn't quite believe, because of her low self-esteem—that when Philip made that comment about her hair, she made the mistake of confusing rudeness with honesty. Since Philip keeps criticizing her, she thinks that he loves her for herself, and not for what she considers to be her flawed looks. She's so busy trying to please Philip that she never stops to ask herself what she's doing with someone who treats her so badly. And to keep this dynamic working, Philip needs to criticize Camilla more and more—he's worried that if he tells her how attractive he really finds her, she'll leave him, because what she was initially attracted to was his rudeness. Camilla's problem, ironically, is that the nice guys don't approach her—they're too intimidated by her beauty.

What to Do Instead: Allow Men Their Natural Nervousness on Your First Dates

When Zoe met Adam, he was in his local bar, surrounded by friends. He'd been drinking there for years, knew all the bartenders, and had a reputation as a big raconteur. He seemed incredibly confident and popular, and Zoe was very attracted to those qualities. Adam and Zoe got talking and hit it off, though they were continually interrupted by Adam's friends, making jokes, wanting Adam to entertain them with his funny stories and imitations (he was a gifted mimic).

Adam didn't ask Zoe out that evening, but he said that he was a regular at that bar and suggested she come back another night. Zoe did, and they got into a pattern of hanging out together and flirting, with Zoe getting to know all of Adam's friends. Zoe was waiting for Adam to ask her out, but after two weeks, he still hadn't done it. Zoe couldn't figure out why—he clearly liked her, was always happy to see her, bought her drinks, and made sure she had a seat next to him. Also, his friends were teasing him about her in her presence, and jokingly calling her "Adam's girlfriend," which he seemed happy about. So why wasn't he asking her out?

Finally, Zoe bit the bullet and suggested that she and Adam go to see a movie one night. Adam accepted, and they went out on a date. Quickly, Zoe understood why Adam hadn't had the nerve to ask her out before. He was so used to being the star of his group, the one who entertained everyone and was the life and soul of the party, that he was nervous and insecure when he found himself one-on-one with a woman, without his friends around him making him look good. The loud, boisterous, fun man she had met in the bar was surprisingly shy and quiet when alone with her, and a lot more tentative.

Zoe might well have decided that Adam wasn't the person she had thought he was and called it quits after that first date. But instead, she decided to give him more of a chance. She realized that the side of him she had seen in the bar would be pretty exhausting to live with twenty-four hours a day, and this quieter, shyer side was actually charming—because his nervousness demonstrated that he liked her a lot.

Zoe set herself to encouraging Adam and making him feel that he actually didn't have to be a perpetual entertainer. She showed him that she really enjoyed his company, and when he walked her home she stressed what a nice time she'd had, and then leaned into him, encouraging him to kiss her good night. Adam was sure that the date had been a failure—he was so used to thinking that unless he was talking all the time and making everyone laugh, he wasn't being a success—and was amazed when he found that Zoe was willing to kiss him good night, and go out with him again. Gradually, they dated more and more. Adam found himself calming down as a result when out with his friends—he felt he had less to prove now that Zoe was showing him that she liked him in his quieter moods, too. And he also became more ebullient when out with Zoe, as his confidence grew. By giving Adam a chance and getting to know the person underneath the façade, Zoe found the man for her; although she was initially attracted to Adam's more superficial, show-offy side, the person she fell in love with was the real Adam.

SUMMARY

Do

- *Look beneath the surface.* Just because he's pretty on the outside, he may not necessarily be pretty on the inside. Try not to be overly distracted by his good looks.

- *Check out how people treat others, not just you.* They may be good to you at first, but if they treat other people badly, that's how they'll end up behaving to you as well.

- *Cut your losses if necessary.* If someone initially dazzled you with his good looks and charm, but now you see beneath his façade and realize that the man underneath is not someone you can respect or have things in common with, don't stay with him just because the sexual attraction is still strong. It will never be the kind of relationship you're looking for—he will never change into the man you mistakenly thought he was.

Don't

- *Be fooled by charm.* I can't say this often enough—someone who's too good to be true probably is. Take time to get to know him, and be wary of a man who's presenting himself as perfect.

- *Date someone who's treating you like arm candy.* You'll know soon enough what his true motive is—he won't ask questions about your life, your interests, or anything that really defines you as a person, not just a pretty face.

- *Date someone because he has qualities you wish you had.* Being with someone more gorgeous, or charming, or extroverted than you can be very seductive. But if you're doing it because you think you're lacking in those qualities, it will only make you feel more insecure—because he has what you think you don't. Work on your own self-esteem instead, and don't try to artificially boost yourself through your boyfriend.

❖　　❖　　❖　　❖

Tips for Telling If a Man Is Only Using You as Arm Candy

✦ He regularly tells you that you should dress more sexily—miniskirts, high heels, revealing tops.

✦ He pressures you to go to the gym.

✦ He criticizes you if you order fries or any other fattening foods.

✦ He loves to show you off in public places and will keep his hand on you (on your arm or the small of your back) as he steers you around a room, indicating that you're his "property."

✦ He never shows much interest in your life or your work—the conversation tends to be all about him.

SIX

LOOK FOR SOMEONE
WHO CAN BRING OUT YOUR
BEST QUALITIES

A more equal match might have greatly improved
[Charles Musgrove]; and . . . a woman of real
understanding might have given more consequence to his
character, and more usefulness, rationality and elegance
to his habits and pursuits. As it was, he did nothing with
much zeal, but sport; and his time was otherwise trifled
away, without benefit from books, or any thing else.

PERSUASION

AMONG A CERTAIN GROUP of my friends, one
married couple is legendary for their fighting. No
one wants to go to their house, or hang out with them
except in a large group, because they squabble constantly
and nastily. It isn't anything like fun, playful banter—she
insults him for being lazy and boring, he calls her control-

ling and bitchy. And that's when they're just warming up. They have been together for seven years and have just had a baby—whom everyone who knows the parents pities profoundly. But they seem, if not happy together, to have found a balance that, in its awful, twisted way, works for them. It's not uncommon for people who come from families that fight incessantly to find partners with whom they can do the same. If not the most comfortable situation imaginable, it's at least familiar—and plenty of people settle for what they know, rather than make changes, which are always scary. Still, this couple, for whatever reason they've decided to stay with each other, are living a very unpleasant life. They're both bitter and perpetually complaining about the other. Instead of having found a partner to help them become the best people possible, they've managed to find the exact opposite. Don't follow their example!

MARY AND CHARLES MUSGROVE

"Mary is good-natured enough in many respects . . .
but she does sometimes provoke me excessively,
by her nonsense."
—*PERSUASION*

The Musgroves, of *Persuasion*, don't have the worst marriage in the world. They get along reasonably well, all things considered, with money and time enough to indulge their interests. Charles likes hunting and shooting, and Mary has her hypochondria and her perpetual complaints to keep her busy. But they're not a particularly well-matched couple. Charles is good-natured and easygoing, if a little selfish; Mary is the worse of the two, snobbish, unkind, and self-absorbed. The quotation at the start of this chapter illustrates all too clearly Jane Austen's view of the Musgroves' marriage. Charles is capable of being a better person, but his marriage to Mary has trapped him in a perpetual boyhood, with little sense of responsibility and little hope of becoming a man in any meaningful sense of the word.

Charles originally proposed to Mary's sister Anne, the heroine of the book. But Anne rejected him, being still in love with Captain Wentworth, her ex. Austen indicates that Anne would have been an ideal wife for Charles—and, indeed, his family feels the same way. Charles's sister Louisa even tells Captain Wentworth as much: "We do so wish that Charles had married Anne instead . . . I wish she had accepted him. We should all have liked her a great deal better . . ."

Charles isn't still carrying a torch for Anne. Any disappointment he felt has long since evaporated, and he has settled down well enough with Mary. He's even, in Anne's opinion, fairly heroic in his tolerance for Mary's annoying ways: "He had very good spirits, which never seemed much affected by his wife's occasional lowness; bore with her unreasonableness sometimes to Anne's admiration; and, upon the whole, though there was very often a little disagreement . . . they might pass for a happy couple."

Mary, on the other hand, is very hard work. She needs constant attention and fuss to make her happy: "While . . . properly attended to, she had great good humour and excellent spirits; but . . . inheriting a considerable share of [her family's] self-importance, was very prone to add to every other distress that of fancying herself neglected and ill-used." She is constantly complaining about every little thing, and is rude and dismissive to Anne. When Mary and Charles's son has an accident and dislocates his collarbone, Mary fights with Charles about which one of them should go to the dinner party they have been invited to that evening.

Charles declares that he will go, and Mary then manages to bully Anne into staying with the child so that Mary can attend the dinner party without guilt. "I am more unfit than any body else to be about the child," she tells Anne. "My being the mother is the very reason why my feelings should not be tried. I am not at all equal to it . . . You, who have not a mother's feelings, are a great deal the properest person."

Charles, who is basically much nicer than Mary, protests to her: "This is very kind of Anne . . . but it seems rather hard that she should be left at home by herself to nurse our sick child." Anne, who has her own reasons for not wanting to go out, convinces him that she is happy with the arrangement. But we can see from this episode that Charles's instincts are better than Mary's. If he had been married to Anne, or someone like her—free from Mary's snobbery, lack of maternal instincts, and self-indulgence—he would have been a significantly better person. As it is, Mary's self-ishness has correspondingly encouraged his own innate self-centeredness, and he has ceded to it instead of struggling not to let it get the better of him. Mary is irredeemable, but Charles's poor choice for a wife has done his own character no favors.

LESSON TO BE LEARNED

DON'T BE INFECTED BY THE BAD QUALITIES
OF THE PERSON YOU'RE DATING

What Not to Do: Don't Duplicate Each Other's Faults

Brad's new girlfriend, Louise, was a slob. When they first met, Louise seemed well put together; she was nicely dressed and made up. Brad was taken aback by the state of her apartment, however, the first time Louise invited him round. It was unbelievably messy. There were clothes strewn everywhere, half-full coffee cups on every available surface, open magazines on the floor, dirty dishes stacked in the kitchen sink, and the bathroom was none too clean. Brad didn't mind this too much—as a man who was used to being nagged by his girlfriends because his place wasn't tidy enough, he actually found the chaos in Louise's apartment reassuring. Here was a girl who would never complain if he didn't wash up the dishes straight after they'd eaten.

But as Brad and Louise became a couple and spent more and more time together, Brad became increasingly affected by Louise's cavalier attitude toward tidiness. He had always made token efforts to straighten up, but now he didn't really bother; Louise never noticed. If his couch was covered with stuff, she would just shove it onto the floor so there was room for her to sit down. Louise was effectively giving Brad permission to indulge his own inner slob.

After a year or so, Brad and Louise moved in together. Their apartment rapidly became a byword among their mutual friends; it was an absolute tip. Dirty laundry lay in piles on the bedroom floor, they only did the washing up when they had run out of plates—and they actually preferred to eat directly out of the take-out containers—Louise's cat covered every surface in hair, and they could never find the remote because it was always buried under layers of magazines, newspapers, and all the other detritus in the living room. Brad's male friends thought it was cozy at first, and that Brad was incredibly lucky to have found a woman who didn't bother him with the usual female crap about cleaning up on a regular basis, but as the apartment descended further and further into chaos, even they were a little disgusted by it.

Before moving in with Louise, Brad had always been pretty

good about paying his bills on time. Now, as soon as the bills arrived, they disappeared into the stacks of stuff piled up on the kitchen table, and Brad could never find them again. Louise, too, had always somehow managed to get her bills paid, even if she did end up waiting for the final notice that threatened to cut off her electricity before she ever bothered to do a search for her checkbook. The two of them together, though, had a very bad effect on each other. They always assumed that the other one would get around to taking care of the bills—and of course that meant that nobody did. When their cable was cut off for nonpayment, Brad and Louise had a huge fight, both of them blaming the other. Brad suggested that they shift their payments to an automated system that would take the money directly out of one of their bank accounts, but he never got around to arranging it.

Brad and Louise are still slogging through a sea of mess and disorder—and fighting with increasing frequency about all the things that get lost or mislaid as a result. But they don't seem to be able to pull themselves out of it, tidy up their place a bit, and organize some sort of system for paying the bills—let alone buy a laundry basket to put the dirty laundry in. The apartment is so cluttered now that even they are slightly embarrassed by it, and they don't want to invite friends over. But they've got stuck in this pattern and can't get free. Brad and Louise have brought out the most juvenile, slobby characteristics in each other; they are much more messy together than apart. And they are starting to resent each other for it.

What to Do Instead: Set a Positive Example, Using Humor to Help It Along

There is no perfect person for you. There is only the man who is good enough. Which means that anyone you meet is going to have qualities that get on your nerves. The trick is to work out whether you can tolerate the occasional annoyances in return for all the good things that he brings to the relationship.

Gary and Lucy are a study in contrasts. Lucy is pleasant and easygoing, whereas Gary is a full-blown neurotic worrier. He's always convinced that he has contracted some terrible disease—this week, for instance, it's gout—that they will both be sacked and have to sell their house, or that the sky will fall on their heads. Gary's previous girlfriends tended to mother him. They would take his concerns very seriously and try to argue him out of them. As a result, they got sucked into Gary's neuroses, because the more his worries were fed, the more they grew.

When Lucy met Gary, she decided to take a very different tack. When Gary announced that he had gout, or that the market was going to crash and he would go bankrupt, Lucy would agree with him instead of arguing. Gout? That's terrible, sweetie, you should see the doctor straightaway, and maybe get yourself a crutch. You're going to default on our mortgage? Oh well, never mind, I'll still date you even if we have to live in a one-room shack on the railroad tracks.

With her combination of validation and gentle teasing, Lucy always managed to calm Gary down. Because Gary, like most perpetual worriers and hypochondriacs, was actually perfectly healthy, and he had an excellent job—his finances were in a very good state. Gary just needed to let off steam by voicing his worst fears, and by not taking them too seriously, Lucy actually gave him the reassurance he needed. The girlfriends before her never understood this, and as a result, Gary's fears grew exponentially—the more those fears were taken seriously, the more attempts were made to argue him out of them, the stronger they grew.

Naturally, this was a very annoying trait of Gary's. But Lucy decided that she could tolerate it because, fundamentally, Gary was a wonderful boyfriend: loyal, faithful, supportive, and madly in love with her. He would do anything for her, and she knew it. Lucy's previous boyfriends weren't half as trustworthy, reliable, and attentive as Gary, and she felt very lucky to have him. Their friends were very impressed by the light, easy way she dealt with his worrying. But to Lucy, it was just one of those compromises you need to make to have a healthy relationship. The more she got to know Gary, the more she realized his true worth and the more she fell in love with him.

Of course, he drives her crazy at times, but she knows she has qualities that Gary finds irritating, too. Charles Musgrove could take a lesson from Lucy—if he tolerated Mary's hypochondria and complaints, both validating them and teasing her about them lightly, instead of dismissing them, she would feel much more loved and understood and would be a considerably nicer, more good-natured person as a result.

ELIZABETH BENNET AND MR. DARCY

"She is tolerable, but not handsome enough to tempt me;
and I am in no humour at present to give consequence to
young ladies who are slighted by other men."
—PRIDE AND PREJUDICE

These are Darcy's first words about Elizabeth, when his friend Mr. Bingley suggests that he ask her to dance because she doesn't have a partner. Certainly, the people at the ball who find him "proud, above his company and above being pleased" are absolutely right. Darcy, at the beginning of *Pride and Prejudice*, is without question rude, stuck up, and egotistical. If he had married someone like Miss Bingley, who shares all of these character traits, he would have become a monster. But Darcy has better instincts than that, even though he is not quite aware of them himself. Notwithstanding his dislike of her vulgar family, he finds himself strongly drawn to Elizabeth. He discovers that, despite his early dismissal of her looks, he finds her very attractive; and "in spite of his asserting that her manners were not those of the fashionable world, he was caught by their easy playfulness."

This will be the key to Darcy's falling in love with her, more even than her physical attractiveness. Elizabeth loves to tease; she is witty, spirited, and, as she is thrown into contact with Darcy, enjoys poking good-humored fun at him, because she finds him a little pompous and thinks he needs to lighten up. The words Jane Austen repeatedly uses to describe Elizabeth's behavior to him are "arch" and "playful," and Darcy, used to women who flatter him, is completely charmed by someone who, instead, refuses to take him very seriously. When they are staying for a few days at Bingley's house, Netherfield Park—Elizabeth has come to visit her sister Jane, who is ill—Elizabeth teases him thoroughly after dinner one night. She even thinks for a moment that she may have gone a little too far, but he responds so nicely that she's taken aback: "Elizabeth, having rather expected to affront him, was amazed at his gallantry; but there was a mixture of sweetness and archness in her manner which made it difficult for her to affront anybody; and Darcy had never been so bewitched by any woman as he was by her. He really believed, that were it not for the inferiority of her connections, he should be in some danger."

It is crucial to notice that the reason Darcy falls for her is that Elizabeth is behaving completely naturally. She isn't flirting with him or teasing him as a studied tactic to catch his attention: she's simply being herself. She loves to joke and laugh, and she is utterly spontaneous. She describes herself well when she tells Darcy: "Follies and nonsense, whims and inconsistencies *do* divert me, I own, and I laugh at them whenever I can . . ."

Darcy has begun to banter with her, even in his rather grave, serious way. She is slowly, without realizing it, bringing out the lighter and more playful side of his own character. And he is enjoying it. In the course of a conversation about people's characters, Darcy tells her: "There is, I believe, in every disposition a tendency to some particular evil, a natural defect, which not even the best education can overcome." Elizabeth immediately retorts: "And *your* defect is a propensity to hate everybody." She's teasing him, but she's hinting, too, that his haughtiness makes people think exactly this: that he does despise everyone who isn't at his social level. And Darcy reacts very well. Instead of being offended, and snubbing her, he says "with a smile": "And yours is wilfully to misunderstand them."

The banter is going so well that Miss Bingley, jealous, interrupts to break it up. Elizabeth is bringing Darcy out of his shell. He senses instinctively that she is the woman who can teach him to take things more lightly, laugh at his own faults and hers, and make him smile despite himself. Elizabeth is showing him that he doesn't need to stand so much on his pride and social status—that if he cracks loose a little, the world won't come tumbling down around his ears, and he'll have much more fun besides.

And Darcy applies the lesson well. He humbles his pride enough to bribe Wickham (a man he has his own well-founded reasons for disliking) to marry Lydia, Elizabeth's sister; and he does it for Elizabeth's sake, with no assurance that she will ever return his love. He learns to act unselfishly, and Elizabeth is very moved when she learns of it, realizing that he has changed. "She was proud of him. Proud that in a cause of compassion and honour, he had been able to get the better of himself." She doesn't know how much she has influenced this change; but later, when she has agreed to marry him, she asks him if he fell in love with her principally because she teased him: "Now, be sincere," she says; "did you admire me for my impertinence?"

"For the liveliness of your mind, I did," he replies.

That's exactly what Darcy finds in Elizabeth, and what he needs so badly in a wife: someone with a lively mind who will take him down a peg, in the nicest possible way, whenever he gets on his high horse. Elizabeth has a bit of a task ahead of her, and it won't always be easy; Darcy will doubtless return repeatedly to his old haughtiness, and she will need to curb it. But she is also lucky to have found Darcy, who is steady and solid and won't encourage her tendencies to make snap judgments of people's characters and to speak before she thinks things through. Darcy and Elizabeth have found a very good balance.

LESSON TO BE LEARNED

YOU SHOULD LIKE WHO YOU ARE WHEN
YOU'RE WITH THE PERSON YOU LOVE

What Not to Do: Don't Close Your Eyes to a Bad Pattern of Behavior

Lacey was very serious about her boyfriend, Mark. He was loving, supportive, and a whole lot of fun. It had taken them a while to get together, because Mark was a real party animal, and he would take Lacey to parties and to bars with his friends where they would hang out in large groups and not spend a lot of time getting to know each other one-on-one. Eventually, though, Mark did suggest that he and Lacey go out to dinner, just the two of them, and after a couple of evenings spent alone together, they rapidly grew close.

At first, Lacey loved that Mark was so social and outgoing and knew so many fun people. But as they started dating seriously, she realized that it would be hard for Mark to limit his social engagements so that they could spend time together as a couple. Even more important, because of his busy social life, Mark's plans were constantly changing. It made making arrangements to see him difficult: they would agree to go to a movie, then Mark would call Lacey at the last moment to suggest that they go to a party instead. Or he would show up and whisk her off for an evening quite different from the one she had planned—he would have tickets to see a baseball game when Lacey had thought they were having a romantic dinner and had dressed accordingly. She felt stupid at the stadium wearing a little black dress and heels when everyone else was in jeans and sweats, but Mark brushed aside her complaints.

In itself, this showed a lack of consideration for her, which wasn't a great sign. But Lacey was still serious about Mark, and she thought that when they settled down together things would change. Mark asked Lacey to move in with him, and she was more than happy to agree. However, once she had moved in, Mark's unreliability worsened. Now that he felt more secure of Lacey, he messed her around more and more. He would change the time they were meeting at the last minute, come home much later than he had said he would, and occasionally even stand her up. Lacey closed her eyes to this and made excuses for him because she was so keen on him; she told herself that Mark was just adjusting to living with her, and she should let him be. But once, after six months of living with Mark, he came home in the small hours. Lacey had been ringing him, but his cell phone was turned off. She was furious with him because she had been so worried that something might have happened to him.

Lacey wasn't jealous. She didn't have any sense that Mark was cheating on her. It was his unreliability, his juvenile behavior, on such a regular basis, that made her so angry. She shouted at Mark and they had a huge fight. Mark tried to calm her down, and finally succeeded. After that, though, the pattern was set. Mark would change his plans at the last minute and Lacey would complain bitterly. Lacey gradually turned into someone she didn't like—a nag who watched how much her boyfriend drank and tried to get him to leave early, or rang frequently when he was out to remind him not to come home late. The less control Lacey felt she had over the situation, the more she tried to enforce it; it became a vicious circle.

Mark didn't mind Lacey's nagging; in fact, it quite suited him. It allowed him to feel rebellious and naughty, as if he were always disobeying rules. In a way, he turned Lacey into a sort of mother figure. But Lacey was bitter and angry because she felt that Mark was perpetually refusing to meet her halfway. One day, complaining to friends of hers about the situation, Lacey realized with horror that she sounded exactly like her mother, who also used to nag her father. Lacey had fallen into the same pattern of behavior that she had hated when she was growing up. This was a real wake-up call to Lacey. Mark had brought out very bad qualities in her—qualities that had been latent in her but needed someone as unreliable as Mark to bring out.

As soon as Lacey noticed this, she couldn't go on with the relationship. She knew that Mark would never change, and she couldn't bear the thought that she was repeating the same mistake that her mother had made. She didn't like the person she had become. She told Mark that she was leaving him, and hard though it was, she never looked back, mainly because she made a conscious decision not to blame Mark or to harbor a grudge toward him. All the warning signs had been there from the beginning; with open eyes, she had chosen a man who brought out the latent nag in her character. Mark had never tricked her or pretended to be anything he wasn't. By letting any blame go and focusing on the future, Lacey freed herself from the mistake she had made and concentrated on finding a man who was more responsible and reliable, who wouldn't trigger her nagging tendencies.

What to Do Instead: Listen to Your Boyfriend When He Genuinely Tries to Help You

Kate had a long history of anorexia, which had started when she was about fourteen. She was in recovery, but still very cautious about what she ate, and she kept herself very slim. Blond, thin, and pretty, she was obviously in great demand by men, and she tended to date ones who appreciated her precisely because of those qualities. They approved of her scanty eating, because it would keep her weight down and she would remain the thin, blond trophy girlfriend they were looking for.

When Kate met Lee, she didn't realize at first that he was different from the men she usually dated. However, after a few weeks, Lee began to comment on the small quantity of food she ate. He knew she worked out a lot and said that he was worried she wasn't getting enough nutrition. Kate was so taken aback that she didn't know how to respond. Eventually, she asked Lee if he thought she was too thin, and he said yes: she was lovely, but she was just skin and bones. Normally, Kate would have taken this as a compliment, but she was confused by Lee's attitude. They went on dating, and Lee noticed how strict Kate's rules for herself were: no dairy, very few carbs, hardly any sugar. Concerned, he went out and bought some books on nutrition, which he gave her as a present. He said, for instance, that because of her no-dairy rule, he was worried that she wasn't getting enough calcium, and that her bones would be weak when she was older.

Kate exploded. She was furious, because Lee's concern made her feel tremendously insecure. The rules by which she had lived for most of her adult life were under attack, and so was her body image, which, naturally, as a recovering anorexic, was fundamental to her. She dumped Lee that evening, telling him that she didn't want to be with someone who didn't love her the way she was.

Lee was hurt and full of guilt; he felt that he had put Kate under pressure and had pushed her too much. He took all the blame and sent her a series of apologetic e-mails, saying that he hadn't meant to be critical and promised never to do it again.

For about a month, Kate refused to answer his e-mails or to see him. But she spent a lot of time thinking about Lee, about how different he was, how he seemed to care about her as a person and not just as a trophy girlfriend, and how threatened that made her feel—the idea of going out with someone who really cared about her. Eventually, she decided to tell Lee about her anorexia and see if he could deal with it. She told him all about how she had been hospitalized several times, and the struggle it had been to put some weight on, something she had never revealed to any previous boyfriend. Lee was hugely sympathetic, and apologized again for his clumsiness.

Kate and Lee got back together and with his encouragement, Kate went to see a nutritionist. She managed to put on a few pounds and she started taking regular supplements. Food issues will never be easy for Kate, and she does feel sometimes that Lee watches what she eats too closely, which makes her uncomfortable. But Lee is also making a huge effort to trust Kate and not pressure her about her eating habits. Kate feels happier than she ever has before: she knows that she can trust Lee with her secret, and that he supports her. And she also has the security of knowing that he loves her for herself, and not her thin body. Lee is someone who loves to take care of people, and in Kate he's found a good match. And Kate has found a man who has brought out a sense of confidence in herself that she didn't know she was capable of; she no longer defines herself just by her eating disorder or how much she weighs that morning, because Lee has made her feel she has a value far beyond that.

EMMA WOODHOUSE AND FRANK CHURCHILL

"I think there is a little likeness between us . . . There is
a likeness in our destiny; the destiny which bids
fair to connect us with two characters
so much superior to our own."
—*EMMA*

When Frank Churchill meets Emma Woodhouse, the heroine of *Emma*, he immediately starts to flirt with her. Frank's motive, however, is not simple attraction. He is using his flirtation with Emma to disguise the fact that he is secretly engaged to Jane Fairfax, a beautiful and reserved girl he met on holiday in Weymouth. Jane is now in Emma's village visiting her relatives, Mrs. Bates, an elderly lady, and Miss Bates, her spinster daughter, a very sweet middle-aged lady who is famously garrulous—she absolutely can't stop herself from pouring out every fleeting thought that comes into her head.

The first time Emma meets Frank, she is struck by the fact that he tends to say what will please people, without much regard for whether it's the strict truth. He flatters his own father, who he's visiting, by saying how much he's always wanted to come and see him—yet Frank hasn't visited his father till now, and Emma finds his protestations a little disingenuous. "That [Frank] should never have been able to indulge so amiable a feeling [of visiting his father] before, passed suspiciously through Emma's brain; but still if it were a falsehood, it was a pleasant one, and pleasantly handled."

This is the best indication of Frank's character we can have. Without being a completely bad person, he adores to dissemble and flatter people. He even goes so far as to criticize Jane to Emma, playing his own secret game to disguise his real love for Jane. "Miss Fairfax," he tells Emma, "is naturally so pale, as almost always to give the appearance of ill health. A most deplorable want of complexion." When Emma describes Jane as "reserved," he immediately agrees: "It is a most repulsive quality indeed," said he. ". . . There is safety in reserve, but no attraction. One cannot love a reserved person." And later: "Miss Fairfax's languid dancing would not have agreed with me, after yours."

Again and again in *Emma*, Frank says the absolute opposite of what he means. And he brings out the worst in Emma herself; in talking to Frank, she becomes her bitchiest self, mirroring him.

The way they discuss their mutual acquaintances is a little cruel. Mr. Knightley, himself in love with Emma, sees this and disapproves of it—and he's jealous of Frank and Emma's bond.

Frank exploits Emma's liking for him and uses it for his own selfish reasons. When he has a fight with Jane, he immediately starts flirting even more strongly with Emma, as if to punish Jane. "You order me, whether you speak or not," he tells Emma. "And you can be always with me. You are always with me." Frank is very lucky that Emma doesn't fall for this; though she doesn't know it herself, her heart is really with Mr. Knightley, and that keeps her safe. But the way Frank courts Emma, it would have been completely understandable for her to think that he was on the verge of proposing to her.

And that would have been a very bad idea. Frank and Emma bring out the worst in each other. They tap into each other's sarcastic, careless side, and it leads them to behave badly. Frank's encouragement even leads Emma to be rude to poor, talkative Miss Bates, mocking her for her inability to stop prattling. Miss Bates is very hurt, and takes the blame on herself: "I will try to hold my tongue," she says to Mr. Knightley. "I must make myself very disagreeable, or she would not have said such a thing to an old friend."

When Emma comes to terms with what she has done to Miss Bates, she is absolutely mortified. It's her own fault, but without Frank's egging her on to excess she would never have said such a thing. If Emma and Frank married, it would be very bad for both of them; they would be a nasty, judgmental couple, constantly mocking and criticizing the people around them. Frank's character is worse than Emma's; he's the one who initiates the secrecy and the games about his concealed engagement. When the engagement becomes public, everyone is outraged: "Very abominable sort of proceeding. What has it been but a system of hypocrisy and deceit,—espionage, and treachery?—To come among us with professions of openness and simplicity, and such a league in secret . . ." Emma exclaims. And Mr. Knightley, as usual, sees the prospective marriage very clearly. Jane has the worst of the bargain, as far as character goes: "I am sorry for *her*," he says. "She deserves a better fate." But he thinks Jane will be the making of Frank: "He may yet turn out well.—With such a woman he has a chance."

Married to Jane Fairfax and Mr. Knightley respectively—quieter, more morally responsible people who can calm them down—

Frank and Emma have a strong chance of emphasizing the good sides of their characters, rather than the bad. But if they had got together, they would have been toxic.

LESSON TO BE LEARNED

DON'T DATE SOMEONE WHO ENCOURAGES
YOUR SELF-DESTRUCTIVE IMPULSES

What Not to Do: Don't Mistake Danger for Excitement

Kara, a supervisor for AT&T, had never met anyone like Rob. He was a wild free spirit who picked her up in a bar, took her along to an after-hours club, and then brought her home with him for a night of incredible sex. She couldn't believe that Rob wanted to go on seeing her, but he did. Rob was a guitarist in a rock band; he had piercings, several tattoos, and cropped purple hair. Kara was completely bowled over by him. She spent every minute she could with him, going along with every crazy suggestion he made.

Rob lived a very nocturnal existence. He never got up before noon; then he'd meet his band members for practice and go out in the evening till very late, either to play a gig or to see friends of his who were playing at clubs in the city. He drank plenty, smoked pot, got to bed about four every morning, and he expected Kara to join him in all these activities.

At first it was very exciting for Kara. Rob took her into a world that she knew existed but had never been able to enter. He was completely unlike all the more conventional men she'd dated before, and she was absolutely infatuated with him. But gradually, Kara's time with Rob started cutting into her regular life. She was exhausted in the mornings because she'd drunk too much the night before, smoked pot, and hadn't had enough sleep, and her work was suffering. Her bosses started to complain. And her friends were also complaining because she wasn't spending any time with them.

Kara tried to talk to Rob about all of this, but he brushed it off, laughing at her. She asked him if they could spend some quiet evenings together and have some early nights, particularly during the week, because she needed to get up early for work. Rob just told her that she was being boring. He wanted a girlfriend who was fun, a party animal, not a staid workaholic who valued her corporate job more than having a good time with him. This tore Kara up. She couldn't face the idea of losing Rob—to her, he represented everything that was exciting and different and sexy.

Kara couldn't see that Rob really didn't care about her at all; if he had, he would have made compromises in his life to meet her halfway. Instead, his attitude was "my way or the highway." Either Kara fit in with his life or he would find a woman who did.

Kara couldn't bear to lose Rob. She did her best to keep up with him and also do her job. But inevitably, her work suffered. And when she told Rob she couldn't go out with him on a particular weeknight, he complained angrily and made her jealous by telling her about all the groupies who were after him. This, of course, made Kara so insecure that she couldn't concentrate on the work she had taken home that evening, or get a good night's sleep; she was too worried about what Rob might be up to, and she pestered him with phone calls.

Eventually, the inevitable happened. Kara got into serious trouble at her job and was given an official warning. When she told Rob, he brushed it off and told her she was better off without a boring corporate job anyway. Even then, Kara couldn't break up with him. She was too into him and the excitement he provided. Kara did throw herself into her work, frightened that she would be fired, and this meant that she couldn't go out with Rob as much. After a few weeks, it was Rob who dumped her. He said she'd got dull now that she was working so hard and he didn't want to see her anymore.

Kara pleaded with Rob, but he wouldn't listen. He told her that he was already seeing someone else, and he wouldn't answer her phone calls. Kara was destroyed. She went to see his band play, meaning to confront him and beg him to take her back, but Rob had a new girl hanging all over him, and Kara slipped away, crying her heart out. She managed to keep her job, but it took years for her to fully get over Rob. She was never able to see that Rob had been very bad for her, that he had encouraged her to neglect her work, her friends, and her responsibilities. If she had been able to see the relationship as it really was—and Rob as a very negative force in her life—she might have been able to muster the courage to break up with him, or even just to recover faster from the emotional impact he had made on her.

What to Do Instead: Pick a Boyfriend Who's a Good Influence on You

Beverley was always the life and soul of the party. She was full of high spirits, and people loved to be around her. But sometimes, with a large appreciative audience egging her on to tell jokes and be outrageous, Beverley would go over the top—usually when she'd had one or two drinks too many. Her banter would get a little too personal, her jokes a little too risqué, her voice a little too loud. Most people encouraged her, but a couple of her close friends would try to tell her that maybe she needed to tone it down just a bit, because sometimes, without meaning it, Beverley could upset the person she was teasing.

Beverley didn't really listen to the warnings. But then, through work, she met Ed. Ed was much more quiet and self-contained than Beverley. She didn't usually like quiet people, preferring ones who, like her, were outgoing and noisy, but she could tell that Ed's quietness wasn't shyness or lack of confidence. He was simply a very calm person, and Beverley, to her surprise, felt herself drawn to precisely that quality in him. Ed, meanwhile, was drawn to Beverley's strong, extroverted personality, and soon he asked her out. They started dating, and Beverley introduced him to her friends.

They didn't quite know what to make of Ed at first; he seemed so composed and didn't say that much in large groups, unlike them, who were all pretty riotous. But then Beverley's closest friends, the ones who'd tried to tell her to tone things down a bit, began to notice what a good effect Ed had on her. Beverley was still loud and jokey, but she didn't go over the top anymore. Ed's calm presence seemed to take the edge off her teasing and her need for attention. Beverley noticed it as well, and she liked it. Ed was different from her previous boyfriends, who had been much more like her. With Ed in her life, she felt a sense of calm and balance that she had never had before, and it meant that she was able to control her wildness much more successfully.

It was a very good match. Ed got something out of it as well, of course: he loved Beverley's energy and drive, and was happy to be the quieter one in the relationship. He enjoyed going out with Beverley and her friends; he found it great entertainment, and didn't feel pressured to join in and be someone he wasn't. But the effect on Beverley was more profound: with Ed to give her balance and security, she didn't have those extra drinks that tipped her over the edge into humor with too much of a bite. She was a nicer person when she was with Ed, and she really appreciated it.

SUMMARY

Do

- *Keep your own values.* If someone doesn't have the same fundamental value system as you—and, worse, if they try to sway you from what you know to be right—you are not in a good relationship.

- *Choose someone who brings out the best in you.* Your boyfriend should help you to strengthen your positive qualities and suppress the negative ones.

- *Support him as much as he supports you.* It's a two-way street. If you're both helping each other to reach your goals in life and be nicer, happier people, you have a much greater chance of maintaining a successful, strong relationship.

Don't

- *Try to change your boyfriend in major ways.* Either decide you can put up with his annoying quirks, or leave him. If you start trying to change him, you will turn into a nag, and you will end up hating yourself.

- *Be influenced by his bad behavior.* Don't get sucked into doing things that you feel aren't good for you. Don't stay around someone who wants to drag you down.

- *Put all the blame on him.* You chose him, after all. If he's not good for you, why did you pick him in the first place? Instead of blaming him, spend your time more usefully by figuring out why you made that mistake so you won't repeat it in the future.

❖   ❖   ❖   ❖

Tips for Telling If You're with Someone Who Brings Out Your Worst Qualities

❖ You're stuck in a rut of criticizing each other, without the situation ever improving.

❖ You feel irritable most of the time you spend with him, without being able to put your finger on exactly why.

❖ You change your outfit or your hair five times before going out on a date with him, never sure whether you've picked the image of yourself that will please him.

❖ You disagree with a lot of his core values, but you tell yourself that it doesn't matter, because they have nothing to do with your relationship.

❖ You find yourself doing things when out with him that you would never normally do—things you don't mention to your friends because you know they would disapprove.

SEVEN

DON'T SETTLE—DON'T MARRY FOR MONEY, OR CONVENIENCE, OR OUT OF LONELINESS

Mr Collins, to be sure, was neither sensible nor agreeable;
his society was irksome, and his attachment to her must be
imaginary. But still he would be her husband.—Without
thinking highly either of men or of matrimony, marriage
had always been her object; it was the only honourable
provision for well-educated young women of small fortune,
and however uncertain of giving happiness, must be their
pleasantest preservative from want. This preservative she had
now obtained; and at the age of twenty-seven, without
having ever been handsome, she felt all the good luck of it.

—PRIDE AND PREJUDICE

I KNOW SOMEONE WHO, ten years ago, settled for a nice, rich man who loved her. She has a baby and a toddler now, and she keeps having affairs. She's bored out of her skull—the full-time housekeeper and the nanny take care of everything around the home—and since she never really loved her husband, she doesn't much look forward to his coming home from work at the end of each day. Basically, she accepted his proposal because she was scared of being alone, and she liked the fact that he could support her in high style. She was more concerned about getting a ring on her finger, and the fabulous wedding she would have, than thinking beyond the wedding day to what her life would be like afterward with a man she didn't love. It's always scary to be alone; in our weak moments we've all thought "I'll be alone for the rest of my life," and been tempted to settle for something less than a supportive relationship based on love. But if we're wise, we don't tie ourselves down to a man for whom we don't have feelings strong enough to carry us through the inevitable problems and obstacles we'll all face in life, someone who will help us through ours and let us help him through his.

CHARLOTTE LUCAS AND MR. COLLINS

"I am not romantic, you know . . . I ask only a comfortable home."
—PRIDE AND PREJUDICE

Though Charlotte and Mr. Collins's marriage is only a subplot in *Pride and Prejudice,* it is one of the saddest little stories in the whole of Jane Austen's work. Charlotte Lucas, "a sensible, intelligent young woman" of a good family, has so far failed to find a husband, which, ironically, is her only chance for any sort of independence. An old maid in the society in which she lives is a lonely figure, pitied by everyone, usually existing on a small income and taken in on charity by luckier, married relatives. Charlotte is determined to avoid that fate at all costs, but she pays a heavy price for her decision.

She targets as a husband the dire Mr. Collins, a vicar and a cousin of the Bennet sisters. He has just unsuccessfully proposed to his cousin Elizabeth, and is in search of a wife—not because he wants to get married on his own account, but because the patroness he toadies to, Lady Catherine de Bourgh, has told him that he should. On Elizabeth's refusal, Charlotte immediately sets out to show Mr. Collins that she herself would be disposed to accept him, and he proposes the very next day.

Mr. Collins is one of Austen's best-drawn comic characters, a pompous, silly ass, overdeferent to people of a higher social status: "Mr Collins was not a sensible man . . . The subjection in which his father had brought him up, had given him originally great humility of manner, but it was now a good deal counteracted by the self-conceit of a weak head . . . [He was] altogether a mixture of pride and obsequiousness, self-importance and humility."

Charlotte has previously been fairly cynical on the subject of marriage—probably because as an unmarried twenty-seven-year-old woman, she is very aware of being on the shelf. "Happiness in marriage," she says to Elizabeth early on in the book, "is entirely a matter of chance. If the dispositions of the parties are ever so well known to each other . . . they always continue to grow sufficiently unlike afterwards to have their share of vexation; and it is better to know as little as possible of the defects of the person with whom you are to pass your life."

With this, Charlotte is essentially announcing her intention to marry the first man who asks her and who can provide for her reasonably well. Still, Mr. Collins is such a bore, so arrogant and simultaneously so smarmy, that it's impossible for Elizabeth to imagine for a moment that Charlotte's marriage will be happy. "[Elizabeth] had always felt that Charlotte's opinion of matrimony was not exactly like her own, but she could not have supposed it possible that . . . [Charlotte] would have sacrificed every better feeling to worldly advantage. Charlotte the wife of Mr Collins, was a most humiliating picture!"

But Charlotte does become the wife of Mr. Collins, and after a few months, Elizabeth goes to visit her. She finds that Charlotte has adjusted to the awfulness of her husband by ignoring the stupid comments he comes out with: "When Mr Collins said any thing of which his wife might reasonably be ashamed, which certainly was not unseldom, [Elizabeth] involuntarily turned her eye on Charlotte. Once or twice she could discern a faint blush; but in general Charlotte wisely did not hear."

Charlotte, being sensible, has also taken a less comfortable sitting room in the house for her own use, calculating that if she sits regularly in the cozier one, her husband will be in there a lot more often. This way at least she gets some distance from him. Elizabeth works this out quickly, and gives Charlotte "credit for the arrangement." Life with Mr. Collins clearly requires Charlotte to avoid or ignore her husband, as politely as she can, most of the time. It is a depressing picture. Still, she has made the best of a bad situation and has plenty of things to keep her busy—and also away from Mr. Collins. On leaving, Elizabeth reflects that Charlotte has "chosen [her life] with her eyes open; and . . . did not seem to ask for compassion. Her home and her housekeeping, her parish and her poultry, and all their dependent concerns, had not yet lost their charms."

LESSON TO BE LEARNED

BE STRONG; DON'T SETTLE
FOR LESS THAN LOVE

What Not to Do: Don't Believe That Being Married Is Necessarily Better Than Being Single

It's tough to be in a position where, like Charlotte, you feel you're getting on, you're still unmarried, and you're beginning to panic about your chances of ever meeting someone. Nicole was in exactly that situation when, at the age of thirty-six, she decided to settle. She had been a professional ballerina for years, never rising beyond the corps de ballet in a series of second-rate ballet companies. It wasn't a particularly successful career, but dancing had always been her life, even though the salary she earned was very small and didn't allow her to save. At thirty-two she had to retire—a dancer's working life is short at the best of times, and Nicole suffered a couple of injuries that didn't allow her to go on dancing professionally.

She took a secretarial job, but, again, it didn't pay very well and didn't offer any future but more of the same. Nicole was panicking not only about her chances of getting married, but also of making any money that would allow her to save for her old age. She had a long-standing friend and admirer, Brad, whom she had known for years. Nicole had never been attracted to Brad, but he had always made it clear that he was in love with her and would propose in a moment if she said the word. Brad was a dentist, with a good income, a stable, solid man she knew would provide for her and look after her. Finally, out of desperation, she agreed to marry him.

Nicole made a bargain with herself: for security, she would trade her independence and her potential to have a marriage with someone she loved. But she never felt secure. Brad married Nicole knowing that she wasn't in love with him, and once the excitement wore off, he quickly came to despise her for it. Brad found that once he had married the woman he had been fruitlessly courting for years, the trophy he had won wasn't as valuable to him as he had thought it would be. He wasn't happy with the bargain he had made, either. Nicole had always been out of reach to him, an impossible fantasy; once he had her, he realized that fantasies coming true weren't all they were cracked up to be. He didn't spend much time at home, coming home late from work and going golfing on weekends. Nicole was left to run the house, all alone in suburbia, not even looking forward to the eventual return of her husband from the office or the golf course. It was a disaster. They started sniping at each other, and then the sniping turned into full-on fights. After just one year of marriage, they decided to call it quits. The divorce was nasty and Nicole is now back where she started, having lost a friend in Brad, and more depressed than ever about the state of her life.

What to Do Instead: Listen to Your Heart as Well as Your Head

After a bad breakup, Linda was nagged by her friends until she agreed to sign up for an Internet dating service. Linda had been dumped by Terry, a boyfriend she was madly in love with and had hung on to for a long time, hoping against hope that his declared antipathy to commitment and settling down would change. It never did. In fact, the longer Linda clung to him, the more Terry took her for granted. Linda finally left him as a last ploy, thinking that maybe when he was without her he would realize how much he missed her and ask her to marry him. It didn't work. In fact, Terry immediately went on to meet someone else, whom he proposed to a mere three months later. Linda was understandably devastated by this, and her friends wanted her to meet someone else as soon as possible to take her mind off Terry. They sat down with her, helped her write her profile and choose some nice photos, and wouldn't leave till the profile was posted.

Linda received several replies, and went out on dates, but she didn't click with anyone for a while. Then she met Sam, a nice solid guy who fell for her like a ton of bricks. Sam, unlike Terry, was responsible and stable, with none of Terry's freewheeling, freeloading characteristics. And he was very serious about Linda. Sam was such a change from Terry that at first Linda was swept away by him; he brought her flowers, he always rang the day they had a date scheduled to confirm what time he would be picking her up, he made a real effort to find out her tastes, and arranged dates he thought she would enjoy.

Linda thought a man like Sam was just what she wanted. But after a few months, she began to have doubts. She had been so happy to meet Sam, and to feel attractive again after years of being neglected by Terry, that she hadn't stopped to think about whether she was in love with Sam. When she took time to analyze her doubts, she knew that she wasn't. She had been attracted to Sam mainly because he was so attracted to *her,* and because he was so different from Terry. Linda had been in a relationship for several years, and she realized that what she actually wanted was to be free for a while, date around, not rush into another relationship. Getting serious with Sam would have been settling for the sake of having a steady boyfriend, a guaranteed date for Saturday nights, a man in her life so she didn't feel sad, lonely, and rejected. It wouldn't be because she actually loved Sam for himself.

As soon as Linda understood this, she knew what she had to do. She told Sam she wasn't ready, and continued dating men she met through the Internet service. She took the time that she needed to recover from the damage Terry had done, and didn't let anything get too serious until she was ready. And a year later, she met someone she really fell in love with . . . and they're very happy.

MARIA BERTRAM AND MR. RUSHWORTH

Being now in her twenty-first year, Maria Bertram was
beginning to think matrimony a duty; and as a marriage
with Mr Rushworth would give her the enjoyment of a
larger income than her father's, as well as ensure her the
house in town, which was now a prime object, it became,
by the same rule of moral obligation, her evident duty to
marry Mr Rushworth if she could.

—*MANSFIELD PARK*

Like Charlotte Lucas, Maria Bertram goes into a boring marriage with her eyes open. But, unlike what we feel for Charlotte, we have little sympathy for her. Maria isn't on the shelf and desperate; she is young, with good looks and a substantial dowry, and could pick and choose between suitors. Maria agrees to marry Mr. Rushworth, "a heavy young man, with not more than common sense," of whom the best that can be said is that "there was nothing disagreeable in his figure or address," simply because he is very rich indeed. Rushworth is boring and stolid, with no idea of how to win a woman's heart. Conversations with him are limited and uninteresting for Maria, "doomed to the repeated details of his day's sport, good or bad, his boast of his dogs, his jealousy of his neighbours . . . and his zeal after poachers, subjects which will not find their way to female feelings without some talent on one side, or some attachment on the other."

Thus, when the seductive Henry Crawford comes upon the scene, Maria, with no emotional attachment to her fiancé, falls head over heels for his wiles. As we have already seen, Henry has no serious intentions toward Maria, and, after flirting madly with her under Mr. Rushworth's nose, leaves the neighborhood without making the proposal of marriage that she hoped for. Disappointed in love, Maria is doubly determined to marry for money, even though her father, Sir Thomas, can tell that she is not in love with her fiancé, and asks her if she wants to call off the engagement. Sir Thomas, having become better acquainted with Mr. Rushworth, finds him "an inferior young man, as ignorant in business as in books," and sees also that his daughter's "behaviour to Mr Rushworth was careless and cold. She could not, did not like him."

Concerned about this situation, Sir Thomas reassures Maria that she need not feel herself bound to an engagement she may have made in too much haste. "Advantageous as would be the alliance, and long-standing and public as was the engagement, her happiness must not be sacrificed to it . . . the connection [would be] entirely given up, if she felt herself unhappy in the prospect of it. He would act for her and release her."

But Maria is set upon her course. She assures her father that she is ready to marry Mr. Rushworth, and her decision is made entirely to spite Henry Crawford. "[He] had destroyed her happiness, but . . . he should not destroy her credit, her appearance, her prosperity too. He should not have to think of her as pining . . . for him, rejecting . . . London, independence and splendour for his sake." So she marries Mr. Rushworth, but promptly arranges to take her sister, Julia, with her on their honeymoon in Brighton, for fear of being bored senseless by having to spend the whole time with her dull husband.

It's not exactly the ideal beginning to a marriage. Maria has everything she could ever want financially, but her husband grates on her, and when she meets Henry Crawford again, she is as ripe for the picking as ever. They start an affair, and eventually she pesters him into running off with her. Henry doesn't love her, but she clings on tenaciously for a while: "She hoped to marry him, and they continued together till she was obliged to be convinced that such a hope was vain, and till the disappointment and wretchedness arising from the conviction, rendered her temper so bad, and her feelings for him so like hatred, as to make them for a while each other's punishment, and then induce a voluntary separation."

Poor Maria; one can't help feeling sorry for her at this point, and still more so when one contemplates her eventual fate, exiled far away from her family home because of the scandal, with her annoying Aunt Norris, "remote and private," where they both rub on each other's nerves till "their tempers became their mutual punishment." But one has to remember that when Maria made the fateful decision to marry Rushworth, she was young and very eligible. There was no reason for her to agree to marry a man she didn't love. And again, when her father offers her a way out, and she refuses to take it, she condemns herself to unhappiness because of pride and pique. All she had to do was return Rushworth's ring and wait till she met someone she had feelings for. Instead, however, she snatched at the money and social status— and paid the price.

LESSON TO BE LEARNED

MONEY WON'T BUY YOU HAPPINESS

What Not to Do: Don't Assume Financial Comfort Will Bring Emotional Fulfillment

Thank God, we are no longer subject to the social mores of Regency England. Nowadays a woman is as able as a man to establish her economic independence without needing to get married to achieve it. And yet there are still plenty of people out there—men and women—marrying people they don't love for money and social status.

Josie was twenty-four, single, and determined to get married. She rang and e-mailed every girlfriend she had, asking them to set her up with someone. And how did she describe the man she wanted to meet? "A Harvard lawyer under thirty." That was it. Nothing about his being nice, or funny, or sweet, or compatible with any of her interests or hobbies. One of her friends did set Josie up with a twenty-eight-year-old Harvard lawyer, Josh, and a year later they got married.

Josie is now thirty-two, with two children. She and Josh live in Connecticut, and Josh, who works in Manhattan, has a long commute to work every day. Josie hardly sees Josh; he leaves the house at six in the morning and gets back after eight at night, when the children are about to go to bed, exhausted from his long day's work and his commute. Josh did suggest to Josie that they buy a smaller house, closer to the city, so that he could spend more time with her and the children, but Josie overrode him; she wanted the big house. Josh has recently been promoted, which means he needs to work even longer hours, and he talked to Josie about the promotion, saying that he was willing to turn it down—again, so that he could have more time with his family. Josie insisted that he take the promotion. She had given up her job as soon as she got married, and she wanted Josh to provide financially as much as he could.

Josie has already had two affairs; since she never really loved Josh, but thought of him more as a means to an end, she's still looking for a great love, but hasn't found it yet with the married guy and the golf pro she had flings with. She is considering Botox because, despite her comparatively young age, she is noticing frown lines on her forehead that indicate her dissatisfaction with her life. She sees a therapist, to whom she complains every week about the boredom and repetitiveness of her daily routine. Her doctor prescribes Prozac for her, but it doesn't seem to be helping much. She has regular blowouts, manicures, and pedicures, and she spends more money than she and Josh can really afford on trips to the mall and catalog shopping.

Josie, in short, is discovering that marrying for money has its pitfalls. As a certain TV talk-show host says, "Marry for money and pay for it every day of your life." She has nothing in her life that fulfills her, apart from her children, and because she's not happy with herself, it's hard to take happiness in them. She got pregnant because it was the next thing on the list she had mapped out for herself as checkpoints to prove she was successful (after "Marry a Harvard lawyer," of course), not because she truly wanted them. Josh knows she's unhappy, but not what to do about it— they fight, but the issues behind their fights are never resolved. He works harder and harder, hoping that material things will help. But, of course, they don't deal with the underlying problem. Josie has never done anything in her life that gave her a sense of autonomy and achievement. She thought marriage would be the solution, but it was just a temporary fix. Josie thought she wanted to live a 1950s life, provided for by a rich husband. But she forgot—or never knew—that a union between two people shouldn't be a financial transaction.

What to Do Instead: Clarify Your Priorities— Sometimes You Can't Have It All!

Angela and Jason met as struggling actors in their twenties. They were immediately attracted to each other and soon were in a relationship. Neither of them, naturally, had any money, and they lived together in a small studio apartment. After several years of living on the breadline, they decided to set up their own children's theater company. They traveled to schools, doing educational theater for which they received grants, and over the school holidays they would put on shows at local theaters.

Working and living together wasn't the easiest thing in the world, but Angela and Jason managed pretty well. Once they had made the decision to go into children's theater, they became more settled and happy; they weren't constantly going on rounds of humiliating auditions, and though their income was small, it was at least regular. Gradually the company became known and their advance bookings grew.

Still, Angela and Jason will never be rich, or even financially very stable. Recently, Jason proposed, and Angela had to confront the fact that if she stayed with Jason for the rest of her life, she would never have a high quality of life; they would always be living hand-to-mouth, dependent on grants and school budgets for their bookings, unsure about where the next month's rent was coming from. Angela's mother had always been hostile to Jason, because she didn't want Angela to have such an insecure financial future, and she encouraged Angela's doubts.

Angela needed to think things over and decide what she wanted out of life. She took a week away, staying with a girlfriend, leaving Jason alone in their apartment and telling him not to contact her. Over that week, Angela went for long walks, talked to her friend, and gradually worked out how she felt. She realized how much she missed Jason, and how important he was to her. Not only that, Jason had always encouraged her to do what she wanted in life. He wasn't afraid of being comparatively poor as long as he was doing something that satisfied and fulfilled his artistic side, and he gave

Angela the strength to see that she, too, felt the same way. Angela had been wondering whether she should pack in their theater company and go back to the temporary secretarial work she had done as a struggling actress to maintain herself. After a week, she decided that this wasn't what she wanted to do. She wanted to be with Jason, running their company, and she was willing to accept a lower standard of life in order to do it.

Angela went back to Jason and told him that she wanted to marry him. They are planning to get married next summer. Because she took the time to think things over and make a sincere decision, she is happy with the life she is living.

Josie and Josh, on the other hand, have set themselves a high standard of living to maintain, and they're frightened of slipping below it. Also, because their marriage is founded, in Josie's case anyway, on financial motives rather than a strong mutual love, they have much more invested in their financial well-being. Josh certainly senses, even if he won't admit it to himself, that his value to Josie lies principally in his being a good provider. If he loses that, his marriage will be in trouble.

Angela and Jason will never have that worry. They know that their marriage will be based on love and compatibility. Neither of them was looking to marry someone rich who could take care of them; theirs is an equal partnership, and though they would both love to make more money—and fantasize about it regularly—it's by no means the most important thing to them. They have had to borrow money from both sets of parents to help them buy an apartment, and that grates on them. But still, they wouldn't alter the way they run their joint lives. Neither wanted a corporate job, and they accept the compromises and strains that come with the lifestyle they have chosen.

ELIZABETH BENNET, COLONEL FITZWILLIAM, AND MR. DARCY

"A younger son, you know, must be inured to self-denial
and dependence . . . In matters of greater weight, I may
suffer from the want of money. Younger sons cannot marry
where they like . . . Our habits of expense make us too
dependent, and there are not many in my rank of life who
can afford to marry without some attention to money."
—PRIDE AND PREJUDICE

When Elizabeth Bennet goes to visit her friend Charlotte, now married to Mr. Collins, she meets Mr. Darcy again, together with his cousin Colonel Fitzwilliam, who immediately takes a liking to Elizabeth: "Mrs Collins's pretty friend had . . . caught his fancy very much." A gentlemanly, well-bred man with open, friendly manners, he and Elizabeth get on very well from the first moment they start talking, and they chatter away like old friends. Enjoying each other's company, they spend plenty of time together. But Colonel Fitzwilliam is not a Frank Churchill or a Henry Crawford, who amuse themselves by making women fall hopelessly in love with them; he takes care to caution Elizabeth quite clearly that she cannot hope for a proposal of marriage from him, because he can't afford to marry a penniless wife. As a younger son, he stands to inherit little, as the English system gives practically all the family money to the oldest son, as the principal heir.

Elizabeth blushes at his hint, but manages to recover quickly, saying "in a lively tone, 'And pray, what is the usual price of an Earl's younger son? Unless the elder brother is very sickly, I suppose you would not ask above fifty thousand pounds.' "

Colonel Fitzwilliam takes her lead, and they treat the subject as a joke, rather than dwelling on the seriousness of his warning. Elizabeth knows perfectly well, as she did with Wickham, that a man with no money cannot afford to marry her, as she has practically nothing of her own. But even when Darcy, with a reputed ten thousand a year, proposes to her, she turns him down flat without thinking for a moment about how rich she would be as his wife.

Elizabeth refuses Darcy, badly offending him because of the strength of her words, because she dislikes and distrusts him. She isn't tempted for a moment to marry for money—or for social status, since Darcy's family is much more aristocratic, and move in much higher society, than her own. Still, months later, when she is touring Derbyshire with her aunt and uncle, they suggest taking a tour of Mr. Darcy's house, Pemberley. Once Elizabeth has assured herself that Darcy is away, she agrees. Pemberley House is described in the most glowing terms that Jane Austen ever lavished on a stately home. And Elizabeth is amazed by its beauty. "Elizabeth was delighted . . . and at that moment she felt, that to be mistress of Pemberley might be something! . . . 'And of this place,' thought she, 'I might have been mistress! With these rooms I might now have been familiarly acquainted!' "

Exclamation marks, comparatively rare in Austen, dot the text profusely here to indicate how much Elizabeth is dazzled by the thought that, in accepting Mr. Darcy, all this might have been hers. It's a perfectly natural reaction, and Austen gives it to Elizabeth to make a specific point—after all, the girl is only human. Elizabeth and Darcy bump into each other at Pemberley; Darcy has returned unexpectedly, and both of them are very embarrassed by the meeting. But Darcy is already a changed man. He is very polite and welcoming to Elizabeth and her relatives, despite the fact that he cited her vulgar family as one of the reasons he was reluctant to propose to her. Over the next few days, Darcy shows he is making a real effort to change; he does everything he can to be the opposite of how Austen described him at the beginning of the novel: "haughty, reserved, and fastidious, and his manners, though well bred . . . not inviting." By the time Elizabeth finds out that he is the one who arranged Lydia and Wickham's marriage, bribing Wickham to marry Lydia, her opinion of him has changed so much that she is more than ready to marry him when he proposes again. Financial considerations aren't a part of it; she is marrying Darcy because she has come to know him well and can see that under his haughty reserve is a good, caring heart. Lucky Elizabeth! She gets both the right man for her, and, as an extra, a lovely way of life!

LESSON TO BE LEARNED

MEN ARE PEOPLE, NOT WALKING,
TALKING BANK ACCOUNTS

What Not to Do: Don't Measure His Worth in Carats

In Austen's time, as I have said, marrying was practically the only way for women to achieve lives of their own. Ironically, Austen repeatedly uses the word "independence" to stress what women gain by marriage—and even more ironically, she doesn't mean it, as one might think, in any ironic sense! It was considered much better for a woman to have her financial needs provided for by her husband rather than her family. The act of marriage was seen as achievement enough; a woman had demonstrated her worth and value by securing a husband, even if she had no legal rights to any of the money she brought to the marriage (the Married Women's Property Act

didn't come into law till the late 1800s), unless her family was intelligent enough to tie it up by settling it on her so that her husband
couldn't spend it all on gambling and loose women.

But now we live in a much more enlightened age, and women
are perfectly capable of earning good livings for themselves. I am
always surprised by the number of women who give up their careers as soon as they marry, as if they had only gone to law school
or college to snag a husband with a good potential earning capacity.
Elizabeth Bennet lived in a time when women weren't supposed to
have careers. And yet, when she marries Darcy, she will have
plenty to do. There's a huge mansion, Pemberley, to run, the children they will hopefully have to bring up, and also the main emotional job she's taken on: softening and humanizing her husband,
reining in his tendency to haughtiness and social snobbery. In this
way, Darcy needs Elizabeth much more than she needs him. Their
marriage is by no means a one-way street.

Even if, like Elizabeth, you have the good fortune to fall in love
with someone rich, you are still going to have to think about what in
your life will give you satisfaction and a feeling of achievement. Too
often nowadays, women still focus on how much money the man
they're dating earns, and how much he is willing to give them,
rather than his other good qualities. My boyfriend recently reported a scene he had witnessed at work: a woman in his office had
just got engaged, and the other women were gathering around her
to ooh and aah over the ring. He was surprised to hear them commenting solely on how many carats the diamond was, what the setting was like, and speculating on how much her fiancé had paid for
it. None of them asked a question about the proposal itself: where
did he take you, did he get down on one knee, what words of love
did he use to ask you to marry him? Instead, they were concentrating only on the financial value of the ring he had given her.

My friend Sabina got engaged last year to her long-term boyfriend, Francis. Francis had been working at a large brokerage firm and had a very well-paid job. However, after several years, Francis decided that he wasn't satisfied in his work, and what he really wanted to do was become a doctor. He had considerable savings from his salary, which he used to fund the costs of medical school, but naturally that was very expensive, and he and Sabina had to live in a modest way during his training. When Francis proposed, he and Sabina looked at expensive rings—Francis was quite prepared to spend a lot of money on an engagement ring, even if they were being careful with money. But Sabina didn't want him to spend a fortune—she told him that even had he still been working at his previous job, she wouldn't have wanted a $50,000 ring. It just wasn't her style. Instead, they settled on a much less pricey one, a really pretty band with white and blue diamonds (the latter being the precise color of her eyes).

Sabina loves her ring and is very happy with it—she says it's exactly the one she wanted. But, going out with them to parties, I have regularly observed women come up to her to see the ring, having heard about the engagement, and commiserate with her about how small the stones are, making comments like: "You should have gotten him to propose when he was still a broker—you'd have got a big rock then" or "That's what you get for marrying a medical student," or the worst one of all, "Oh, but it's so tiny!" Sabina, Francis, and I laugh about this kind of comment. But it's horribly indicative of the way a certain kind of woman thinks—the kind who is more interested in the bank balance of a man, rather than his great qualities. Francis is a loving, caring, faithful guy who any woman would be lucky to have, a hard worker who is doing really well at medical school and has great prospects. Still—"that's what you get for marrying a medical student"! It's very scary.

And then there's the woman at a party who told me how she broke off with her long-term boyfriend. Shortly after he proposed, she realized, confronted with the prospect of being with him for the rest of her life, that he wasn't the one for her. She did the right thing to break up with him—but she didn't when she kept the ring he had given her. The poor sap is still making payments on that ring. She actually presented her decision to keep the ring in terms of personal empowerment—as if she had somehow got the best of him. If he had broken the engagement—and her heart—this might have been understandable. But under these circumstances, it was outrageous behavior. Men were not put on this earth to maintain women. A relationship or marriage should be an equal partnership between two human beings. What goes around comes around, and that girl who hung on to the ring and made her ex-fiancé keep paying for it is storing herself up a lot of very bad karma indeed . . .

What to Do Instead: Value Yourself More Than Their Money

Amy was determined to marry someone with money. But she also wanted to find someone she loved. Following the old Yorkshire proverb, "Dunna marry for money, but go where money is," Amy targeted places she might expect to find men who were well off. With a girlfriend on the same quest as her, she hung out in bars where Wall Street brokers went to wind down; she dressed smartly and pleaded with check-in staff at airports to get upgrades on flights to sit in business class, where she might hope to meet single men traveling for work; she took up scuba diving and took shorter holidays so she could afford the expensive resorts where, again, there might be rich single men.

Amy, in short, did everything according to those books that tell you how to meet rich guys. She kept herself in very good shape, saved up for designer clothes, and never went out without expertly applied makeup and her hair nicely styled. And her efforts paid off. Amy did meet a very rich man, James, who fell for her. They dated for a few months and then James proposed. But the snag was that he wanted her to sign a prenup.

Rather ironically, Amy was hurt by this. She and James had a big fight about it, but James wouldn't back down. Amy debated with herself about whether she would take the risk of marrying James, even without the prenup. But the more she thought about it, the more she realized that she really wasn't in love with James; she had been swept away by the lavish holidays, the presents, the attentions he showered on her, and the glamorous lifestyle he could provide for her.

Amy wasn't at heart a bad person. She remembered that she had made a resolution to marry not just for money, but for love; she had gone where the money was to meet James, but the second part of the equation wasn't there. She told James she wouldn't marry him. James was so shocked that he did actually end up telling Amy that he would tear up the prenup. He was in love with her; he had just tried to be cautious financially, but he didn't want to lose her.

Faced with the possibility of marrying James without a prenup in place, Amy made the best decision of her life. She turned him down once again, telling him that she just wasn't in love with him enough to marry him. Amy couldn't quite believe she was doing this, but she knew in her heart that it was the right thing to do. She didn't have a massive moral turnaround after this incident; she was still sure that she wanted to marry a rich guy. But she knew that she didn't want to settle for someone she didn't care about. Amy continued with her program of haunting places where she could expect to find a man with a substantial bank account. Every so often she did regret turning James down, and she came close to ringing him several times. But then she met someone she really liked—an executive she sat next to on a flight from Denver to Chicago. They have been dating for two months and the relationship is going very well. Amy looks on course to get both the rich man she wants, and the love she needs.

SUMMARY

Do

- *Have faith that you will meet the right person.* There are so many people out there to meet—you don't need to compromise for less than love.

- *Marry primarily for love*—and all the other important values we're discussing in this book. But if money comes along with love, by all means enjoy it!

- *Be positive about being single.* Sure, you want a relationship—but you want the right one, and it's only sensible to be choosy. You're better off single than in an unsatisfactory relationship or marriage.

Don't

- *Settle.* It will only make you discontented and restless, and it's not fair to the person you're settling for.

- *Expect money in itself to make you happy.* It won't.

- *Treat men like cash cows.* It's lovely when they take you out to dinner, or on holiday, or buy you nice presents. But treat them as people and give them respect, because you want to be respected in return. And no one has respect for a gold digger.

✧   ✧   ✧   ✧

Tips for Working Out Whether You Are Settling, or Interested More in a Man's Money Than Him

✧ You talk to your girlfriends about how much he makes and the nice places he takes you, not about his good qualities.

✧ You spend a lot of time planning your fantasy wedding—the dress, the centerpieces, the setting—but the face of the groom is always hazy.

✧ You are so excited when someone well off asks you out that you don't stop to ask yourself how much *you* really like *him*.

✧ You have a preformed idea in your head about the kind of man you will end up with, and it's more about the lifestyle you will have together than anything else.

✧ You are desperate to have a baby, and see marriage as a means to that end, rather than something you want for itself.

✧ You focus more on a man's financial status than his compatibility with you.

EIGHT

BE WITTY IF YOU CAN, BUT NOT CYNICAL, INDISCREET, OR CRUEL

"I have been pained by [Miss Crawford's] manner this morning, and cannot get the better of it . . . the influence of her former companions makes her seem, gives to her conversation, to her professed opinions, sometimes a tinge of wrong. She does not <u>think</u> evil, but she speaks it—speaks it in playfulness—and though I know it to be playfulness, it grieves me to the soul."

—*MANSFIELD PARK*

THIS CHAPTER IS FOR anyone who suspects that they might be using humor as a defense or as a way of hiding from their true feelings. The Jane Austen heroines we warm to most of all—Emma Woodhouse and Elizabeth Bennet—are sympathetic because they are open and lively and love to joke. They have characteristics that we identify with; we would love to be like them—playful, funny, and charming. But in this chapter we will look at how well Elizabeth manages her sense of humor, using it to get to know people and endear herself to them, and how Emma sometimes goes over the top with hers and has to train herself to rein back its worst aspects. No gift is completely positive: you have to learn how to use everything for good, to make sure you're not putting off the very people you want to attract the most!

MARY CRAWFORD

"It is her countenance that is so attractive. She has a wonderful play of feature! But was there nothing in her conversation that struck you . . . as not quite right?"

—*MANSFIELD PARK*

Mary and Henry Crawford are clever, funny, charming, and attractive, possessing all the qualities anyone could wish to have. But, brought up by their uncle, Admiral Crawford, and his wife in a fast set in London, they have been corrupted by an atmosphere of careless behavior and poor morals (when the wife dies, Admiral Crawford, "a man of vicious conduct," moves his mistress into his house). By the time they visit the Mansfield Park area to stay with their aunt, Mrs. Grant, they are already lost souls, their values permanently contaminated by the life they have lived in London.

It's crucial to stress here that the morals of the nineteenth century were very different from our own. By contemporary standards, it is much more understandable to us that a man in a long marriage might well have a mistress on the side, even if we don't approve of it. But in Jane Austen's day, she couldn't have expressed more strongly how appalling his behavior was than by telling us that he actually moves the mistress into a house where he had lived with his wife—and where his niece and nephew are still in residence. It would be almost a parallel today, for instance, if Admiral Crawford had regularly beaten his wife and abused his nephew and niece. If you see it in these terms, you will understand how damaged Henry and Mary are by the lives they have lived. Mary refers to the "vices" she has seen at the admiral's house, and she is clearly talking not just about his conduct after the death of his wife, but during her entire upbringing, surrounded by his friends, who were as depraved as he. Thus, Henry and Mary have emerged from this environment with their core values completely warped, with little sense of morality or good conduct, and few goals but selfish short-term pleasure.

We have already seen how Henry messes up himself and most women around him by his hobby of making women fall in love with him for his own amusement. His sister, Mary, is not quite as bad as he, but she also suffers from the same moral corruption. Mary intends to marry a rich man, and is initially attracted to the older son of Mansfield Park, Tom Bertram, simply because he is the heir to the house and baronetcy. She initially ignores Edmund, the second son, because he will be much poorer than Tom and won't have the title. Mrs. Grant tells Mary that, living with her aunt and uncle in London, she has been in "a bad school for matrimony," and Mary knows this is true; having seen the admiral's treatment of his wife while she was alive, Mary has had a terrible model of marital happiness on which to base her own ideas. "My poor aunt," she agrees, "had certainly little cause to love the state; but however, speaking for my own observation, it is a manoeuvring business." Mary has learned to see marriage not in terms of love, but strategy. Mrs. Grant disapproves: "You are as bad as your brother, Mary; but we will cure you both. Mansfield shall cure you both . . ."

And Mansfield Park, in the person of Edmund Bertram, does indeed offer Mary the possibility of a cure. Edmund is quiet, gentle, caring, and strong. He is immediately attracted to Mary, and admires her sharp sense of humor, even though he sees from the first that she is too free with her rather scandalous opinions, and too careless of how they may seem to others. Still, he defends her against Fanny's criticisms: he says that when Mary speaks too freely she has "the right of a lively mind . . . seizing whatever may contribute to its own amusement or that of others; perfectly allowable, when untinctured by ill humour or roughness; and there is not a shadow of either in the countenance or manner of Miss Crawford, nothing sharp, or loud, or coarse. She is perfectly feminine, except in the instances we have been speaking of . . ."

And Mary begins to fall for Edmund. "Without any of the arts of flattery or the gaieties of small talk, he began to be agreeable to her. She felt it to be so, though she had not foreseen and could hardly understand it; for he was not pleasant by any common rule, he talked no nonsense, he paid no compliments, his opinions were unbending, his attentions tranquil and simple. There was a charm, perhaps, in his sincerity, his steadiness, his integrity . . ."

Mary is horrified to learn that Edmund plans to be a clergyman; she has no intention of becoming a vicar's wife in a small country parish. Her ambitions are much larger. And yet Edmund's appeal grows on her, to the point that she is ready to marry him even though he is the opposite of the rich, charming titled man she always thought would be her husband. Meanwhile, Edmund is so seduced by her charm and wit that he is desperate to marry her, even though he knows that she is morally flawed—"That uncle and aunt!" he complains to Fanny. "They have injured the finest mind!—for sometimes . . . it does appear more than manner; it appears as if the mind itself was tainted."

Edmund is right. Mary isn't capable of learning from him and letting her better feelings come to the fore. She has enough of those to realize that Edmund is the man for her, but not enough to suppress her worldliness and cynicism. Shockingly, when Edmund's brother Tom falls very ill, Mary's thoughts immediately leap to the prospect of Edmund's becoming the heir to his father's estate and title. She even writes to Fanny that she hopes that Tom will die of his illness—not in so many words, but her intent is clear: "Poor young man!—If he is to die, there will be *two* poor young men less in the world . . . And now, do not trouble yourself to be ashamed of either my feelings or your own. Believe me, they are not only natural, they are philanthropic and virtuous. I put it to your conscience, whether 'Sir Edmund' would not do more good with all the Bertram property, than any other possible 'Sir.' "

If Edmund had seen this letter, he would have dumped Mary in an instant. But he is soon to be faced with an instance of her hypocrisy and cynicism that he cannot ignore. When his sister Maria runs off with Henry Crawford, Edmund goes to see Mary, and her attitude to the scandal is so worldly and cynical that he is forced to realize that he can never marry her. She takes the matter too lightly for him, suggesting that Maria must stay with Henry so that he will eventually feel himself under an obligation to marry her. Edmund is horrified at this; he sees it as condoning adultery, and Mary should surely know that to speak this way to a clergyman is idiotic. Again, the course of action Mary proposes for Maria may seem understandable to us. But by the standards of Austen's time, it's as if Mary were suggesting that Maria become a prostitute. Seeing it in this way will make us understand how profoundly shocked Edmund is, and why he cannot propose to Mary—her values are much too corrupt for him. And it shows, too, how self-centered Mary is: common sense should dictate to her that even if that's what she secretly thinks, giving that opinion to a man like Edmund—about his own sister!—will irretrievably ruin things with him. Mary is incapable of seeing anyone else's perspective but her own.

Recounting the meeting to Fanny, Edmund describes Mary's take on the scandal: "She saw it only as folly, and that folly stamped only by exposure . . . I do not consider her as meaning to wound my feelings. The evil lies yet deeper . . . She was speaking only as she had been used to hear others speak, as she imagined everybody else would speak. Hers are not faults of temper . . . Hers are faults of principle . . . of blunted delicacy and a corrupted, vitiated mind."

Edmund leaves Mary forever, and marries Fanny. But Mary still yearns for him; she "was long in finding . . . anyone who could satisfy the better taste she had acquired at Mansfield, whose character and manners could authorise a hope of the domestic happiness she had there learnt to estimate, or put Edmund Bertram sufficiently out of her head."

LESSON TO BE LEARNED

CYNICISM WILL DAMAGE YOU BADLY
IF YOU LET IT TAKE YOU OVER

What Not to Do: Don't Be Ruled by Negative Images from the Past

After growing up in the shadow of his parents' messy and bitterly fought divorce, Colby—like Henry and Mary—was deeply cynical about relationships in general and marriage in particular. He didn't believe that it was possible for two people to love and trust each other for any length of time—his parents had cheated on each other, and he had also seen their post-divorce relationships being plagued with problems. Colby had learned from an early age to hide his real feelings behind a mask of imperturbability—having read the book *The Man in the Iron Mask* when he was young, he used this image as a way to help him through his parents' fighting. He closed himself down and wouldn't let anyone in. Colby was determined not to be hurt again.

However, he still had a need for love and physical contact. Colby had brief-lived affairs in college and after he graduated and got a job, but they all foundered for one of two reasons: either Colby found the girls too needy, or they wanted to take care of him. Colby was so determined to be independent, not to need anyone, that if a girl tried to be at all nurturing to him, he pushed her away.

Then Colby met Lily. Lily was the sister of a work colleague of Colby's, and she came into his office to meet her brother one day. Lily was strong, smart, and independent—she was self-employed because she wanted to run her life in her own way, without answering to a boss. Colby was immediately attracted to Lily, not only because she was very pretty, but because of all those qualities that indicated to him that she wouldn't be needy, wouldn't cling to him, and wouldn't try to change him, because she was happily focused on her own life and needs.

Colby wasn't by any means a ladies' man, but he did manage to ask Lily out. She agreed; Lily, too, was looking for a man who wouldn't cling to her, who would respect her independence, and Colby seemed perfect. Lily and Colby grew closer and closer, and after a few months they were very much in love. Lily traveled a lot for work and she was grateful that in Colby she had found someone who wasn't jealous, who understood that she needed to take frequent business trips without pressuring her to stay at home more, and didn't fuss about the possibility that she might have a fling with another man while she was away. Lily had no intention of cheating on Colby, and she appreciated his trust and his understanding.

Still, there were warning signs about Colby's character that Lily chose to ignore. Though she gave him the keys to her apartment, he didn't reciprocate by giving her his. He was happy to bring her into his life, introducing her to his family and friends, but showed no interest in reciprocating by getting to know hers; when they did occasionally go out with her friends, he was stilted and obviously uncomfortable. He wanted her to share his interests, taking her to baseball games that she didn't enjoy but made an effort to understand for his sake; but he refused to accompany her to the concerts and plays that she liked. Colby was acting very selfishly. He would let Lily into his life to some degree (though not going so far as to give her keys to his place!) but wouldn't enter or be a part of hers.

Loving Colby as she did, Lily closed her eyes to these imbalances in the relationship. But after a year, Lily began to wonder where things were going with them. Colby and she hadn't made plans to move in together, or even discussed it. She tried to broach the subject with Colby, but he didn't want to talk about it. Lily let it go, hoping that she had planted a seed and that Colby would think about it and bring it up himself. But Colby never did. After another six months, Lily raised the subject again, but she could see from Colby's reaction that he was very opposed to any discussion about living together. She knew that Colby loved her, but she was beginning to realize that he just wasn't capable of committing to her any more than he already had.

Lily spent the next few months in a lot of pain. She loved Colby and wanted to marry him, but she didn't believe that he would ever want to move ahead to the next stage—living together and talking about marriage. She knew that theirs was the only serious relationship that Colby had ever had, and while in the beginning she had liked the fact that there were no ex-girlfriends to be jealous of, now she started to realize that it had actually been yet another danger sign. Colby had never had a serious relationship before because he wasn't capable of it. Lily's independence and strong character had allowed him to be more committed to her than he had managed to with another woman, but now he had reached his limit.

Lily told Colby that she had to break up with him unless he could fully commit to her. Colby's heart was broken. He was completely in love with Lily and didn't want a life without her. If he could marry anyone, it would be Lily. But he just couldn't do it. His childhood experiences had damaged him too much, and he wasn't brave enough to get some professional help to work through the issues with which it had left him. Colby and Lily cried in each other's arms for several days before Lily got up the strength to leave him.

Lily has moved on and met someone else, though it took her a year and a half to recover from Colby. But Colby hasn't seriously dated anyone since. His broken relationship with Lily has only deepened his cynicism; instead of taking the pain he went through as a wake-up call, he has retreated even further behind the iron mask he adopted in childhood for safety. Lily made the right decision, but if she had managed to look out for the signs earlier, she wouldn't have got so involved with Colby; the breakup would have come sooner; and she would have spared herself a lot of pain. If she had been strong enough to call him on the imbalances in their relationship earlier, she would have understood Colby's limitations and been able to break things off with him before falling so deeply in love and getting so badly hurt.

What to Do Instead: Learn to Move On and Put the Past Behind You

Two years after his painful divorce, Scott was still wary of getting involved. He wanted to be married, but his marriage had gone so badly wrong that he didn't think he could trust anyone again deeply enough to propose to her. However, he missed the physical companionship and closeness, and had started to date, though as soon as he started to get close to a woman he would make excuses to himself as to why it wouldn't work out, and would dump her.

Jerri had been warned by her friends that Scott wasn't ready for a serious relationship. So, although she found him attractive, she steered clear of getting too close to him. Scott was very interested in Jerri, and asked her out, but she turned him down nicely. Even without her friends' warning, she felt that Scott was sending her mixed messages; he would pay her compliments and be attentive, but at the same time he would seem to be pulling away—he would go to get her a drink at the bar when a group of them were out, but then come back twenty minutes later, having forgotten her drink. Or he would make a comment about women that he meant to be funny, but it had a bitter edge, and was completely inappropriate to the subject they were discussing. Once he invited her to a party some of his friends were giving, and seemed happy to see her, but then disappeared immediately after greeting her, going out to get some take-out food, and leaving Jerri on her own for half an hour in a group of strangers. All these indications showed Jerri that she couldn't afford to like Scott too much, because he was unreliable. So she protected herself by pulling back.

Over the next six months, Scott would ring Jerri up occasionally and ask her out, when he had tickets to something he thought might interest her. It was very occasional—every few weeks or so. Sometimes Jerri did agree, because he'd caught her at a weak moment, and they would go to the theater or to a concert and then maybe for drinks afterward. Scott was nice on these outings, and they would have good conversations, but he never tried to kiss her at the end of the evening, partly because he wasn't ready, and partly because Jerri didn't encourage him. She was careful with him, feeling that there was still sometimes a harsh edge to his conversation, and she didn't want to get romantically involved with someone like that.

Jerri did date other men during this time, but nothing worked out. Scott, meanwhile, was gradually beginning to feel a change in himself. As the damage from the divorce faded away, he was less cynical; he was finding the old Scott coming through again, the person he had been before the divorce, someone who was more open and less bitter about women. Slowly but surely he began to accept that his ex-wife had been just one woman, not representative of the entire sex; just because he hadn't been able to trust her didn't mean that all women were equally untrustworthy. And he respected Jerri for not pushing him when he wasn't really ready—she had never called him, and in retrospect, as he began to recover from the aftermath of the divorce, he realized that Jerri had been right to be wary of him and not initiate contact. He looked back and saw that he had not been the kind of man that any sensible woman would want to go out with.

On one of their evenings out, after six months or so, both Scott and Jerri felt a change in the atmosphere. Things were much easier and more relaxed. Before, when they'd gone out, they had liked each other but the communication had been snarled; it was as if there were a maze between them and it would be almost impossible for them to find a way through to each other. Now that maze was disappearing, and the lines of communication were much more straightforward. They really clicked that evening, and Scott rang Jerri only a week later to ask her out again. This time things were even better. They began seeing each other much more regularly. Scott was still tentative and Jerri, sensing that, went slowly, too. But she could feel the difference in him and was encouraged by it. She started to call him every so often, instead of leaving it all up to him, and Scott responded well to that. After a couple of months of this slow-and-steady dating, they kissed for the first time, and it was great.

Scott discovered that he really liked Jerri. He understood that he was going to have to put his cynicism aside and learn to trust again if he was ever going to have the kind of relationship he wanted. He could also see that she was a sensible woman who had truly responded to him only when he had been showing the real Scott, the open, easygoing person he had been before his divorce had embittered him. He made a real effort to open himself up to her, to take a risk, and the rewards were huge. Jerri and Scott have now been a steady couple for more than a year, and Scott is seriously considering proposing to her.

ELIZABETH BENNET VS. MISS BINGLEY

"Undoubtedly . . . there is meanness in all the arts which
ladies sometimes condescend to employ for captivation.
Whatever bears affinity to cunning is despicable."
—*PRIDE AND PREJUDICE*

We have already seen how Mr. Darcy falls in love with Elizabeth because of the way she teases him, her playfulness, her bubbling sense of humor. Elizabeth doesn't suck up to him; she isn't using her teasing as a way to flatter him or grab his attention. She is simply being herself, and that's what attracts him so much. Of course, he also finds her very pretty, and when he expresses this to Miss Bingley, the latter immediately becomes jealous.

Miss Bingley is the sister of Mr. Bingley, Darcy's best friend, and she intends to marry Darcy if she possibly can. Jane Austen uses Miss Bingley to contrast with Elizabeth, showing how Elizabeth always gets it right, while Miss Bingley invariably makes a mistake. Where Elizabeth is light, Miss Bingley is heavy-handed; Elizabeth is playful, while Miss Bingley studies everything she says in order to make its best effect on Darcy; Elizabeth teases, while Miss Bingley is bitchy.

And Miss Bingley is one of the nastiest bitches in the whole of Austen's oeuvre. Practically as soon as she opens her mouth for the first time, we hear her criticizing Elizabeth and Jane Bennet—even though Jane is supposed to be Miss Bingley's new best friend. Jane is ill and staying with the Bingleys because she's too sick to be moved home. Elizabeth walks over to visit her, and Miss Bingley immediately starts in on Elizabeth. In classic Miss Bingley style, the negative comments start the moment Elizabeth is out of the room: "Her manners were pronounced to be very bad indeed, a mixture of pride and impertinence; she had no conversation, no style, no taste, no beauty." Miss Bingley complains that, in her haste to see her sick sister, Elizabeth has taken a shortcut across some fields and got the hem of her dress muddy: "What could she mean by it? It seems to me to shew an abominable sort of conceited independence, a most country town indifference to decorum . . . I am afraid, Mr Darcy . . . that this adventure has rather affected your admiration of her fine eyes."

"Not at all," Darcy replies; "they were brightened by the exercise."

As well as being nasty, Miss Bingley is also a fool. This is the first time she has criticized Elizabeth to Darcy, and she gets slapped down. But she is incapable of learning from her mistakes; she continues putting down Elizabeth to him every chance she gets. When she, Elizabeth, and Darcy start a conversation about the accomplishments that every young woman should possess, it's clear that Miss Bingley is doing so in order to point out how many she has, and how many Elizabeth lacks. Elizabeth refuses to engage in competition; instead, she makes a joke of it, saying that nobody could possibly be the model of perfection Miss Bingley is describing. When Elizabeth leaves the room, Miss Bingley turns on her at once (as usual—Miss Bingley's very big on talking badly about people as soon as they're out the door), saying to Darcy: "Eliza Bennet . . . is one of those young ladies who seek to recommend themselves to the other sex, by undervaluing their own . . . A paltry device, a very mean art."

But Darcy again won't hear Elizabeth criticized. "Undoubtedly," he says, "there is meanness in *all* the arts which ladies sometimes condescend to employ for captivation. Whatever bears affinity to cunning is despicable."

Miss Bingley understands this enough not to answer him, but she isn't clever enough to perceive that cattiness is not the way to Darcy's heart. Miss Bingley, in fact, confuses cruelty with wit. She isn't capable of seeing the real difference between her behavior and Elizabeth's; that Elizabeth is never bitchy; that she jokes spontaneously, for the pleasure of amusing and being amused; while Miss Bingley is always calculating the effect of what she says on her listener. There's no spontaneity there, no pleasure in bantering. She even describes Elizabeth's wit to Darcy as "that little something, bordering on conceit and impertinence."

Miss Bingley's idea of seducing a man is to flatter him, to agree with everything he says (Austen calls her Darcy's "faithful assistant" at one point), and to be unpleasant about any other woman he may praise. Unsurprisingly, these tactics don't work. When Elizabeth suggests to her, in Darcy's hearing, that he needs to be taken down a peg—"Teaze him—laugh at him.—Intimate as you are, you must know how it is to be done . . ." Miss Bingley recoils in horror, choosing her words in a way that she thinks will flatter Darcy to the utmost: "But upon my honour I do *not*. I do assure you that my intimacy has not yet taught me *that*. Teaze calmness of temper and presence of mind! No, no—I feel he may defy us there."

Elizabeth makes it clear that this is absolute nonsense. "Mr Darcy is not to be laughed at! . . . That is an uncommon advantage, and uncommon I hope it will continue, for it would be a great loss to *me* to have many such acquaintance. I dearly love a laugh."

And that's why Darcy falls in love with her. If she had just been a pretty girl with those "fine eyes" he praises, he wouldn't have noticed her beyond that. But Elizabeth's liveliness, her wit, her love of laughing, are just what he needs, while he is quite capable of seeing through Miss Bingley. It's a shame for Miss Bingley that she is too self-important to understand that he's giving her a heavy hint when he refers to "meanness" and "cunning."

LESSON TO BE LEARNED

BE FUNNY, IF YOU CAN, BUT NOT MEAN

What Not to Do: Don't Bolster Yourself by Putting Other People Down

From an early age, Jenna had always been very good at making acute, bitchy comments about people. It was something she had learned from her mother, a classic Miss Bingley type, motivated by jealousy and insecurity, whose favorite sport was criticizing the people she knew behind their backs. Jenna's ability to poke fun at people's weak spots soon made her well known at school, and she had a coterie of girls who hung round with her. Jenna considered these girls her friends, but actually their association with her was out of fear rather than friendship: they wanted to get on Jenna's good side, for fear of what she might say about them if she turned against them. And they spent so much time with her because, again, they were nervous about what might happen if they didn't. They'd seen how Jenna would rip on someone as soon as she left the room, or did something Jenna didn't like; they didn't want to end up with one of the nicknames Jenna bestowed on people, nicknames that always stuck because they managed to pinpoint so accurately a physical oddity or embarrassing habit that her targets had. Jenna—pretty, well groomed, and well dressed— was one of those Queen Bees described by sociologists who study girl groups, keeping her "court" together by intimidation and fear.

The sycophancy of her courtiers taught Jenna that being bitchy was the way to get friends. And she thought she was being funny, because they would always laugh at her nastier comments. Still, she didn't understand that they were laughing more out of nervousness and fear of her turning on them, rather than genuine amusement. At college, Jenna's technique still worked, though slightly less well; college was much larger and the groups people joined for protection at high school were less necessary. She began to notice, though, that she didn't have boyfriends. Girls appreciate bitchiness much more than men do—and nobody wants to date Miss Bingley. Even Darcy would rather marry Elizabeth, despite her low birth, lack of financial advantages, and embarrassing family, than the well-bred but sharp-tongued Miss Bingley. Men who were initially attracted to Jenna would be put off as soon as she opened her mouth.

Jenna is now twenty-five, with a good job—she's smart and competent—but the people in her office give her a wide berth. The tricks that worked in high school to make friends are seen, in the real world, as cruel and destructive. Jenna can't figure out what she's doing wrong. She's increasingly lonely and isolated, but it would take someone who really cared about her to be honest enough to tell her that being cruel and mocking isn't the way to make friends or attract men. Her boss has noticed what's going on, and is thinking about giving Jenna a tactful hint. She finds Jenna a very good worker and doesn't want her to be handicapped by her bad habit. If Jenna's boss finds a way to tell her that she's alienating people, it would be the best thing that's ever happened to Jenna. Because the way she is right now, she's never going to make friends—let alone date a man she likes.

What to Do Instead: Use Your Humor to Make People Feel at Ease

Dennis wasn't particularly physically attractive, but from an early age he had learned to compensate for his lack of hunkiness by making people laugh. Dennis was genuinely very funny, and he loved to joke and entertain people. He was popular and had a good circle of friends, but he was looking to meet someone for a serious relationship, and he had been disappointed in the past when girls he liked, who found him funny and laughed at his jokes, still went off with guys who didn't have as good personalities as he did, but were better-looking.

So when he met Jenny, he was tentative. He liked Jenny very much, and didn't want to be disappointed. In the past, he had tried to make women like him by making them laugh, only to find out that, though they enjoyed his company and sense of humor, they weren't romantically interested in him. Dennis actually held back from getting to know Jenny, because he didn't want to be hurt.

Jenny, however, was very attracted to Dennis. He was good-tempered, happy, and popular, and she very much liked all these qualities and wanted to get to know him better. Jenny had dated men who were good-looking but didn't have much to say for themselves, and once the initial attraction had worn off, she had found that she was bored by them. Dennis seemed like someone who would never be boring. Not only that—Dennis's humor was always generous. He didn't make fun of people, or mock them. This, more than anything, was what attracted Jenny to him. She had been in the habit of dating men who didn't treat her very well, and having realized that, had decided that it was a pattern she wanted to change. Dennis seemed like the exact opposite of the men she had previously dated: he was genuinely nice and open, and didn't have the kind of good looks that often make men arrogant and selfish, because they always have women running after them.

Jenny was also intrigued by the fact that Dennis seemed to avoid her when they were out in a group of mutual friends. As so often when you are attracted to someone, this made her even more interested; she saw Dennis as a bit of a challenge. A pretty girl who was used to getting attention from men, Jenny was curious about the reasons why Dennis was acting a little standoffish with her when he was so friendly and sincere with everyone else. Even when she tried to flirt with him he seemed to back away. Wondering why, she told one of her female friends that she liked Dennis but he didn't seem to like her, and the friend immediately contradicted her. More, she passed the information on to Dennis.

Dennis was blown away by the news that Jenny was attracted to him. He started talking to her and Jenny was totally charmed by him. They went out, and they laughed all evening. Dennis was in very good form, encouraged by the fact that he knew she liked him. Dennis was slow to make a pass at Jenny; in fact, he eventually confided that he felt out of his league with her—she was so pretty, and he just didn't think he was that attractive. Jenny was very touched by this; it made her warm to Dennis even more.

Of course, his insecurity might have put Jenny off. But she was self-confident enough to take it as a compliment, and she reassured him, because she could tell that Dennis's insecurity was only on the surface, and didn't run too deep. She sensed that once he realized her attraction for him was genuine, she wouldn't have to spend all her time repeating the same words of reassurance. Jenny did exactly the right thing; instead of protecting herself or hiding behind humor, she told Dennis frankly that she hadn't been that well treated by previous boyfriends, and one of the reasons she liked him so much was that he seemed so warm, open, and considerate. She told him that she thought he was the funniest, nicest person she had ever met and she really liked his outgoing personality and the way he always saw the jokey side of everything. This allowed Dennis, who had just made himself vulnerable, to see vulnerability in Jenny, too, and it brought them very close. He assured Jenny that he really liked her and wanted to treat her well, and he made good on his words, proving it through his actions. As a result of their opening up to each other, Dennis and Jenny made a real connection. They are now engaged, and they're blissfully happy.

EMMA WOODHOUSE AND FRANK CHURCHILL

*"Our companions are excessively stupid. What shall we do
to rouse them? Any nonsense will serve."*

—*EMMA*

As we have already seen, Emma and Frank have a bad effect on each other. They are too alike; both of them love to use their quick wits to amuse and entertain, but together, under the wrong circumstances, they can become toxic. They push each other to new heights of wit, gossiping about the people they know and being very playful. This in itself is no bad thing; a couple that loves to laugh together and shares a similar sense of humor has a very strong base for their relationship. But Emma and Frank end up pushing each other into doing things they know are wrong, and wouldn't have done without the other's encouragement.

Frank bitches about Jane Fairfax—the woman he loves—to Emma. It starts as a tease to himself; he loves Jane so much that he takes a perverse pleasure in criticizing her to Emma, because, since the engagement is secret, he can't praise her openly. Frank is hugging to his heart the secret that he loves and is loved by Jane. He wants to talk about her any way he can, and this is the solution he finds—criticizing the very qualities in Jane that he secretly finds so attractive, like her calmness of mind. Miss Fairfax's reserve, he says to Emma, "is a most repulsive quality indeed . . . there is safety in reserve, but no attraction. One cannot love a reserved person."

And Emma—who resents Jane because the latter is beautiful and gifted—is immediately led on to bitch about Jane in return: "Intimacy between Miss Fairfax and me is quite out of the question. I have no reason to think ill of her . . . except that such extreme and perpetual cautiousness of word and manner . . . is apt to suggest suspicions of there being something to conceal."

Poor Jane does indeed have something to conceal: her secret engagement to Frank. But her fiancé, instead of defending her, "perfectly agreed" with Emma, and continues, with Emma as a willing accomplice, to find opportunities to tease and embarrass Jane. On one occasion, when they are all playing a game, Frank gives Emma and Jane a word puzzle whose solution he knows will upset and embarrass Jane. Mr. Knightley, who is in love with Emma, notices this, and confronts Emma about it: "Pray, Emma, may I ask in what lay the great amusement, the poignant sting of the last word given to you and Miss Fairfax? I . . . am curious to know how it could be so very entertaining to the one, and so very distressing to the other."

Emma is embarrassed, and says it was "a mere joke." But Mr. Knightley won't let her off the hook. "The joke," he replied gravely, "seemed confined to you and Mr Churchill."

Even this gentle hint to Emma doesn't rein her in; she continues to tease Jane, and ends up—as we have already seen—being very rude to Jane's aunt, poor garrulous Miss Bates, under Frank's encouragement. Frank and Jane have had a fight, and Frank punishes Jane by flirting openly with Emma on a disastrous afternoon picnic where a group of them are gathered. "Every distinguishing attention that could be paid, was paid to [Emma]. To amuse her, and be agreeable in her eyes, seemed all that he cared for . . ." Frank is described at the picnic as being so overexcited that "[his] spirits rose to a pitch almost unpleasant," and his humor becomes positively cruel.

Together, Emma and Frank have a nasty tendency to use their wit to amuse themselves at the expense of others. They both need to find partners who will calm them down, not overstimulate them to the point of going over the top and taking their high spirits out on vulnerable targets.

LESSON TO BE LEARNED

BE AWARE OF THE IMPACT YOUR JOKES HAVE ON OTHER PEOPLE

What Not to Do: Don't Use Humor as a Shield to Hide Behind

Karen always has the people she knows in stitches. She's quick-witted and funny and her colleagues at work are often gathered around her desk, hearing her take on the day's events and gossip. Karen finds it very easy to make new friends and meet men; people are attracted to her lively personality and her love of laughing. She regularly hangs out in the bar around the corner from her home, where she knows all the bartenders and most of the locals and has a great group of friends. Karen is a real live wire. But her humor is a defense mechanism, born out of insecurity and anxiety about her weight. She is a little overweight and doesn't consider herself that attractive; she was teased in school for being pudgy, and learned then that if she made jokes and teased people back, she could carve out a role for herself as the class clown, someone people hung around with because she made them laugh. If she laughs and jokes and rips on people, she thinks that will mean that they won't notice her extra pounds, and will want to be with her purely because of her personality.

Joe, a friend of a regular in the bar, was instantly attracted to Karen when he saw her at the center of a group of people, laughing and talking. He didn't care that she was a little overweight; in fact, he had always preferred women who were more curvy and rounded than the socially accepted norm. He liked her energy and her popularity. Karen seemed like someone who would always be up and happy and see the positive side of life. He got his friend to introduce him to her, and they got on very well. Karen found Joe very attractive and they clicked immediately. They hung out in the bar, and eventually Joe asked Karen out on a date. They went out and things just kept going very well.

After a month or so, Joe wanted Karen to meet some of his friends. He was very excited about introducing her to them—he thought Karen could be the one. And at first, his friends really liked all the qualities about her to which Joe had been attracted. But then Karen started doing what she was used to—making snide comments about the other people in the bar, pulling them to pieces, commenting on how badly one girl was dressed, making fun of another group. When Karen was on her home turf, she had all of her friends around her, egging her on and rewarding her bitchy comments by laughing at them. Karen had done this when she was out with Joe, too, but he was so physically attracted to her that he hadn't really noticed the edge and the bitchiness behind her humor. His friends, however, did—and now Joe started seeing Karen through their eyes.

One of Joe's friends mentioned to Karen that she was being pretty mean to the girl she was criticizing, but Karen laughed it off. After that, though, Joe began to notice how negative a lot of Karen's humor was. He tried to talk to her about it, but Karen got very offended. She said that she was just having a laugh, and Joe was taking it much too seriously. In fact, Joe's comments provoked Karen into being even more bitchy. She took the attitude that Joe had liked her in the beginning for who she was, and now he was trying to change her.

There was some truth in that. Joe had been too dazzled by Karen to really see that her humor was founded on pulling other people down; he had gone along with her circle of friends, laughing with her, instead of taking the time to study her behavior and realize that he didn't actually like this crucial aspect of it. But now Joe tried to point out to Karen that she didn't have to mock other people in order to be funny.

It didn't work. Karen blew off his criticism. She said that was just the way she was, she didn't mean any harm by it, and Joe was taking her much too seriously. Joe was disturbed by the fact that Karen just didn't seem to get why he was concerned about this. They continued to date, but now every time Karen made one of her catty comments, Joe called her on it. Obviously, this caused a lot of friction, and their relationship started to deteriorate. Karen didn't have the courage to admit to Joe that the reason she ripped on people was self-protection, that her insecurity about her weight had led her into this pattern of behavior. It was a real shame, because if she had been brave enough to do so, Joe would have given her all the reassurance she could have wanted: he would have told her that he found her very attractive just the way she was and that he didn't want her to lose a pound. They could have built a relationship based on honesty, and Joe's words would have caused Karen to calm down and no longer feel the need to use her sense of humor in a negative way.

Joe and Karen eventually broke up. Karen blamed Joe: she told all her friends that he didn't have a sense of humor. But she had really liked Joe, and it caused her a lot of pain. Joe was suffering, too—he had been very into Karen. But he didn't want to spend his life with someone who tore down other people. Joe made the right decision. It's always hard to hear criticism, but it's a shame that Karen couldn't listen to what Joe was telling her. It wouldn't have hurt her to moderate her humor, to make it slightly less cruel, and it would have meant that she would have kept a boyfriend who was very good for her. She should have realized that she no longer needed to use her sense of humor to protect herself from her insecurities about her physical appearance, because Joe had clearly demonstrated that he liked her body just the way it was.

What to Do Instead: Be Serious When Necessary—
Don't Make a Joke When It's Not Appropriate

Charlotte's entire family was quick-witted and they loved to tease one another. Charlotte had grown up in an atmosphere of endless joking and affectionate mockery, and she was the quickest-witted one of all. She was never at a loss for a snappy comeback or a silly joke. She loved to entertain people and had a big circle of friends, who were always encouraging her to say something outrageous and funny.

However, Charlotte, like Emma, could go over the top sometimes. She had never learned to recognize the limits, and occasionally she would go too far and hurt someone. But she was working on it. First of all, her sister took her aside one evening and said that she had just made a wisecrack that had really hurt one of her friends. Charlotte was shocked and mortified at the time, but it didn't sink in beyond that evening. The second time, her closest friend told her severely that she was going much too far in mocking the outfit of a woman sitting close to them; the woman had heard her and been very upset. Charlotte's friend was harder on her than her sister had been, and it was a real wake-up call. Charlotte determined that she was going to keep better control of herself in the future. She also took time to think over what she was doing, and realized that her humor was born to some degree out of arrogance. She tried to be a little more humble, to not think she was better than everyone else because she was so quick-witted.

When she met Jonathan, she was doing well in keeping to this resolution. But Jonathan made her nervous, because she was so attracted to him, and Charlotte's usual way of coping with her nervousness was to go into full-on joking mode. Because she was working hard on not being bitchy, she didn't put Jonathan off with ill-judged comments about people around them. But she did end up keeping him at a certain distance; Jonathan liked her and wanted to get to know her better, but he found it hard to get through Charlotte's barrage of funny comments. He sensed that she used her humor as something of a shield. He loved the fact that Charlotte was so open and funny, but he wanted to get to know the person behind the shield as well.

As Charlotte got more comfortable with Jonathan, she began to relax and let him get to know her a bit better. Jonathan walked her home one night and kissed her at her front door. It was such a great kiss that it made Charlotte nervous, and because she was used to filling silences with her jokes, she made a wisecrack about it. To her surprise, Jonathan got really cross. He said that he really liked Charlotte, that he loved her humor, but there was a time and a place for it and he wanted to be able to kiss her without feeling that she needed to make a joke immediately afterward. Charlotte protested that she had just thought of something funny and wanted to say it, but Jonathan told her that she wasn't being honest with herself; she had made a joke because she was scared of getting close to him, and sometimes, you needed to be serious.

Charlotte was taken aback by what he had said. But when she thought about it later, she admitted that he was right. She *had* felt very serious about the kiss; why had she deflated the moment with a wisecrack? She also realized that the people she cared about—her sister, her best friend, and now Jonathan—were those who were strong enough to tell her when she needed to rein herself in. Jonathan was right. She shouldn't use her sense of humor as a defense. She rang him up and said that she wanted to see him again. Jonathan helped Charlotte to calm down and not fall back on cracking jokes when they weren't appropriate, and Charlotte gave the quieter, more restrained Jonathan the energy and fun that came with dating the live wire that she was. They balanced each other out very well indeed.

SUMMARY

Do

- *Be spontaneous.* That's where the best humor comes from.

- *Find someone who makes you laugh.* That's the best way of making sure you feel relaxed with him. And it will make a bond that lasts for the rest of your life.

- *Laugh at yourself!* This will stop you from taking yourself too seriously. And surround yourself with people who can laugh at you affectionately, too.

Don't

- *Be bitchy.* If you really have to make snarky comments, save them for your friends. Cattiness will turn off a man who's attracted to you.

- *Use humor as a defense.* If you do, it will stop you from getting as close to someone as you want. Defensive humor will deflect the honesty and simplicity that are crucial for building a relationship.

- *Be cynical.* This seems attractive in books—particularly in the heroes of Jane Austen–imitating romance novels!—but doesn't work in real life. You have to open up and be loving to be loved.

❖ ❖ ❖ ❖

Tips for Seeing If You're Using Humor or Cynicism as a Defense Against Your Insecurity

❖ You're never short of a wisecrack—you are always filling awkward silences with a joke, especially when those silences might lead to an honest declaration of your feelings.

❖ When a man gives you a compliment, you immediately wonder what he wants from you, instead of simply enjoying it.

❖ You feel that it's your job to "entertain" everyone, as if people will only like you while you keep them laughing.

❖ If you're quiet or thoughtful, people ask you what's the matter—they're used to you always being "up."

❖ When you recount to your friends a compliment your boyfriend paid you, you have to dismiss it jokingly immediately afterward—"he really needs to get his eyes checked!"—as if you don't quite feel you deserve it.

NINE

BE PREPARED TO WAIT FOR THE RIGHT PERSON TO COME ALONG

"It is a period, indeed!
Eight years and a half is a period!"

—*PERSUASION*

I'M CERTAINLY NOT ADVOCATING following the example of Anne Elliot, who has to wait more than eight years to see the man she loves again, and then hope that he'll still be free and thinking romantically of her! But poor Anne lives a very secluded life, without the chance to meet many eligible men. Thank goodness that nowadays women don't have to live in such restricted circumstances, dependent on their families for the ability to move around and meet new people. Still, just because we have a freedom in the twenty-first century of which a girl in the Regency period couldn't even dream, that doesn't mean that we should overcompensate by grabbing at every dating possibility that comes along. Surrounded by the multiple ways to meet men that we have in the modern age—parties, bars, the Internet, singles events—we have to take a deep breath, learn to pace ourselves, and learn to discriminate between Mr. Right Now and Mr. Right. And when we meet a prospect we really like, that's when the real work of pacing ourselves starts. If you throw yourself crazily at someone, you may scare him so much that he steps aside and you find yourself smacking into the wall behind him instead.

COLONEL BRANDON AND MARIANNE DASHWOOD

Colonel Brandon was now as happy, as all those who best loved him, believed he deserved to be;—in Marianne he was consoled for every past affliction . . .
—*SENSE AND SENSIBILITY*

In *Sense and Sensibility*, Colonel Brandon falls for Marianne Dashwood almost as soon as he lays eyes on her. Marianne reminds him very much of the young woman he loved years ago, who for financial reasons was forced to marry his brother instead. Colonel Brandon sees, however, that Marianne is not interested in him. She considers him "an absolute old bachelor, for he was on the wrong side of five and thirty . . . 'He is old enough to be *my* father; and if

he were ever animated enough to be in love, must have long outlived every sensation of the kind.'"

Marianne is far more attracted to the young, dashing
Willoughby than Colonel Brandon, who, after all, is more than
twice her age. Elinor, Marianne's sister, sees Brandon's love for
Marianne and knows him to have no hope against such a rival. "She
saw it with concern; for what could a silent man of five and thirty
hope, when opposed by a very lively one of five and twenty? . . .
She liked [Brandon]—in spite of his gravity and reserve . . . His
manners, though serious, were mild . . ."

Colonel Brandon is no fool. He can tell that Marianne is too infatuated with Willoughby to have any interest in him. He doesn't
try to court Marianne, but he does make sure, by talking to Elinor,
that there is no hope for him. "Is everything finally settled?" he asks.
"Is it impossible to—? But I have no right, and I could have no
chance of succeeding."

He's quite correct: with Marianne in her wild, emotional state
of love for Willoughby in particular and a fairy-tale idea of romance
in general, she would never look twice at Brandon. But he stays
around, as a friend to the family, in the most perfect and tactful
way. Brandon isn't creepy about it, like some hopeful suitors. He is
respectful and doesn't impose his love on Marianne, who is never
even aware of it. When Willoughby jilts her and she gets very ill,
Brandon is there to help, by rushing off to bring her mother to her
sickbed. But he doesn't make her feel obligated or try to claim
points for it with her. And thus, when Marianne recovers, and
learns all about Willoughby's sordid past—he ran off with Colonel
Brandon's ward and then abandoned her without marrying her—
she is ready to be courted by Brandon, because he hasn't been pushy
up to that point. In fact, when she finally realizes his love, Austen
describes it like this: "with a conviction of his fond attachment to

herself, which at last, though long after it was observable to every-body else—burst on her." He has kept her unaware that he loves her, which is very sensible—she doesn't feel that he's been hover-ing over her, not giving her a chance to breathe.

We also learn that Colonel Brandon challenged Willoughby to a duel to avenge his ward's honor, even though neither of them were hurt; Brandon isn't passive or wet. He is a man, capable of taking the necessary actions, according to society's rules, for attempting to punish bad behavior.

Although it takes time for Marianne to recover from her love for Willoughby, when she eventually marries Brandon, Austen makes it clear that she isn't just accepting him to have a rich hus-band. Sobered by her past experiences, her love for him isn't the "irresistible passion" she had for Willoughby, but it is love nonethe-less. "Marianne could never love by halves; and her whole heart be-came, in time, as much devoted to her husband, as it had once been to Willoughby."

Colonel Brandon is rewarded for his patience with Marianne's hand and heart. And "reward" is exactly the right word. He has done everything right all along the way, so that when Marianne does get over Willoughby, she doesn't feel pressured by Brandon, who gives her the time and space to find her own feelings for him.

LESSON TO BE LEARNED

DON'T BE PUSHY WITH THE PERSON YOU LOVE

What Not to Do: Don't Ruin a Good Possibility with Bad Timing

Sophie had always had a mad crush on Eric, her brother's best friend—a crush that, unfortunately for Sophie, wasn't reciprocated. Eric had never thought of Sophie romantically; though he liked her, he had always treated her like a sister. He found it easy to be around her, and enjoyed her company, but never thought of her as a girlfriend prospect. Eric dated a lot and had plenty of girlfriends, but for three years he had been in a steady relationship. When his girlfriend dumped him, he was devastated. He told his best friend, Sophie's brother, that his heart was broken and he'd never recover.

Sophie immediately saw her opportunity. When Eric went out drinking with her brother, she did her best to come along, sympathizing with the grieving Eric, and encouraging him to confide in her. Her brother realized what was going on and advised her not to make a move on Eric for a long time; he was still very much in love with his ex and not ready to get involved with anyone.

Sophie didn't listen, however. It's possible that she might have stood a chance with Eric, but we'll never know, because she messed things up so badly that she blew any possibility she might have had of getting together with him. Only a month after Eric's breakup, she was out at a bar with him and her brother. The latter left at ten, as he needed to get up for an early meeting, and Sophie and Eric stayed on at the bar, drinking steadily. Sophie eventually suggested that Eric crash at her place, which was nearby (she had chosen the bar with that in mind) and Eric was too tipsy to realize that it wasn't a good idea. They ended up falling into bed together.

Sophie was over the moon. But the next morning was very

awkward. Eric woke up with a raging hangover and the knowledge that he had done something wrong. He didn't realize that Sophie had deliberately tried to seduce him; he thought it was his fault. He apologized to her, grabbed his clothes, and shot out of her apartment as if it were on fire.

Sophie was hurt by this. She was so in love with Eric that she had lost any sense of perspective; she had actually convinced herself that Eric's agreeing to come back to her place meant that he wanted to get involved with her. Refusing to read the signs he was giving her—because a man's apologizing after having had drunken sex with you is never a good sign!—she pestered Eric with phone calls. Eric felt terrible that he had—as he saw it—taken advantage of his best friend's little sister. He didn't initially answer her calls, and when she finally got hold of him and asked him out, he turned her down. He apologized again, told her he had been drunk, and said it was all his fault. Sophie assured him that she wasn't offended and said she wanted to see him again. Eric realized with horror that Sophie thought their one-night stand was the start of a relationship. He did the decent thing—instead of telling her over the phone, he took her out for a drink to break the news to her that he didn't think of her romantically. Sophie, still misreading the signs—because, after all, Eric had neither called her nor even picked up the phone on the several occasions she had left messages for him—was shattered. She had conned herself into thinking that Eric's taking her out for a drink meant that he was interested in her.

Eric told her that, as she knew, he had only just had a bad breakup and wasn't remotely ready for a relationship. If Sophie had managed to play it cool, she might have salvaged something; if she had laughed this off and stayed friends with Eric, she might have been able to bide her time and make a successful move on him in, say, six months' time, or whenever she felt that he was sufficiently over his ex. They did have a lot of things in common, and the sex, though drunken, had actually been pretty good. But Sophie didn't manage to control her emotions. She burst into tears and there was a terrible scene. Eric felt hugely guilty, and his guilt meant that he avoided Sophie like the plague from that moment on. A few months later, he did meet a girl he liked, and they gradually started dating. Eric took things slowly, and the girl was willing to let him do that. They got serious about each other with time, and are now in a steady relationship. Sophie is still very upset by what happened with Eric, and she is incapable of seeing that she completely ruined any prospect she might have had with him by moving much too fast— and confusing drunken sex with any kind of serious commitment.

What to Do Instead: Let Things Simmer Till They're Ready

Carrie dated Ben briefly, several years ago, but much as she liked him, she could tell that he just wasn't ready to settle down yet. Carrie was very keen on Ben and knew that if she went on dating him, she would fall for him in a big way, while Ben just wouldn't be able to return her feelings. Ben had been a bit of a geek in high school and college, but in his mid-twenties he had really come into his looks, as some men do. Because of this, he was making up for lost time, having fun dating the women who wouldn't have looked at him earlier, and he simply hadn't sown enough wild oats to be able to commit to just one woman.

Carrie broke things off with Ben very cleverly. She told him that she wasn't ready for a serious relationship, effectively turning the tables on him. Though it wasn't true, it intrigued Ben, because usually he was the one to say that to women. Since she handled it this way, she and Ben were able to stay friends after the breakup—

as Carrie had intended—and though Ben occasionally suggested that they have sex for old times' sake, Carrie managed to resist the temptation. As a result, Ben saw Carrie as the one that got away.

Carrie dated other men; she wasn't just hanging around waiting for Ben. But as far as she was concerned, he was the one—though she never let him know it. She kept in touch with Ben, hoping that one day he would realize that they were meant to be together, and that he wouldn't meet someone else he wanted to settle down with. Maybe Carrie's constant presence in Ben's life meant that he never fully committed to the other girls he dated; she was careful to keep herself just out of reach, which naturally intrigued him.

Recently, Ben hit thirty, which was something of a wake-up call for him. He decided that it was time for him to take life more seriously. He had had a wild time in his twenties, but now most of his friends were in steady relationships, and he was getting bored with the bar scene. He started thinking about Carrie, who had always been in the back of his mind. When he rang up Carrie to ask her out, she could tell that things were different. Holding on to her self-control, she managed not to get too excited and throw herself at Ben. She kept a little aloof, and made Ben chase her. Gradually, Ben started asking Carrie out more and more often, and she noticed that he was asking her questions to see if the attitude she'd told him she had when they broke up—that she wasn't looking for a serious relationship—had changed. Instead of telling him that yes, it had, Carrie let him persuade her into it, so he felt that he had convinced her. Carrie had no wish to mess with Ben's feelings, or make him feel insecure. But she knew that she needed to think tactically if she wanted to reach her goal of having Ben as her boyfriend, and she had enough self-control to manage it.

Ben finally came clean and told Carrie that he wanted to go out with her, and he wanted it to be serious. Carrie was ecstatic. They've been together ever since, and Carrie managed never to mention marriage—which caused Ben to propose a few months ago.

ANNE ELLIOT AND CAPTAIN WENTWORTH

"All the privilege I claim for my own sex . . . is that of loving longest, when existence or when hope is gone."
—*PERSUASION*

Anne Elliot, as we've already seen from our analysis of *Persuasion*, made a big mistake in turning down Captain Wentworth, whom she loved very much, eight years before the book starts. Now, almost a decade later, Captain Wentworth comes back into her life, and Anne is still as much in love with him as she was all that time ago.

But Captain Wentworth isn't thinking about Anne. He was wounded by her refusal to marry him, and also thought she was weak for being persuaded to turn him down just because he wasn't yet settled in his career. He is looking to get married, but wants someone who has a good strong character—after his disappointment with Anne, he wants someone who knows her own mind.

Anne doesn't want to chase after Captain Wentworth when she meets him again. And Captain Wentworth doesn't pay much attention to her; he's busy flirting with Anne's sisters-in-law, Louisa and Henrietta Musgrove, who are both applying Rule 1—If You Like Someone, Make It Clear That You Do—very successfully. Wentworth is particularly attracted to Louisa, who has the strong personality he's looking for. "Your sister is an amiable creature," he tells Louisa, "but *yours* is the character of decision and firmness . . . It is the worst evil of too yielding and indecisive a character, that no influence over it can be depended on . . ."

Anne overhears this, and is hurt. She feels, rightly, that Wentworth is really talking about her. But Wentworth is beginning to learn that he may have misjudged Anne—that her character is stronger than he thinks. Louisa lets slip that Anne has actually turned down a marriage proposal from Louisa's brother Charles, and Wentworth is very struck by this. Later, the family group goes on a trip to Lyme Regis, and Louisa, headstrong and overexcited, insists on jumping from some steps and being caught by Captain Wentworth. She jumps too soon, and Wentworth isn't in time to catch her; she hits her head and knocks herself out.

It's up to Anne, who sensibly doesn't panic, to send someone for a doctor and look after Louisa. She later hopes that Wentworth, who has been impressed by her keeping her head in a crisis, will "question the justness of his own previous opinion as to the universal felicity and advantage of firmness of character; and whether it might not strike him, that, like all other qualities of the mind, it should have its proportions and limits. She thought it could scarcely escape him to feel, that a persuadable temper might sometimes be as much in favour of happiness, as a very resolute character." In other words, Wentworth is learning that Louisa's wild impulsiveness and insistence on doing what she wants, without listening to others' advice, may not be the best personality traits for someone with whom you want to spend the rest of your life.

It's crucial to note that Anne isn't trying to change her personality to appeal to Wentworth. All through the book, she behaves in character. Hearing that he wants a strong-minded woman, she doesn't start coming out with decided opinions in his hearing. She stays herself and hopes that her subtler, more balanced character traits will win through. And Wentworth comes to realize that Anne does have her own brand of quiet strength. As he spends more and more time with her, she gently encourages him, but following his lead, dropping hints that she is still in love with him:

"I am not yet so much changed," she says, and later—again, following Rule 1—she says in his hearing that she believes that women, once they have truly loved, are always emotionally faithful to that love.

It's as clear a hint as she can give; and Captain Wentworth responds to it, leaving her a letter in which he tells her that he still loves her, too: "Tell me not that I am too late," he writes, "that such precious feelings are gone for ever. I offer myself to you again with a heart even more your own, than when you almost broke it eight years and a half ago . . . I have loved none but you. Unjust I may have been, weak and resentful I have been, but never inconstant."

Anne has won back Captain Wentworth by waiting it out, by not forcing herself on his attention but allowing his desire and love for her to grow. Much as she always loved him, he had to find his love for her again and not be pressured by her throwing herself at him; he needed time to reconnect with his old feelings and not be rushed by her.

LESSON TO BE LEARNED

DON'T BE IN A HURRY

What Not to Do: Don't Treat a New Prospect Like a Settled Boyfriend Too Early On

Eleanor was very excited when she met Cooper, who seemed to be everything she was looking for. Cooper was very cool and funny and, most important, keen on her. He called her up regularly to ask for dates, and didn't make her feel insecure by not ringing when he said he would or canceling at the last minute.

Unfortunately, this went to Eleanor's head. She became over-confident about Cooper, and boasted about him to all of her friends when the two of them had only had a few dates. She invited him out to meet her friends almost immediately, and, though Cooper coped with it well, and her friends liked him, it was a bit too soon. Eleanor started treating Cooper as her boyfriend almost from the beginning; she had him to her apartment every time they met, she let down a lot of boundaries and told him a lot about herself, and she confided in him about problems that she was having at work and with her family.

None of this would have been too bad if Eleanor had done it in small doses. But instead she gave Cooper the whole package, much too soon. She skipped the essential courtship stage, where both parties get to know each other gradually, building trust and mutuality, and went straight into behaving as if they were an established couple.

While Cooper was gentlemanly and polite, Eleanor's enthusiasm meant that things were much too skewed to her side of the equation. Not only did they end up at her apartment after their dates, they also went out with most of her friends. Cooper didn't introduce Eleanor to his friends—though he liked her a lot, he felt that it was too early. He wanted to get to know her first before he showed her off publicly. Eleanor had no such inhibitions, and it began to worry Cooper. He thought that she might be a little desperate: if she let him into her life so quickly it didn't show much discrimination, because he felt that he hadn't known Eleanor long enough for her to trust him this way. Also, he liked the courtship stage, the gradual letting down of one's guard, the excitement and thrill every time you meet the new person, the spaces in between when you don't see each other, which build desire. Eleanor didn't give Cooper the chance to experience much of this; she rushed him, and it was fatal. Because he was being so reliable, she took him for granted, which is always a mistake—especially in the early stages of a relationship.

After a few weeks of this, Cooper did cancel a date he had made with Eleanor. He didn't say he would call her soon, but she assumed he would. Cooper never rang Eleanor again. He had liked her, but she had made him so uncomfortable by rushing him that he didn't want to date her anymore. Cooper wasn't trying to play games, or looking for a woman who would treat him mean and keep him keen. He just wanted someone who was confident enough in herself and her own attractiveness that she wouldn't fasten on him before either of them knew the other well enough to be able to make any kind of commitment.

Eleanor was extremely upset. Looking back, though, and discussing what had happened with her friends, she was able to see what she had done wrong. She resolved that the next time she met someone, she would take things much more gradually, letting desire build, rather than forcing it, and giving them both enough time to feel the mutuality of their attraction and compatibility.

What to Do Instead: Pace Yourself

Like Eleanor, Jack had been burned before by going too fast with women. When his long-term relationship broke up, Jack was devastated—ending it had been the right thing to do, since his ex had moved to a different state for work and Jack didn't want to leave his home and his friends. The decision was more or less mutual. But Jack really liked being in a relationship; he hated the insecurity and mind games of dating, and after only a short time he felt he was absolutely ready to meet someone.

Jack, however, wasn't as ready as he thought he was. He overwhelmed women with too much attention in the beginning, and they felt pressured by it. Even though they liked Jack, the women he courted so hard were scared off by his overfrequent phone calls. Although women are responsive to men who are both romantic and reliable in the early stages of dating—calling when they say they will; asking, at the end of a date, for another one; bringing flowers; taking the trouble to find out the kind of restaurants and movies they like—women, just like men, are wary of dating people who seem too needy and desperate.

Then Jack met Cheryl, who fell for him almost immediately. She and Jack had a great deal in common, and she loved that he was so attentive. However, she also, like the women he had seen before her, felt that he was pushing her much too hard. After their first date, Jack called or e-mailed her every day. His calls and e-mails were lovely and friendly, but Cheryl felt that it was just too much. She was also worried that if they rushed into a relationship, the way that Jack seemed to want to do, it would burn itself out because of the sheer speed with which they had got together. Cheryl really enjoyed the courtship process—the fluttering of excitement as you get dressed up for a big date, the walks home, kissing on every street corner, the increasing desire and excitement as you slowly build up enough intimacy to decide to go to bed together—and she felt that if she got together with Jack too quickly, she would miss out on all of that. She didn't want to find herself in a mere month's time in a relationship where they saw each other almost every day and began to take each other for granted; she wanted the whole buildup. Cheryl knew that if she and Jack did make a go of it, they would have the rest of their lives to be domestic together and have arguments about whose turn it was to buy the toothpaste or do the laundry. She felt that couples need to have a "honeymoon" period of pure love and lust before they fall into a settled domestic routine, and if she let Jack rush her, they wouldn't have time for that.

So she decided on a strategy of keeping Jack to some degree at arm's length. She made up a story about having had a recent difficult breakup, which meant that she needed to take things slowly. It wasn't true, but it worked. Jack understood this, having had a difficult breakup himself. Cheryl didn't accept every invitation to go out with him; in fact, she threw herself into her work and her own social life, booking herself up so that she wasn't able to see Jack four or five times a week, as he wanted. In this way, she protected herself from the temptation to see him too often—because she *was* tempted, as she liked him so much. Every time she did see Jack, though, she was very encouraging to him, showing him how much she enjoyed his company and spending time with him. As a result, she didn't make Jack feel insecure (which, despite what other dating books may say, is never a good emotion to provoke in a genuinely nice man!). Jack knew that Cheryl really liked him and wasn't seeing other men; she just needed to take things slowly. With heroic effort, Cheryl managed to pace herself and Jack, and when they did finally go to bed together and begin to build a solid relationship, they had had enough time to get to know each other. After only a couple of months, Jack proposed. He felt Cheryl was the one and didn't want to waste any more time. Cheryl told him to ask her again in three months. Her strategy of pacing them had worked so well that she wasn't going to fall at the final hurdle and let Jack rush her now; she needed a little more time, and also she was scared that Jack would panic, having proposed much too fast, and pull back.

Cheryl was absolutely right. When Jack proposed again after the three months were up, he told her how much he loved her, but also thanked her for having made him wait. He said that though he'd thought he had been ready when he had previously asked her to marry him, he now realized that he hadn't been. Before, he had worried that if his ex moved back to the city where he lived and asked him to take her back, he would have agreed. Now he saw that he had moved on, and that he wasn't still secretly fantasizing about getting back with his ex. The space that Cheryl had imposed had given him time to fully get over his ex, and he was now free of the past. Cheryl accepted him immediately, and they are blissfully happy.

FANNY PRICE

"You must be aware, Fanny, that it is every young woman's duty to accept such a very unexceptionable offer as this."
—*MANSFIELD PARK*

Ever since childhood, Fanny has been in love with her cousin Edmund, the only member of her aunt and uncle's family, with whom she lives at Mansfield Park, who has ever taken care of her or been thoughtful about her needs. But Edmund, for his part, is in love with the fascinating Mary Crawford, and it looks as if he will propose to her any minute—which sends Fanny into "disappointment and depression."

When Henry Crawford, Mary's brother, proposes to Fanny, she strongly rejects him, as we've already seen. Fanny has seen so many instances of Henry's flirtatious behavior with her cousins Maria and Julia that she just doesn't feel she can trust him, even if Edmund weren't in the picture. She isn't tempted to marry the wildly eligible Henry to escape from her uncomfortable home, where she is continually patronized and treated like a servant by her aunts; she isn't tempted, either, to agree to marry Henry simply to spite Edmund. Even before Henry has proposed, Fanny has been suspicious of his intentions toward her: "He evidently tried to please her—he was gallant—he was attentive—he was something like what he had been to her cousins; he wanted, she supposed, to cheat her of her tranquillity as he had cheated them," and she is absolutely right. Henry originally intended only to flirt with Fanny and leave her miserable. As we've already observed in Chapter Four, Fanny is right to trust her instincts.

Though Henry's decision to ask Fanny to marry him does come from the better part of himself— "[he] had too much sense not to feel the worth of good principles in a wife"—it's also fostered by Fanny's obvious refusal to engage in the kind of flirting games he played with her cousins. Henry likes a challenge, and wants the one girl who doesn't want him. Poor Fanny is absolutely tortured by Henry's proposal, because of the pressure that's put on her by her relatives. As far as they can see, Fanny is refusing a very eligible match, and they do everything they can to make her accept him.

" 'This is very strange!' said Sir Thomas [her uncle], in a voice of calm displeasure . . . 'Here is a young man wishing to pay his addresses to you, with everything in life to recommend him; not merely situation in life, fortune, and character, but with more than common agreeableness, with address and conversation pleasing to everybody . . . I am half-inclined to think, Fanny, that you do not quite know your own feelings . . . Have you any reason, child, to think ill of Mr Crawford's temper?' "

Fanny says no—but she "longed to add, 'but of his principles I have.' " But she couldn't explain this without telling her uncle that his daughters flirted wildly with Henry, and she won't betray them. Fanny "had hoped that to a man like her uncle, so discerning, so honourable, so good, the simple acknowledgement of settled *dislike* on her side, would have been sufficient. To her infinite grief she found it was not."

Her aunt Lady Bertram, Sir Thomas's wife, also enters the fray, giving Fanny "almost the only rule of conduct, the only piece of advice, which Fanny had ever received from her aunt in the course of eight years and a half"—that it is her duty to make such an eligible match. Even Edmund, usually her only ally, tries to convince her to accept Henry. When Fanny says that she and Henry have nothing in common, he disagrees: "You have moral and literary tastes in common . . . . there is a decided difference in your tempers, I allow. He is lively, you are serious; but so much the better; his spirits will support yours. It is your disposition to be easily dejected, and to fancy difficulties greater than they are. His cheerfulness will counteract this . . . Your being so far unlike, Fanny, does not in the smallest degree make against the probability of your happiness together; do not imagine it. I am myself convinced that it is rather a favourable circumstance."

And then there's Mary, who tries a rather different tack, telling Fanny that she should be over the moon because she has succeeded in conquering Henry, when so many other women have set their caps at him and failed to win him: "the glory of fixing one who has been shot at by so many; of having it in one's power to pay off the debts of one's sex! Oh, I am sure it is not in woman's nature to refuse such a triumph."

Heavy weapons indeed are being brought against Fanny: her sense of duty; a doubt that she really knows her own feelings; well-reasoned intellectual persuasion; an appeal to her pride, that she has made a conquest that many other young women failed to achieve. And yet she holds absolutely firm, even when the Bertrams send her away to the comparative squalor of her mother and father's house in Portsmouth, banishing her from Mansfield Park in the hopes that she will learn through the contrast to appreciate all the creature comforts that a marriage to Henry could give her. Henry comes to visit, and behaves very well. But even this doesn't help his chances. Fanny becomes "quite persuaded of his being astonishingly more gentle, and regardful of others, than formerly." But this, instead of softening her resolve not to marry him, only makes her hope that he will stop putting her under pressure. "So anxious for her health and comfort, so very feeling as he now expressed himself, and really seemed, might not it be fairly supposed, that he would not much longer persevere in a suit so distressing to her?"

We already know what happens next. Henry runs off with Maria, Mary disgusts Edmund by her overcynical attitude to the scandal, and Edmund, chastened, eventually falls in love with Fanny. She has her reward for not settling for Henry. But even if Edmund *had* married Mary, Fanny would still have been right not to have taken Henry, who would no doubt have cheated on her and whose lack of morals would have made her very unhappy. In resisting the pressure from her family and holding out for a man she can respect—even if Edmund isn't available—Fanny, as always, does the right thing.

LESSON TO BE LEARNED

DON'T BE RUSHED BY OTHERS' EXPECTATIONS

What Not to Do: Don't Grab at Security, and Sacrifice a Chance for True Love

After Emily's last relationship fizzled out, her mother set her up with Seth, the son of one of her friends. Seth, on paper, was perfect: the same age as Emily, nice, stable, attentive, attractive, looking to settle down and have kids. Seth was relaxed and easygoing, and Emily really enjoyed his company. They started dating on a regular basis and Emily was very impressed by Seth's reliability; he called when he said he would and never played games with her to make her feel insecure, which was a welcome change from her last boyfriend, an aspiring video director who had repeatedly canceled dates at the last minute by texting her phone to say he was busy or tired.

Seth was such a pleasant change from the would-be video director that Emily found herself liking him more and more. Almost imperceptibly, they slipped into a steady relationship. Emily didn't have the same passion for him as she had had for her ex-boyfriend, but she told herself that this was because the ex had been completely impossible, and she had been feeling all the passionate desire that we perverse humans often do for someone we can never have. Seth, by contrast, was the real thing, she thought; it was cozy rather than wild, but that's what you want in a long-term relationship. Both of their mothers were overjoyed that Seth and Emily were dating, and Emily's friends also really approved of Seth — they were happy to see Emily with a nice guy who didn't jerk her around.

After nearly a year of dating, Seth proposed, and Emily accepted. She was happy to be settled; most of her friends were married or in steady relationships, and she was grateful not to feel that she was on the shelf. But as the wedding preparations gathered speed, Emily began to have serious doubts. She realized that she had been keener on the idea of getting married than she actually was on Seth. When she tried to confide in her mother, her doubts were brushed aside; her mother said that it was normal to feel scared before you got married, that Seth was clearly the right man for Emily, and she was not to panic, just take deep breaths and not think about things too much.

Though Emily tried to follow this advice, it got harder and harder. Her friends weren't that supportive either when she confided in them; their analysis of the situation was that she had been through some bad relationships with unreliable men, and now that she had found a nice one, she was getting cold feet, because she was hooked on the thrill of the impossible chase. Although this made sense to Emily, she still couldn't deny the fact that she had a sinking feeling every time she thought about being married to Seth. She stopped wanting to have sex with him. Seth was understanding, but that didn't help, either. She just didn't feel there was enough chemistry between them to sustain her for the rest of her life.

Emily rang up her ex, went out with him, and had sex with him that evening. She knew she was never going to get back together with him; she wanted to have a last moment of rebellion before she settled down. But that night didn't do what she had hoped. She realized she wasn't in love with her ex, but she realized, too, that she wasn't in love with Seth, either. Only a few weeks before the rehearsal dinner, she had to tell Seth that she didn't want to marry him. He argued with her, of course, but Emily was absolutely sure that she was doing the right thing.

Seth's heart was broken. Emily felt hugely guilty. Her mother was furious and berated her, not only about dumping Seth, but about the cost of the wedding arrangements and the mess she had created by breaking up with him so close to the wedding. Emily was shocked that her mother was so unsympathetic to her feelings and the pain that she was going through; she considered that she had done the right thing by being honest and not going through with a wedding to someone she just didn't love enough. She realized that her mother was more concerned with marrying her off than with her happiness, and that she shouldn't have listened to her mother when the latter dismissed her prewedding doubts as nervous jitters. Emily had nearly allowed herself to be pushed into marriage with the wrong man because her mother and her friends played on her fears about being single forever, and she hurt Seth very badly along the way.

What to Do Instead: Wait for Intimacy and Sex Till the Right Person Comes Along

Ed had been single for a year when he met Brittany, a friend of a friend, when a group of them went out for the evening. Brittany was cute and funny and Ed was attracted to her enough to get her number and call her to ask for a date. They went out and had a very nice evening. Ed called Brittany again, and over the next couple of weeks they saw each other a few times. Finally, they ended up back at Brittany's apartment, and started making out.

Though they had fun, Ed didn't feel a major spark between them. But Brittany obviously did—she made it clear to Ed that she wanted to have sex with him. Ed was tempted, but it was late, and he decided to go home, much to Brittany's disappointment. Over the next couple of days, he did a lot of thinking. Brittany rang him, but he didn't pick up and let her leave a message. He felt that he was behaving badly, but he was confused and unsure. He eventually decided that he ought to feel more strongly about Brittany if he decided to have sex with her. He wasn't sure if it was that he didn't have enough chemistry with Brittany, or if he just wasn't ready to get more serious with someone, but he eventually figured out that even if he had sex with Brittany, he didn't think he would want to have a relationship with her.

Brittany was much more into Ed that he was into her—she rang him again, and again Ed didn't pick up the phone. He knew that if they did get more involved, it wouldn't be fair to her—he would just be using her for sex, and he was mature enough to feel that this would be the wrong thing to do. He wanted to hold out for something more. So he e-mailed Brittany to say that he was busy at that moment, and would call her eventually. It was a cowardly thing to do—Ed would have done better to be honest with her and tell her that he wouldn't be getting in touch with her again. But Brittany got the message, and stopped calling.

She was, naturally, angry with him—she felt that he had led her down the garden path, and Ed could certainly have handled things better. But at least he had nipped things in the bud before he slept with her and made her feel even more let down. Ed decided to wait till he met someone he was so attracted to that he felt carried away by it, someone he felt could be the one. And though she went through pain and disappointment on Ed's account, Brittany was saved from the harsher disappointment she would have felt if he had slept with her a few times and then told her it wasn't going to work out. Brittany recovered and went on to date someone who did feel she was the one. Ed is still waiting for his Ms. Right, but his experience with Brittany has shown him that he's doing the right thing by holding out.

SUMMARY

Do

- *Let him know that you can't be rushed.* He will respect you that much more than if you show him you're so desperate for a relationship that you will let him sweep you off your feet in a mere couple of weeks.

- *Be brave.* Hold out for someone you really love, with whom you are compatible. There are millions of people out there—the odds are that you're going to find the right person, as long as you don't settle for something less.

- *Pace yourself.* You can ruin a budding relationship by being in too much of a hurry. Remember—enjoy the moment!

Don't

- *Stay with someone out of fear of being alone.* It's bad for you—you keep yourself from meeting the real Mr. Right—and it's equally cruel to the man you're settling for.

- *Be persuaded by others against your own instincts.* You're the only one who can judge whether your relationship is giving you what you need. Just because your mother likes him doesn't mean he's the right one for you!

- *Be desperate.* Keep reminding yourself that you are fabulous and valuable, and that finding the right match sometimes takes time.

❖　❖　❖　❖

Tips for Telling If You Are in Too Much of a Rush with Your New Man

✦ You're doodling your first name and his surname over pieces of paper to see what it looks like.

✦ You want to show him off to your friends before you've even had a chance to get to know him properly.

✦ All your friends know his name, his shoe size, and the team he supports after your third date—you have to swear them to secrecy when they meet him in case they let slip how much information they already have about him.

✦ After a few dates, you are planning gourmet dinners you can cook for him, featuring his favorite foods, to show him what a good wife you'll make.

✦ You bone up on the bands he likes and his favorite TV programs so you can talk to him about them and show him how compatible you two are.

✦ Every time he e-mails you, you spend hours composing a reply that you hope will please him.

✦ You keep buying him presents—CDs and books by people he's mentioned he likes, or a sweater you saw in a shop window he seemed to admire.

TEN

IF YOUR LOVER NEEDS
A REPRIMAND, LET
HIM HAVE IT

"Your reproof, so well applied, I shall never forget:
'had you behaved in a more gentlemanlike manner.'
Those were your words. You know not, you can scarcely
conceive, how they have tortured me."

—*PRIDE AND PREJUDICE*

THERE ARE ALWAYS GOING to be times, in any good relationship, when your lover is driving you crazy and you have to say something to him about his behavior. Nobody is perfect. And the way he and you handle this kind of situation will teach you a lot about whether the relationship is viable in the long term. For example: I have a friend who had been dating a woman for seven months, and everything was going wonderfully, when they had their first fight, about something very trivial. They had a good yell at each other and she stormed out of his place. The next day she rang him to say it was over; she couldn't bear the fact that they'd had a fight at all. Apparently, she came from a family that never openly fought with one another—instead they just perpetually let their grudges fester, creating an atmosphere of grumpiness and gloom. A good open fight made her feel so insecure that she couldn't continue the relationship. My friend was very upset and tried to argue her out of it, but she wouldn't budge. He was at least grateful that he'd found out this crucial fact about her sooner rather than later; if they had been further along in the relationship, it would have been even harder for him to recover from the breakup. Any relationship is going to have its ups and downs, and it's very important not to bear grudges that can poison it, but lance the wound cleanly at the time by speaking out about what's bothering you and trying, together, to find a solution that will allow you both to move forward. It will also allow you to see what aspects of behavior your boyfriend can change and which ones he can't—and this way you can see whether or not you are prepared to make the necessary compromises to adjust accordingly.

ELIZABETH BENNET AND MR. DARCY

"My behaviour to you . . . had merited the severest reproof. It was unpardonable. I cannot think of it without abhorrence."

—*PRIDE AND PREJUDICE*

Almost as soon as Elizabeth meets Darcy in *Pride and Prejudice*, she is giving him hints that his proud, haughty, judgmental behavior needs to be toned down. "It is particularly incumbent on those who never change their opinion," she tells him at a dance, "to be secure of judging properly at first." This is a nice foreshadowing of Darcy's growing attraction to her: having said in her hearing that he didn't consider her good-looking enough for him, he will come to believe that she is the most attractive woman he has ever met. But it also sets the stage for their relationship. Darcy falls for Elizabeth because, unlike Bingley and Miss Bingley, she isn't overwhelmed by his imposing personality. She stands up for herself, doesn't let him cow her, and tells him the truth as she sees it.

By the time they meet again at Rosings, his aunt's house, Darcy is already conscious of a deep attachment to her, which grows precisely because she makes playful fun of him and gently points out his faults. In front of his cousin, Colonel Fitzwilliam, she teases Darcy about being standoffish at the ball where they met, when he refused to dance with anyone but Miss Bingley and her sister. Darcy defends himself, saying, in effect, that he's shy: "I certainly have not the talent which some people possess, of conversing easily with those I have never seen before. I cannot catch their tone of conversation, or appear interested in their concerns, as I often see done."

But Elizabeth doesn't let him get away with this. She tells him that he must practice to improve his social skills, and she uses the analogy of playing the piano, which she has just finished doing, to make her point: "My fingers do not move over this instrument in the masterly manner which I see so many women's do . . . But then I have always supposed it to be my own fault—because I would not take the trouble of practising."

Darcy smiles, understanding what she's telling him. It's crucial to remember, as we have already seen, that Elizabeth isn't game-playing or mocking Darcy deliberately in order to get his attention. She is spontaneous, she speaks from the heart, and Darcy isn't offended but is attracted to her because of her criticisms, sensing that here is the woman he needs, the one who will soften him up and poke fun at him when he needs it. As Elizabeth's aunt Mrs. Gardiner says later in the book, hinting at the fact that Darcy is very serious about Elizabeth, "he wants nothing but a little more liveliness, and *that*, if he marry *prudently*, his wife may teach him."

Shortly after the conversation at the piano, Darcy proposes. But he does it in such a rude and arrogant way that Elizabeth rejects him outright, as any woman with a healthy dose of pride would do: he begins by telling her that he has done his best to suppress his love for her, feeling that she is not a suitable match for him. "In vain have I struggled," he starts. "It will not do." Darcy goes on to tell Elizabeth that he's willing to marry her despite her vulgar relations and low social status: "His sense of her inferiority—of its being a degradation—of the family obstacles which judgment had always opposed to inclination, were dwelt on with . . . warmth . . ."

Elizabeth is naturally furious. She turns him down. He gets angry—having assumed that merely expressing the wish to marry her would make her fall into his arms—and demands an explanation. So Elizabeth lets him have it. "I might as well enquire . . . why with so evident a design of offending and insulting me, you chose to tell me that you liked me against your will, against your reason, and even against your character? . . . I might have felt [concern] in refusing you, had you behaved in a more gentlemanlike manner . . . From the first moment . . . of my acquaintance with you, your manners [impressed] me with the fullest belief of your arrogance, your conceit, and your selfish disdain of . . . others."

Darcy is mortified, and rightly so. When they meet up again by chance at Pemberley, his house, he is determined to show Elizabeth that he has changed. He behaves very politely to her aunt and uncle (who, fortunately for Elizabeth, are no embarrassment to her, being as well mannered as her parents are eccentric and vulgar), talking to them "with the greatest civility." He asks Elizabeth if he can introduce his sister to her, and when he does, the very next day, Elizabeth sees in him "an accent so far removed from hauteur or disdain of his companions, as convinced her that the improvement of his manners which she had yesterday witnessed . . . had at least outlived one day . . . When she saw him thus civil . . . to the very relations whom he had openly disdained . . . the change was so great . . . that she could hardly restrain her astonishment."

When Darcy proposes to her again, he has worked on himself. He acknowledges his previous faults, and apologizes: "What did you say of me, that I did not deserve? . . . The recollection of what I then said, of my conduct, my manners, my expressions . . . is now, and has been for many months, inexpressibly painful to me."

Elizabeth tells him that she wasn't intending to effect a change on him: she merely said what was in her mind at the time. "I was certainly very far from expecting [my words] to make so strong an impression. I had not the smallest idea of their being ever felt in such a way."

This is crucial. Elizabeth didn't reprove Darcy in the hopes of changing him. It is always dangerous to think that you can change a person's behavior, because it's rare that you can. All you can do is tell him how you feel, see how he reacts, and base your opinion of him on whether he is capable of deciding to make that change.

Now, she apologizes in her turn for having wounded him, and also misjudging him when she accused him of ill-treating Wickham: "Oh! do not repeat what I then said," she begs him. "These recollections will not do at all. I assure you, that I have long been most heartily ashamed of it."

By acknowledging her own faults, and suggesting they put their past quarrels behind them—"Think only of the past," she tells him, "as its remembrance gives you pleasure"—Elizabeth deals with the situation perfectly. Darcy was right to apologize; and now she draws a line under the past so they can be happy in the present without recriminations.

> LESSON TO BE LEARNED
>
> ACCEPT APOLOGIES GRACIOUSLY

What Not to Do: Don't Blow Things Out of Proportion

We all know people who, when you apologize for something you've done wrong, respond by telling you all over again about the fault you originally committed, thus ensuring that you will be a lot less likely to apologize to them in the future—even if you ought to. Our mothers usually do this to us, and we don't enjoy it very much. So try not to do it to other people!

Jackie had been out with Ken three times, and he had asked her out to dinner on Saturday night. Jackie was excited about it, feeling Ken might well be a serious prospect. She booked a hair appointment, got her nails done, and was at home in the late afternoon deciding what to wear when Ken rang to say that he had a work emergency and had to cancel. Ken apologized profusely, but Jackie was extremely angry. Ken's canceling their date made her feel insecure, and that caused her to give him a hard time about it. Like most people, she had had a couple of bad experiences when someone she was dating seemed very into her at first and then suddenly disappeared off the radar. Assuming this was what Ken was doing, she let him have it with both barrels.

Jackie told Ken she was very angry and that he had ruined her

Saturday night— it was too late now for her to make other plans. All this was true, but Jackie's reaction was disproportionate, because it was informed by her assumption that Ken was doing what other men in the past had done to her—blowing her off just as things were going well. Ken was taken aback and upset by her extreme reaction. He kept apologizing, and said he would call her on Monday, when his work crisis would be over.

Ken did ring Jackie on Monday. He understood that it was reasonable for her to be upset that he had canceled a Saturday-night date with her at the last minute, and apologized again. At this point, Jackie should have let it go. It was too early for her to be able to assume that Ken was unreliable, the kind of man who would regularly cancel dates with her. By ringing her promptly when he had said he would, Ken had shown that he was, so far at least, a man of his word. Jackie should have given him the benefit of the doubt. He did ask her out to dinner that week, and Jackie accepted, but her insecurity led her to make a sarcastic comment about hoping he would actually turn up this time, which put Ken's back up. He felt he had already apologized repeatedly, and that should have been enough.

Ken had been planning to bring flowers to their next date, by way of extra apology, but Jackie's comment rankled, and he ended up not buying flowers after all. Their date didn't go well; conversation, for the first time, was strained. Jackie had been expecting flowers and was offended that she didn't get them. Ken felt that Jackie might be too demanding, the kind of girl who would always put her own needs before his, who wouldn't understand that he had heavy work commitments sometimes. The chemistry between them fizzled and Ken didn't call Jackie again.

Jackie took this as a sign that all men are unreliable bastards. But it was her own distrusting behavior that had ruined their budding relationship. Ken had apologized; Jackie should have given him a chance to demonstrate that he really was sorry, and that his canceling their date was, as he had told her, a onetime thing. If she had accepted his apology and waited to see if he would make it up to her, Ken would have met her with flowers on their next date and made a big effort to reassure her on their subsequent evenings out.

What to Do Instead: Help Each Other over Rough Spots in the Relationship

Melissa met Jared only a month after she had broken up with her boyfriend, and she was still a little raw. Jared knew that she had recently had a breakup, and was prepared to go slowly. He didn't want to be Melissa's rebound guy. But Melissa assured Jared that she was more than ready for a new relationship—the last one had ended badly, and she was over it and ready to meet someone new and nice. She pushed for them to see each other more often, and Jared was happy to agree.

Melissa and Jared had a really good connection and saw each other frequently. But Jared couldn't help being bothered by Melissa's repeated references to her ex. Even though they were almost all critical, it made Jared feel insecure. He felt she was harping on her ex too much and not opening herself up to the possibility of a relationship with him.

Jared eventually told Melissa that he didn't like her making comments about her ex. Melissa protested. She said that she was talking about her ex to stress how badly things had gone, and how much better Jared was for her than her previous boyfriend. Jared said that he would really rather Melissa didn't mention her ex at all, even if the comparisons to him were flattering. Melissa tried to argue with him, continuing to insist that Jared should take the comparisons as a compliment, and they had an uncomfortable evening.

Afterward, Melissa talked it over with a couple of her friends.

To her surprise, they sided with Jared. They told her that she shouldn't have been talking about her ex, and that Jared had been right to point it out. Melissa took a deep breath and examined her behavior. She realized that she wasn't fully over her ex, no matter what she had told Jared. Her frequent references to him were a coded way of communicating that to Jared, even if she was doing it subconsciously. She had been rushing into a new relationship before she was ready, but her unconscious had sabotaged her attempts to pretend the past was completely behind her.

She rang up Jared and apologized for making him feel uncomfortable, and she said that she had realized that he had been right when he wanted to take things slowly. She wanted to go on seeing him but she knew it would take some time for her to recover fully from her past relationship.

Jared was disappointed—he had wanted to believe that Melissa was more ready for a relationship than his instincts had told him. But he appreciated her honesty. They decided to see each other only a couple of times a week, and Melissa promised that she would do her best not to mention her ex. She did slip a couple of times, but she apologized straightaway, and Jared was grateful for her efforts. After two months of dating, Melissa realized that she hadn't mentioned her ex for a long time, or thought about him, either. She had taken enough time to recover. And she realized, too, that if Jared hadn't mentioned that her talking about her ex bothered him, Melissa wouldn't have been able to take a good hard look at her emotional state. They would have gone too fast and broken up as a result of it. Instead, their slow-and-steady pace over those first two months was exactly what they needed. Melissa and Jared have just had their first-year anniversary together, and are going strong.

EMMA WOODHOUSE AND MR. KNIGHTLEY

"It was badly done, indeed! . . . This is not pleasant to
you, Emma—and it is very far from pleasant to me; but
I must, I will,—I will tell you truths while I can . . ."

—EMMA

Mr. Knightley has known Emma since she was a baby and has a very protective attitude toward her. This has taken the form of his trying to give her good advice when he sees her going off the rails—which Emma, who is headstrong and convinced that her ideas are always right, has a tendency to do. Emma has dissuaded her friend Harriet Smith from accepting the proposal of a nice young farmer, Robert Martin, because she thinks Harriet can do better. But Mr. Knightley tells Emma that she is being ridiculous: for Harriet—who, though sweet, is fairly stupid, not to mention illegitimate—Robert Martin would be a great match.

"Till you chose to turn her into a friend," he says to Emma, "[Harriet's] mind had no distaste for her own set, nor any ambition beyond it . . . You have been no friend to Harriet Smith, Emma."

Mr. Knightley is right; Emma has given Harriet aspirations beyond her social status, which make Harriet very unhappy for a while. Again, we have to look at the prevailing rules in Austen's time to understand this. While nowadays Harriet's being illegitimate, and not knowing who her parents were, wouldn't be unusual—several of my friends are adopted, and nobody would refuse to marry them on those grounds!—in the Regency period, when birth and class were much more important, this would make it impossible for Harriet to marry into an elevated social status. Though we may, from our modern perspective, see this as awfully snobbish, it is for better or worse the way things worked then, and Emma is being willfully impracticable in imagining otherwise. Mr. Knightley is only telling her the truth, out of concern for Harriet's well-being as much as for Emma's.

But Emma doesn't follow Mr. Knightley's advice, though he does make her doubt herself: "She did not always feel so absolutely satisfied with herself, so entirely convinced that her opinions were right and her adversary's wrong, as Mr Knightley. He walked off in more complete self-approbation than he left for her."

Though Mr. Knightley's quite correct, he can be patronizing to Emma: "I have . . . the advantage of you," he says, "by sixteen years' experience, and by not being a pretty young woman and a spoiled child." Despite the annoyingly superior tone he takes with her, it's to Emma's credit that she does continue to listen to him, because she knows how sensible and intelligent he is. And when she goes too far and makes fun of poor Miss Bates—egged on by Frank Churchill, as we've seen in Chapter Eight—it is Mr. Knightley who steps in and, acting as a good concerned friend, tells her how bad her behavior has been.

"Emma," he says, "I must once more speak to you as I have been used to do; a privilege rather endured than allowed, perhaps, but I must still use it. I cannot see you acting wrong, without a remonstrance. How could you be so unfeeling to Miss Bates? How could you be so insolent in your wit to a woman of her character, age, and situation?"

Emma tries to defend herself initially, but she knows he is right. She is "agitated, mortified, grieved," and the next day does her best to make it up to Miss Bates. Meanwhile, Mr. Knightley has realized he is in love with Emma, his jealousy roused by seeing Frank Churchill flirting with her. And when Mr. Knightley finds out that Frank isn't in fact in love with Emma, nor she with him, he immediately proposes—and does so in a way that declares his intention to stop treating her as a "spoiled child," acknowledging the fact that she is now a grown woman whom he must stop patronizing.

"My dearest Emma . . . If I loved you less, I might be able to talk about it more . . . I have blamed you, and lectured you, and you have borne it as no woman in England would have borne it . . . God knows, I have been a very indifferent lover . . ."

Emma, who has also realized by now that she is in love with Mr. Knightley, accepts his proposal immediately. And Robert Martin renews his proposal of marriage to Harriet, who happily accepts. Emma tells Mr. Knightley how pleased she is to hear this news: "I am perfectly satisfied . . . and most sincerely wish them happy."

"You are materially changed since we talked on this subject before," he comments.

"I hope so—" Emma says, "for at that time I was a fool."

We can see here a good illustration of how both Emma and Mr. Knightley have changed, and how well their marriage will run; because instead of telling her a little arrogantly, as he would have done before, that he's glad she's admitted her fault, Mr. Knightley immediately takes some blame, too.

"And I am changed also," he says, "for I am now very willing to grant you all Harriet's good qualities."

Emma and Mr. Knightley are meeting each other halfway. Doubtless Mr. Knightley will continue to "lecture" Emma every now and then, but he will also admit his own faults. And there is another huge advantage to Emma in marrying a man as mature and reasonable as Mr. Knightley; as well as keeping her down-to-earth, and checking her tendency to go off in wild speculation or be bitchy instead of witty, he also agrees to leave his own house and move in with her, to help look after her hypochondriac father. It's a rare man who would do this. Frank Churchill certainly wouldn't have done it, as his stepmother well knows— Frank is too selfish. "Who but Mr Knightley could know and bear with Mr Woodhouse, so as to make such an arrangement desirable?" she thinks. Mr. Knightley is the best match Emma could possibly find.

LESSON TO BE LEARNED

Speak out—don't let things fester

What Not to Do: Don't Make a Mountain Out of a Molehill

Johanna had been dating Neil for a month, but they had still never gone out on a Saturday night. The reason for this was that Neil, who had been single for a while, had established a regular ritual of going out on Saturdays with his male friends. Johanna was increasingly annoyed by the fact that they hadn't had a Saturday-night date yet, but she didn't know why. When Neil asked her out to brunch one Saturday, but told her he was busy in the evening, she asked him what he was doing later and he explained the situation to her.

Johanna was taken aback. She felt undervalued, despite the fact that she and Neil had agreed to take things slowly. Though she accepted Neil's invitation to brunch, she was grumpy during their date, which Neil didn't understand. And after that, she was more distant with Neil, because she was offended; she took several days to answer a message when he left one on her machine, rather than getting back to him straightaway, as she had done before. Neil was aware that something was wrong, but he didn't know what, because Johanna wasn't telling him. He thought that she was less interested in him, as her behavior seemed to indicate, rather than realizing that she still liked him but wanted to have priority—sometimes, at least—over his standing arrangement with the guys.

This misunderstanding just made things worse and worse. Johanna was hoping that Neil would pick up that something was wrong and would ask her about it. Then she would tell him that she was hurt that he never asked her out for a Saturday night. Instead, however, Neil assumed that she didn't like him as much as he had thought she did. Because Neil was self-employed and worked from home, Saturday nights weren't as significant to him as they were to Johanna—Saturday was just another day of the week to him. Of course, Neil could have been a little more sensitive, and realized that it meant more to Johanna, because going out on a Saturday evening would be a sign that he was taking their nascent relationship seriously. But often men don't understand the things that matter to women until the women take the trouble to explain . . . and to Neil, his nights out with the guys had been very important when his previous relationship broke up. He had got a lot of support from his buddies, and he felt loyal to them.

Johanna became increasingly infuriated by Neil's keeping his Saturday nights sacrosanct, and she began to see faults in his behavior she hadn't previously noticed. Because she was never direct with him, she never gave Neil a chance to put things right. Eventually, the relationship fizzled. Neil wasn't getting the green light from Johanna anymore, and he decided she wasn't that into him. Johanna was getting increasingly offended by what she perceived as Neil's neglect of her. If Johanna had only managed to have the courage to sit down with Neil and simply explain to him why she was hurt by his giving his friends priority over her, Neil would have been surprised—and flattered, because it would have shown that Johanna was coming to care for him. He would have been threatened by Johanna's asking him to completely give up his time with his friends, but he could always have switched them to another night—and his friends would have understood that Saturday night has connotations to a girlfriend that she finds very important. Neil and Johanna might well have gone the distance as a couple. But because Johanna let things fester, her resentment poisoned any possibility they might have had for really forming a good relationship.

What to Do Instead: Listen to Criticism When It's Justified

Lynda was a lovely girl, with many fine qualities. But being on time wasn't one of them. Her new boyfriend, Larry, was rapidly being driven crazy by Lynda's inability to turn up anywhere without being at least half an hour late. He tried to drop hints about it to her, but Lynda dismissed them—she had been running late all her life and by now it was an ingrained habit.

Things came to a head when Larry booked theater tickets, and Lynda turned up so late that they missed the opening of the show. Larry was furious. When Lynda did eventually arrive, he was pacing the steps outside the theater, building up a real head of steam. He shouted at Lynda, telling her that her behavior was totally inconsiderate, that he had been looking forward to seeing the play and she had ruined his evening, and that her habit of being late was an insult to the person she was meeting, who was forced to hang around and wait for her while she took her own sweet time.

Lynda was really shocked at the force of Larry's reaction. But he did exactly the right thing in telling her how strongly he felt about her rudeness to him, and also in doing it at the right time—

it's always better to tell someone that you don't like an aspect of their behavior at the moment it's happening, rather than to wait, simmer, and throw it up at them when they're not expecting it. Lynda tried to be flirtatious and dispel Larry's anger that way, but he wouldn't let her get away with it. He said he was 100 percent serious about this and he expected her to take it equally seriously. He really liked her but he couldn't go on dating someone who treated him so thoughtlessly. He wasn't dumping her then and there, but he was very angry and needed to take a break to think about how he felt.

And with that, Larry called Lynda a cab and said he was going home. Nobody had ever reacted that way to Lynda's lateness—she had always been able to charm her way out of it. She was flabbergasted by Larry's reaction. Still, being so late for the theater that they missed the opening was so egregious that even Lynda had to admit it had been a bad thing to do. She couldn't laugh her way out of it as she did when she turned up late for dinner, or got to the movie theater just in time to rush inside for the start of the movie. At first she was cross with Larry for being angry, but that didn't last long. She knew she was in the wrong. She expected Larry to call her the next day, but he didn't. Lynda realized that she was going to have to make it up to him and promise to change if she wanted to see him again.

The day after that, Lynda rang up Larry and asked him to meet her for a drink. When he got to the bar, she was already there waiting, with a bunch of flowers for him. She apologized and said that she would really try not to be late again—she understood how annoying it was. Larry was overjoyed that Lynda had taken his criticism so seriously. He hadn't wanted to break up with her, but he knew that if he didn't make a stand then, this pattern of lateness would have set in for their entire relationship.

Naturally, Lynda couldn't change her bad habit in one fell swoop—there were times when she did run late, and Larry got cross. But he could see she was making a real effort, and he appreciated it. They also agreed that Larry would ring Lynda before their dates to remind her what time she needed to leave to get there on time, and fortunately they were so into each other that this became a running joke between them, rather than getting on their nerves. After a year of dating, Larry asked Lynda to move in with him. He did it by bringing along his bedside alarm clock to one of their dates, and pointing out that, with the aid of this, Lynda would be much more likely to make it in to work on time every morning. Lynda was ecstatic that Larry wanted them to live together. The combination of Larry's well-timed reprimand, and their joking about it afterward to dispel any lingering resentment that Lynda might have felt about being ticked off by him, set a very good pattern in their relationship. They are able to bring up things that annoy them about the other person without fearing that they will provoke a big fight, because they have learned that they can use humor to make their points and keep the other one on the straight and narrow.

CATHERINE MORLAND AND HENRY TILNEY

"I always hoped you would tell me, if you thought I was doing wrong . . ."
—NORTHANGER ABBEY

Henry Tilney, in *Northanger Abbey*, is one of Jane Austen's most appealing heroes—a clear-sighted, charming young man with a good sense of humor and a nice sense of the ridiculous. When he meets

Catherine Morland, he is attracted to her, partly, as we have seen in Chapter One, because of her obvious preference for him; and he immediately starts teasing her. "Now we shall soon be acquainted," he says to her the first time they meet, "as I am authorized to tease you . . . whenever we meet, and nothing in the world advances intimacy so much."

Catherine, who is visiting Bath for the first time, has never before left her country village, and is young, naïve, and very eager to learn about the world. Catherine is open and ready to learn from the opinions of others with more experience than she has. When Mrs. Allen, with whom she is staying in Bath, tells Catherine that she has agreed to an outing that might not be considered quite proper, Catherine, instead of arguing, immediately becomes worried that she has behaved badly: "Dear madam . . . I am sure if I had known it to be improper, I would not have gone . . . but I always hoped you would tell me, if you thought I was doing wrong . . . this was something of real consequence, and I do not think you would have found me hard to persuade."

Catherine is the perfect target for Henry, who loves to instruct. He picks her up on her use of words, criticizing her gently, for instance, because she's overusing the word "nice" instead of being more specific in her choice of adjectives.

" 'I am sure,' cried Catherine, 'I did not mean to say any thing wrong; but it *is* a nice book, and why should not I call it so?'

" 'Very true,' said Henry, 'and this is a very nice day, and we are taking a very nice walk . . . Oh! It is a very nice word indeed!—it does for every thing . . . now every commendation on every subject is comprised in that one word.' "

Henry has a pleasant, light way of giving his opinions, always tempering them with humor, that makes it easy for Catherine to take them in without feeling directly criticized. She doesn't yet understand how much Henry likes her, and that one of the main reasons he does is that he feels he is a good influence on her. He perceives quite clearly that she is young and naïve, and needs someone older and wiser telling her what to do (if I can be allowed to quote from *The Sound of Music* in this context). And that makes her an ideal match for Henry, who likes the idea of helping to form Catherine's character. If this makes Henry sound appalling, we have to remember that Henry clearly doesn't want a wife who always agrees with him; Catherine is a girl who has her own opinions, and is quite willing to argue with him.

But Henry does his best to show Catherine the difference between real life and the oversensational ideas she has, which come from her reading of lurid Gothic romances. Visiting Henry and his sister at their home, Northanger Abbey, a very Gothic old house full of dark corridors and paneling that might have come straight out of one of Catherine's favorite horror stories, Catherine becomes overwhelmed by the atmosphere and manages to convince herself, absurd as it may sound, that Henry's father murdered his mother years ago. Henry isn't offended by this crazy speculation, but he does see that Catherine needs to be brought down to earth, and he does so in a way that's more serious than usual, knowing that he needs to nip Catherine's tendency for lurid overimagining in the bud once and for all: "If I understand you rightly, you had formed a surmise of such horror as I have hardly words to—Dear Miss Morland, consider the dreadful nature of the suspicions you have entertained. What have you been judging from? . . . Dearest Miss Morland, what ideas have you been admitting?"

Catherine flees, "with tears of shame," convinced that Henry will think she's an idiot and never want to talk to her again. But when she meets him later, "the only difference in his behaviour to her, was that he paid her rather more attention than usual. Catherine had never wanted comfort more, and he looked as if he was aware of it." Knowing how much he has upset her, Henry continues to make a real effort to reassure her that a momentary idiocy hasn't lost her his love: "Henry's astonishing generosity and nobleness of conduct, in never alluding in the slightest way to what had passed, was of the greatest assistance to her . . ." Henry doesn't mention it again, because he sees that his words have made an impression on her. Catherine has been thinking about her mistake and learning from it: "Charming as were all [the Gothic novels she has been reading] . . . it was not in them perhaps that human nature . . . was to be looked for . . . Her mind made up on these . . . points, and her resolution formed, of always judging and acting in future with the greatest good sense, she had nothing to do but to forgive herself and be happier than ever."

Catherine needs to grow up a little—one can't blame her for her naïveté, as she's only seventeen when the book starts—and in Henry, she has found the perfect man to help her. It's important to note, though, that Catherine's openness and willingness to improve herself is crucial: Catherine realizes that in her sheltered little village at home she hasn't had the best educational opportunities and that there is plenty about the world outside with which she needs to become familiar. It makes her very charming to Henry.

Men, bless them, do love to instruct—their status is much more tied to the knowledge they have than women's is (look how men love to argue about sports statistics, for instance). If every so often, you let your boyfriend lecture you on an area he feels he knows all about—whether it's the cell-phone provider with the least roaming charges, the history of 1970s British punk bands, or the recipe for his special barbecue marinade—it will make him feel wonderful. Just nod and look fascinated. Make him happy at the cost of a little light boredom to yourself, every so often. After all, he sits through a lot of stuff that you tell him that doesn't interest him one little bit. Believe me, he does.

> LESSON TO BE LEARNED
>
> A GENTLE REPROOF AT THE RIGHT TIME
> CAN STRENGTHEN A RELATIONSHIP

What Not to Do: Don't Keep Banging the Same Drum

Maureen had been dating Johnny for a few weeks. She really liked him. They were compatible, she found him very attractive, and she also had the reassurance of feeling that Johnny had been interested in her for a long time now—he had been calling her on and off for a year to ask her out. Maureen had actually gone out on a date with Johnny months ago, but he had seemed to give her mixed messages. He was unemployed then and a little gloomy, and though she liked him, she felt that part of him was pulling away; she assumed that was because he wasn't happy about being unemployed and wasn't sure if he wanted to get into a relationship when he wasn't settled with his work situation.

When Johnny called up again, the first thing he told Maureen was that he had a great new job and was very excited about it. Maureen felt much more positive energy from him and decided to accept his invitation to go out to dinner. They had a great time, and Johnny asked her for another date at the end of the evening. At the end of the second date, he asked her for another one. Maureen accepted immediately. Though she wanted to take things slowly and not rush into sex, they started to fool around a bit at the end of the evenings, and she felt that sexually they would be a great match.

Johnny had asked her out for a Saturday-night date and she was really looking forward to it—it would be their fifth date, and she was all fired up.

Then Johnny rang to cancel their date, saying that he was sorry, but he was too tired and busy to go out. This made Maureen nervous, but she tried to remain positive. Johnny e-mailed her all that week, and she e-mailed him back. Then he called, but very late one night when she was out with friends. Suddenly, all the signals were going haywire. If he really liked her, why wasn't he ringing her at a sensible hour and asking her out properly? Maureen told him she was out with friends and couldn't talk. Johnny said he would call her the next day, but e-mailed her instead to say he was sorry, he was tired and busy, again. Then, for the next few days, he e-mailed her every day but didn't call. Maureen was confused and unhappy. She rang him, and they had a nice chat, but then she had to go, and Johnny said he would call her that evening. Yet again, he e-mailed her to say sorry, he was tired, instead of calling.

At this point, Maureen should have let things go. She knew instinctively that Johnny was, for whatever reason, pulling away from her. Instead, she tried to rectify things. She rang him to tell him that she didn't like being e-mailed when he had said he would call. Johnny apologized—but then, Maureen had already had plenty of apologies from him, and she should have known that by this point, they didn't mean all that much. Maureen thought she could change his behavior. She had decided that he felt insecure, he had just started a new job, and he needed reassurance. The situation dragged on for another horrible month. Johnny did call her occasionally, but he also e-mailed a lot, with apologies, and every time he did, Maureen complained. She became increasingly stressed and unhappy. She attempted to "train" Johnny to call her when he said he would by ignoring his e-mails and waiting instead for a call, but it didn't work—it just made her feel more insecure because she was sitting around waiting for his very infrequent phone calls.

Reproofs fall on stony ground when the man you are complaining to doesn't care as much about you as you do about him, and thus has no real impetus to change his behavior for you. Maureen put herself through a lot of pain for Johnny, and it was only when she met someone else that she got up the courage not to call him again. Johnny's e-mails trailed off eventually, and she never heard from him again. For whatever reason, he had decided that the great start they had made together couldn't be sustained. All the signs were there almost from the beginning, but Maureen didn't want to read them.

What to Do Instead: Learn from Your Mistakes

The new guy Maureen met, Chris, was positive and nice—unlike Johnny, he rang when he had told her he would, and he seemed reliable. But Maureen, having been a little scarred by her recent experience with Johnny, was skittish with Chris and not really able to trust him. She was frightened that history would repeat itself and as soon as she got close to Chris he would start pulling away.

As a result, she was the one giving Chris mixed messages. If he said he would call her a particular evening, and he didn't ring till ten, she was standoffish with him, because she considered he had made her feel insecure by waiting that long for a call—when, after all, Chris was only doing what he had said he would do. Chris was confused by this, and couldn't work out why Maureen seemed to like him one minute but then to reject him the next.

After a couple of weeks, he was brave enough to call her on it. He said that he liked her but wasn't sure where things were going, because he felt that he was getting mixed messages. Maureen was horrified that she had been repeating Johnny's behavior, and impressed that Chris was confident enough to bring it up. She realized that she really liked him and would hate to lose him because of her own insecurities. She apologized to Chris and was honest with him in her turn, explaining that she had recently dated someone who had messed her around, and because of that was a little insecure.

Chris understood and reassured her that he was a stand-up guy. But he also said that he didn't want Maureen bringing past history into their relationship—he was doing all he could to reassure her, and in return she needed to put the past behind her.

Maureen knew that this was fair. She made a real effort not to confuse Chris with Johnny or to make him pay for Johnny's sins. And Chris, because he really liked Maureen, was careful to try not to do anything that could trigger her insecurities. He was also on the watch for hints that Maureen was being unreasonable with him, because that would have been a big warning sign that Maureen wasn't over Johnny yet. But Chris's talk with Maureen had opened her eyes, and she was able to move on, as he had wanted. Their relationship is going from strength to strength, because they are staying honest with each other.

SUMMARY

Do

- *Stand up for yourself.* If someone is doing something you really don't like, tell him, and be prepared to end the relationship if it doesn't change.

- *Make your criticisms in the right way.* Reprimanding someone as soon as he behaves badly is the best time to do it, instead of storing up grudges that will only fester. But choose your words wisely and stay focused. Don't exaggerate, and don't drag in other things that have nothing to do with the subject under discussion.

- *Be honest.* Don't be indirect about any problems you may have and hope the person will understand your subtle hints. No man can be expected to read your mind or to figure out why you are doing the classic female thing of seeming offended but saying that nothing's wrong! Be brave enough to tell him about things that really matter to you, even if that means you have to open yourself up to him.

Don't

- *Try to change your lover in vain.* Don't stick around, hoping a man will change, if it's clear that your comments have had no effect on him.

- *Burden a new relationship with problems from the past.* Come to each relationship with as clean a slate as you can manage. If you can't do that, you're not ready to date yet— you need to take more time to recover from the past.

- *Be selfish.* Telling your lover when something isn't working for you is *not* a license to impose unfair demands on him! Make sure that your criticisms are reasonable and that you've taken the time you need to think them through.

❖   ❖   ❖   ❖

Tips for Telling If You Need to Bring Up Something That's Bothering You

❖ It's been on your mind for ages—you've tried to drop subtle hints, but to no avail.

❖ You feel it's something important to you, but he doesn't realize how much it's bothering you.

❖ What's troubling you is something he is capable of changing—like being late, or referring to his ex-girlfriend frequently—not a deeply rooted character trait, which you will never get him to change.

❖ Be wary of trying to get between him and his buddies—don't ask him to cancel his regular weeknight poker rendezvous with the boys, for example. He will think you are trying to take away his freedom, and react very badly.

❖ Talk it over with your girlfriends first to make sure that you are making a reasonable demand: you need to make these requests of him sparingly. You wouldn't like it if he were always on your case about little things you do. Give him the same tolerance you want him to give you.

WHICH JANE AUSTEN
CHARACTER ARE YOU?

Find out what kind of girl you are—and what kind of man you'll be compatible with!

1. You identify with
    a. Sleeping Beauty
    b. Cinderella
    c. Beauty (and the Beast)
    d. The wicked queen in *Snow White*
    e. Tinkerbell
    f. The Little Mermaid

2. Your favorite movie star is
    a. Anyone dark, French, and sexily brooding
    b. George Clooney
    c. Colin Farrell
    d. Matthew McConaughey
    e. Viggo Mortensen
    f. Harrison Ford

3. Your favorite exercise is
    a. Dancing
    b. Yoga
    c. Riding
    d. Walking
    e. Pilates/gym workout
    f. Running

4. Your favorite game is
   a. Charades
   b. Twister
   c. Risk
   d. Card games
   e. Wink Murder/Murder in the Dark
   f. Badminton/tennis/group sports

5. Your favorite romantic movie is
   a. *Jerry Maguire*
   b. *Love Story*
   c. *The Philadelphia Story*
   d. *Dirty Dancing*
   e. *When Harry Met Sally*
   f. *Four Weddings and a Funeral*

6. If you had to pick one reason to turn someone down, it would be because
   a. He's too old
   b. He doesn't laugh at my jokes
   c. He's not emotionally open enough
   d. He's not ambitious enough
   e. He doesn't make me feel secure
   f. He isn't passionate enough
   g. He has a tiny penis

7. You meet a really nice prospect at a bar and get talking. You're feeling frisky that evening. How does it end?
   a. You tell him flirtatiously that he should ask for your number
   b. You exchange numbers
   c. You hope he will ask for your number, but you wouldn't ask for his—you're a little shy

d. You wait till he asks for your number, but don't take his

e. You go dancing together

f. You go home together

8. You've had two really good dates with a man and he said he'd call. It's been four days and he still hasn't called. What do you do?

a. You call him

b. You curse his name and go out drinking with your girlfriends

c. You erase his number from your phone, feeling totally betrayed

d. You go over and over the details of your dates with him, trying to work out what you did wrong

e. You decide he's probably just busy at work and will call you soon

f. You shrug your shoulders and start planning how to find a new prospect

9. You think on-line dating is

a. A great idea—it's hard to meet people and anything that makes it easier is okay with you

b. A terrifying prospect—you don't think you could convey your personality well on a dating site

c. Unromantic—you'd rather meet people in person and feel instantly whether there's a spark

d. A good idea in principle, but people could be telling so many lies about themselves

e. Unnecessary; so far you've managed to meet men just fine without resorting to the Internet

f. Something you wouldn't criticize anyone else for doing, but you would rather wait to meet someone in a more spontaneous way

10. What do you drink?
   a. What have you got?
   b. Champagne
   c. White wine/spritzers
   d. The latest trendy cocktail
   e. Red wine, vodka, and/or brandy
   f. You don't really drink much—a glass of wine or a beer is enough for you

11. You flirt
   a. With anyone who'll flirt back—gender immaterial
   b. With any good-looking man who crosses your path
   c. With men you like, but it's more mutual teasing and quick-witted banter than sexual innuendo
   d. Discreetly—it may feel to you like flirting, but your friends would never call you a flirt
   e. Yes, but you're not comfortable if the conversation gets too sexually provocative
   f. Not really—it's rare that you meet someone you really connect with. But if you like someone, you direct all your attention at him

12. You dress
   a. Down—jeans, sweaters, sneakers. You like to be comfortable
   b. Classy but sexy—you like to be noticed
   c. Attractive, but not flashy
   d. In the latest trends, and you like to show skin—low-rider jeans and a belly-button piercing, if you have the figure for it
   e. Feminine—skirts, pretty tops, kitten heels
   f. To express your personality

13. Your heroine is
   a. Marilyn Monroe—she was such a babe
   b. The Brontë sisters—such imaginative and romantic writers
   c. Susan Sarandon—gorgeous, funny, and wearing her age so well
   d. Kate Winslet—talented, happy with her body
   e. Joanne Woodward—a great actress, and such a happy marriage
   f. Oprah Winfrey—courageous and caring

14. Would you consider seriously dating a single father?
   a. Yes, the more children the merrier
   b. Yes, if he takes good care of his children, it shows what a great father he'll make to those you have together
   c. Yes, as long as you don't come second to his kids—it's important that you and he have a very strong bond
   d. Yes, but it might be difficult to find your place in a family that's already established
   e. No, you're not even sure you want to have children of your own
   f. No, you're not remotely ready to be that responsible

15. Are you a jealous type?
   a. No, you're too busy flirting with other men yourself to notice if your boyfriend's being a bit naughty
   b. You keep an eye out for possible flirtations he may be having—no reflection on him, but you think anyone is capable of straying
   c. You don't like it when other women pay attention to your boyfriend, but you wouldn't say you were a jealous person
   d. Not at all—you believe the best of everybody. Why go looking for trouble?

e. Not really—you're very secure, and your boyfriend is very focused on you

f. Yes—you're very passionate, your boyfriend is everything to you, and you want to be the same to him

Question 1:

   a. 2   b. 1   c. 3   d. 4   e. 5   f. 6

Question 2:

   a. 4   b. 3   c. 5   d. 2   e. 6   f. 1

Question 3:

   a. 5   b. 2   c. 6   d. 1   e. 4   f. 3

Question 4:

   a. 3   b. 5   c. 4   d. 1   e. 6   f. 2

Question 5:

   a. 1.   b. 6.   c. 4   d. 5   e. 3.   f. 2

Question 6:

Yes yes yes, we all picked "g." It was a trick question. Go back and try again.

   a. 5   b. 3   c. 2   d. 4   e. 1   f. 6

Question 7:

   a. 4   b. 3   c. 1   d. 2   e. 6   f. 5

Question 8:

   a. 5   b. 3   c. 6   d. 1   e. 2   f. 4

Question 9:

   a. 3   b. 1   c. 6   d. 4   e. 5   f. 2

Question 10:

   a. 5   b. 4   c. 2   d. 3   e. 6   f. 1

Question 11:

   a. 4   b. 5   c. 3   d. 1   e. 2   f. 6

Question 12:

   a. 1   b. 4   c. 3   d. 5   e. 2   f. 6

Question 13:

   a. 5   b. 6   c. 4   d. 3   e. 2   f. 1

Question 14:

   a. 2   b. 3   c. 6   d. 1   e. 4   f. 5

Question 15:

   a. 5   b. 4   c. 1   d. 2   e. 3   f. 6

If your score is 15–29, you are **Anne**—quiet, composed, and cautious. You need someone straightforward, confident, and sure of his opinions, to balance your tendency to be quiet in company. Your best matches are:

   Captain Wentworth
   Colonel Brandon
   Edmund Bertram

If your score is 30–40, you are **Jane**—sweet and straightforward; you see the best in everyone. You need someone as happy, open, and easygoing as you are. Be careful—someone who plays games will really mess with your head, as you tend to be very trusting about what people tell you. Your best matches are:

   Henry Tilney
   Mr. Bingley
   Colonel Brandon

If your score is 41–51, you are **Elizabeth**—outgoing, funny, and direct. You want a serious relationship, but it's essential for you to find someone you can have fun with or teach to have fun. Your best matches are:

Mr. Darcy
Henry Tilney
Captain Wentworth

If your score is 52–63, you are **Mary**—bitchy, clever, and cynical. You're a tough proposition! You need someone stable, not flashy, to balance you, someone who will be capable of dressing you down when you need it, but who will love your dry wit and your confidence. Your best matches are:

Edmund Bertram
Mr. Knightley
Henry Tilney

If your score is 64–71, you are **Lydia**—flirty, wild, and thoughtless. You're not ready for a serious relationship—what you need is a series of fun flings, and any of these wild boys will do nicely:

Henry Crawford
Willoughby
Wickham

If your score is 72–90, you are **Marianne**—impulsive, reckless, and romantic. Someone your own age—mentally or physically—will be unlikely to suit you, as he will tend to encourage you when you go over the top emotionally. You need a sweet, steady older man who will make you the center of attention and be capable of giving you all the love you need. Your best matches are:

Colonel Brandon
Mr. Knightley

WHICH JANE AUSTEN
CHARACTER IS
THE MAN YOU LIKE?

Find out how compatible you'll be with your current love interest.

1. You try following the Rules with the man you're dating—rarely returning his calls or being available for dates. He:
    a. Stops calling you the first time you don't return his calls
    b. Calls you a couple of times, then gives up
    c. Calls you, but stops being romantic or kissing you good night—the mixed messages you're giving him make him think you only want to be friends
    d. Keeps calling, but the dates don't really go anywhere as he seems very reserved
    e. Keeps calling, but sporadically—he's playing your game, too, being as difficult to get as you are
    f. Keeps calling, but dumps you as soon as you've had sex with him—he was only in it for the chase

2. His ideal movie star is:
    a. Nicole Kidman
    b. Kirsten Dunst
    c. Katie Holmes
    d. Cameron Diaz
    e. Catherine Zeta-Jones
    f. Pamela Anderson

3. He generally invites you:
   a. To artsy European movies with subtitles, or to free gigs of deeply obscure bands his friends are in
   b. Hiking, or to do something sporty
   c. To classical music concerts, museums, or the theater
   d. To the latest trendy bar for cocktails and people-watching
   e. To dinner at expensive restaurants
   f. To late-night clubs

4. At the end of your first date:
   a. He mumbles something about how nice it was and then sketches you a little wave good-bye
   b. You stand there for ages before he finally kisses you on the cheek
   c. He walks you home and kisses you quickly on the mouth
   d. He walks you home, gives you a big hug and an enthusiastic kiss on the mouth
   e. You make out in a dark bar
   f. You don't quite know how it happened, but you're back at his place and suddenly you're not wearing any clothes

5. The first time you have sex with him, it's:
   a. Lots of fun—you both laugh a lot and feel very relaxed
   b. Sweet, but a little fumbling—you may need to help him along a bit
   c. Clear he knows what he's doing and is very considerate
   d. Good, but you sense it's more about his showing you what a great lover he is than his really being into you as a person
   e. Naughty—spanking may well be involved
   f. A revelation—he seemed very self-controlled and you had no idea he was capable of such passion

6. He dresses:
   a. Very conventionally—he looks uncomfortable out of a suit
   b. As though he's still wearing the clothes he had in middle school
   c. Down—he doesn't like to call attention to himself
   d. In cutting-edge fashion
   e. Well—you can tell he thinks about what he wears, but he's not flashy
   f. Pretty sexy—leather trousers, silver jewelry

7. His typical gift to you would be:
   a. Flowers
   b. A book
   c. Jewelry
   d. A CD
   e. Sexy underwear
   f. Schoolgirl or nurse outfits

8. What's he like with other women?
   a. Reserved—but he's very gentlemanly with them
   b. Shy—he blushes when he meets an attractive woman
   c. Fun and joking
   d. Polite and friendly
   e. Automatically flirty with everyone, even waitresses and bar staff
   f. He deliberately plays the attractive ones off against you to make you jealous

9. When it comes to his exes:
   a. He's quite secretive and never talks about them at all—you wish he would; you'd get more of a fix on him
   b. He has a couple of serious ones, but it's all over—they're not hanging around and he doesn't refer to them

   c. They're pretty nonexistent: he hasn't had a serious relationship for a long time

   d. He's friends with several of them, but they've all moved on—it doesn't make you jealous

   e. They're still calling him to let him know about fun parties. You wish they wouldn't—they always sound so sexy on the answering machine

   f. They're numerous, but you don't have time to worry about them—it's the girls he may currently be seeing that really worry you

10. His friends are:
   a. Fun and easygoing
   b. Wild boys who hit on you when he's at the bar
   c. Initially amazed that he's got a girlfriend
   d. A real mixture of types—he'll hang out with anyone who amuses him
   e. Quiet and friendly
   f. Mostly male, and a little deferent to him—he's the alpha of the group

11. He drinks:
   a. At most a couple of drinks a night
   b. You got a beer?
   c. Sambuca—preferably brought to the table on fire
   d. Body shots off hot bargirls at the Coyote Ugly
   e. Dry martinis, or a robust California merlot with hints of tannin and oak
   f. Mint tea

12. He mainly reads:
   a. *Maxim,* leafing through and looking at the pictures

b. Adventure sports magazines, or anything about sports

c. Fantasy novels

d. Serious nonfiction

e. *Forbes/The Wall Street Journal*

f. His little black book of girls' phone numbers

13. If he's at work, he's usually:

a. Flirting with the pretty new assistant

b. Joking with colleagues at the watercooler

c. Quietly and competently getting on with things

d. Running the show

e. Being reprimanded

f. Throwing a TV set out a hotel room window while demanding that the tour manager get the damned dates right for once

14. To him, exercise is . . .

a. A thing of the past—he's too busy now to work out

b. Fun—he plays team sports and/or loves new challenges, like kayaking or rock climbing

c. Important—he stays in shape because he respects his body

d. Crucial for building the muscles that make him a chick magnet

e. Too much of a chore—but he still looks great, damn him!

f. Nonexistent—he doesn't do any, and it's beginning to show

15. His hair is:

a. A bit messy

b. Neatly but basically cut by the local barber

c. Well cut, but nothing too fashionably metrosexual

d. Trendily cut and styled with the latest wax

e. Long, or shaved off

f. Hard to see—he always wears a woolly pull-on hat

Question 1:
   a. 1   b. 2   c. 3   d. 4   e. 5   f. 6

Question 2:
   a. 5   b. 1   c. 2   d. 3   e. 4   f. 6

Question 3:
   a. 1   b. 3   c. 2   d. 5   e. 4   f. 6

Question 4:
   a. 1.   b. 2.   c. 4.   d. 3   e. 5   f. 6

Question 5:
   a. 3   b. 1   c. 2   d. 6   e. 5   f. 4

Question 6:
   a. 2   b. 3   c. 1   d. 5   e. 4   f. 6

Question 7:
   a. 3   b. 1   c. 4   d. 2   e. 5   f. 6

Question 8:
   a. 4   b. 1   c. 3   d. 2   e. 5   f. 6

Question 9:
   a. 4   b. 2   c. 1   d. 3   e. 5   f. 6

Question 10:
   a. 3   b. 6   c. 1   d. 5   e. 2   f. 4

Question 11:
   a. 2   b. 3   c. 5   d. 6   e. 4   f. 1

Question 12:
   a. 5   b. 3   c. 1   d. 2   e. 4   f. 6

Question 13:

   a. 5   b. 3   c. 4   d. 2   e. 1   f. 6

Question 14:

   a. 2   b. 3   c. 4   d. 5   e. 6   f. 1

Question 15:

   a. 3   b. 2   c. 4   d. 5   e. 6   f. 1

If his score is 15–29, he is **Edward Ferrars**—shy, sweet, and hesitant. PROBLEM: he may need a lot of encouragement to bring him up to scratch. SUITABLE FOR: Anne, Jane—as long as you are prepared to help him along in his courtship of you, he will provide stability and faithfulness. UNSUITABLE FOR: Elizabeth, Mary, Lydia, Marianne—I doubt any of you would even look at an Edward! He's too shy for you—you want a guy with more initiative.

If his score is 30–40, he is **Colonel Brandon, Mr. Knightley,** or **Edmund Bertram**—serious, steady, and possibly older. PROBLEM: he may be a little staid. SUITABLE FOR: Anne; Jane; and Elizabeth, Mary, and Marianne, if they are truly looking to settle down and are prepared to take on a guy who is quieter and more sober than the men they usually date. He will provide solid love, balance, and reassurance. UNSUITABLE FOR: Lydia—he won't be nearly flirty or wild enough for her.

If his score is 41–51, he is **Captain Wentworth, Henry Tilney,** or **Mr. Bingley**—straightforward, happy, and looking for love. PROBLEM: if you're used to playing games, you may put him off. SUITABLE FOR: everyone—his happy nature and friendly disposition make him the easiest man to get on with out of the whole list. Mary may mess things up, though, by making him insecure with her game-playing. Lydia and he will have fun, but it will only work if she really wants to settle down and give up other men, as he won't be into her dating others. Marianne wants a deep passion, and if they find that together and have a lot of common interests—very important for her—it should work.

If his score is 52–63, he is **Mr. Darcy**—reserved, seemingly haughty, but with a good heart. PROBLEM: you will always be the one to loosen him up and you may get frustrated with that. SUITABLE FOR: Elizabeth, whose playful ways and sense of fun will balance him perfectly. Mary—as long as she really cares about him—will work, too, as he'll love her flirtiness if she doesn't make him jealous with it. Marianne—Darcy is capable of the kind of intense passion she's looking for, and it will work if he shows it to her! Jane will respond to his gentlemanly courtship, as long as he's not too reserved with her; Jane probably needs someone more outgoing than Darcy. UNSUITABLE FOR: Anne, whose quiet nature is unlikely to attract him, and Lydia— they would drive each other mad.

If his score is 64–71, he is **Frank Churchill** or **Willoughby**— very flirtatious but with a serious core. PROBLEM: unless he decides that you're the One, he will mess you around. SUITABLE FOR: Elizabeth, Mary, Jane, Marianne, and Lydia, though Lydia is unlikely to last with him longer than a brief affair. UNSUITABLE FOR: Anne, who needs someone quieter.

If his score is 72–90, he is **Henry Crawford** or **Mr. Wickham**—a wild, unreliable, bad boy. PROBLEM: he won't ever make any kind of commitment and will make you very unhappy, unless you're inclined to behave equally badly yourself! SUITABLE FOR: Lydia—but only as a fling. UNSUITABLE FOR: everyone else, and anyone looking for a serious relationship!

Compatibility Chart

Once you know which Jane Austen character you are, see at a glance which types you're compatible with!

	Edward Ferrars	Colonel Brandon	Edmund Bertram	Mr. Knightley	Captain Wentworth	Henry Tilney	Mr. Bingley	Mr. Darcy	Frank Churchill	Willoughby	Henry Crawford	Mr. Wickham
Anne	X	X	X	X	X	X	X	*	*	*	*	*
Jane	X	X	X	X	X	X	X	0	0	0	*	*
Elizabeth	*	0	0	0	X	X	X	X	0	0	*	*
Mary	*	0	0	0	X	X	X	0	0	0	*	*
Lydia	*	*	*	*	0	0	0	*	0	0	0	0
Marianne	*	X	X	X	X	X	X	0	0	0	*	*

x = good match

0 = good under certain circumstances

* = bad match

BOOK SUMMARIES

Pride and Prejudice

There are five daughters in the Bennet family all looking for love: Jane, Elizabeth, Mary, Kitty, and Lydia. Jane falls for Mr. Bingley, a rich, eligible, sweet-natured young man, but nearly loses him because Mr. Darcy, his snobbish, haughty friend, thinks that her family is too vulgar and that she herself isn't really in love with Bingley, because Jane is reserved about showing her feelings. Mr. Darcy falls for Elizabeth because of her lively, playful nature, but proposes to her so rudely that she refuses him. Lydia, the wild youngest daughter, runs off with the charming but unreliable Mr. Wickham, and though there is bad blood between Darcy and Wickham, out of love and concern for Elizabeth, Darcy bribes Wickham to marry Lydia. Elizabeth finds this out and is touched by the fact that Darcy still loves her, and that he went to so much trouble on her behalf. She assures Darcy that Jane loves Bingley, and Darcy conveys this to Bingley, who instantly proposes to Jane. Darcy has undergone a big change since falling for Elizabeth, revealing the better side of his nature. When he proposes to Elizabeth again, she realizes this and accepts him happily.

Sense and Sensibility

Marianne and Elinor Dashwood are impoverished sisters: Marianne is all passion and spontaneous emotion, while Elinor is more reserved and self-controlled. Marianne falls madly in love with Willoughby, an alluring, handsome young man, who reciprocates her feelings, charmed by her obvious affection for him. But, though he does love Marianne, he ends up dumping her for a rich girl. Marianne is so upset by this, and the public humiliation, that she makes herself so ill she nearly dies. Colonel Brandon, an older man who has loved her from the first, does everything he can to help, and eventually he and Marianne marry. Elinor is in love with Edward Ferrars, a shy young man dependent on his family for money. Edward loves Elinor but in his rash youth got engaged to the ghastly, scheming Lucy Steele, and thus isn't free to propose to Elinor. Lucy eventually dumps Edward for his rich brother, Robert, leaving the field clear for Edward and Elinor, who get married and settle down in the same village as Marianne and Colonel Brandon. Brandon has given Edward a job as the vicar of the local church, which provides Edward and Elinor with an income to live on. Willoughby, in a loveless marriage, still pines after Marianne, while she has come to love her husband as much as she ever loved Willoughby.

Persuasion

Anne Elliot, a sweet, retiring girl, refused to marry the man she loved, Captain Wentworth, because she was persuaded by her family that he wasn't eligible enough. When she meets him again, soon after the book starts, eight years have passed. She loves Wentworth but he is still angry with her for turning him down, and though he's looking for a wife, he doesn't consider her, flirting instead with Louisa and Henrietta Musgrove, her sisters-in-law. Louisa is his preference, but when she injures herself in a wild jump on a trip to the sea, Anne is the one who keeps her head and takes care of Louisa. Wentworth realizes that he has undervalued Anne's quiet strength and overvalued Louisa's impulsiveness. He comes to love Anne again just as much as he did before. But he is made jealous by the attentions paid to Anne by her scheming cousin Mr. Elliot, and Anne must be brave enough to make it clear to him that he is the one she loves so that he will have the confidence to propose to her once more.

Mansfield Park

Fanny, a shy little mouse living with her wealthy relatives, has been in love with her cousin Edmund for as long as she can remember. Edmund's sisters, Maria and Julia, two pretty, outgoing girls, have always neglected Fanny, and Edmund is the only one who is kind to her. When Henry and Mary Crawford, a glamorous brother and sister, visit from London, Edmund falls for Mary, much to Fanny's distress. And Henry flirts wildly with Maria and Julia. Maria is engaged to the boring but rich Mr. Rushworth, whom she would leave for Henry, but Henry stops short of asking Maria to marry him. In pique, Maria goes ahead with her marriage to Mr. Rushworth. Henry then decides to make Fanny fall in love with him, but Fanny has seen his flirtations with Maria and Julia and is very wary of him. Despite her shy exterior, Fanny has an unexpectedly strong core. Henry, to his surprise, falls in love with Fanny and proposes to her, but she refuses him. Mary is in love with Edmund but is reluctant to marry him as he is only the younger son and he plans to become a vicar, leading a quiet life in a country village, which won't suit her social and financial aspirations. While Henry is courting Fanny, he again pursues a flirtation with the now-married Maria, and, frustrated by Fanny's constant refusals of him, eventually runs off with Maria. Edmund is shocked at Mary's cynical reaction to the situation, and decides that she's not the woman for him. Henry won't marry Maria, even when Mr. Rushworth divorces her, and the disgraced Maria is condemned to an exile in the country, away from her family and friends. Edmund finally realizes that Fanny is the woman for him and proposes to her.

Emma

Emma Woodhouse is a spoiled, snobby girl with a very good heart. She loves to matchmake, and when she takes on a protégée, the sweet but dim Harriet Smith, she discourages Harriet from accepting the proposal of a nice young farmer, Robert Martin, who would be eminently suitable for Harriet. Emma thinks Robert Martin is socially below Harriet, whom she pushes at a lot of men of a higher class. Mr. Knightley, Emma's neighbor and brother-in-law, tells her how silly she's being, but she won't listen to him.

When Frank Churchill, a dashing young man, arrives to visit friends of Emma's, Emma and Frank start a flirtation. Little does Emma know that Frank is secretly engaged to Jane Fairfax, a beautiful, impoverished girl who is also visiting Emma's village. Frank is using his flirtation with Emma as a smokescreen to cover his feelings for Jane—he cannot openly declare his engagement to her, as he doesn't have enough money to get married on yet. Emma doesn't quite fall for Frank, though she's charmed by him. But Mr.

Knightley, who loves Emma, is made very jealous. Frank's rich aunt dies, leaving him a lot of money, so he is free to marry Jane.

Harriet, meanwhile, has developed a crush on Mr. Knightley, which makes Emma jealous in her turn, as she realizes that she, too, loves him. Upon the news of Frank's engagement, Emma tells Mr. Knightley that she never had feelings for Frank, and Mr. Knightley proposes to her and is accepted. Harriet ends up with Robert Martin, and Emma admits that she was wrong to try to prevent that marriage.

Northanger Abbey

Catherine Morland, a young girl who has never been out of her country village, goes to Bath for a holiday with some friends and meets Henry Tilney, a nice young man with a great sense of humor. Catherine falls for him at once, and Henry reciprocates her feelings. Her brother James is engaged to a flighty, pretty girl named Isabella, who upon realizing that the Morland family doesn't have much money, sets her cap instead for Henry's dashing older brother, Captain Tilney. She dumps James, but Captain Tilney was only flirting with her without serious intentions, and he never proposes. Isabella tries to get James back, but to no avail—he has seen through her. Catherine goes to visit Henry's country house, and he and she get on increasingly well—Henry loves to tease her and teach her about the world, and Catherine responds to his attention, while not losing her own sense of self. Despite problems from Henry's father, who thought Catherine had more money than she does and tries to prevent their marriage when he finds out that she doesn't have the large dowry he expected, Henry is true to Catherine, and proposes to her.

CHARACTERS

Elizabeth: Nearly Perfect

Elizabeth Bennet is witty, clear-sighted, charming, and attractive. Of all Jane Austen's heroines, she is the one we would most like to resemble. Elizabeth is unsentimental enough to be able to assess the members of her family honestly. She sees that of her sisters, Jane is the only one with whom she has anything in common. Mary is a bore, while Lydia and Kitty are not only shallow and willful, but so badly behaved that they are a danger to her and Jane's prospects of making good matches. Her mother is foolish and indiscreet and Mr. Bennet, for all his intelligence, is pretty low down in the good-father stakes. The one time Elizabeth's judgment is clouded is by Wickham—but we can hardly blame her for being temporarily taken in by a very good-looking man with a plausible story! Elizabeth is enviably good at expressing herself, forthright and direct, particularly to poor Darcy. The scene where she lets him have it is one of the most enjoyable moments in the whole of *Pride and Prejudice* . . . that, and the time she scores a resounding victory over Lady Catherine de Bourgh. And she's honest with herself. The first time she sees how beautiful Pemberley, Darcy's house, is, she wistfully admits how much she would love to be its mistress. We would all have thought exactly the same, and we give Elizabeth top marks for her sincerity.

Frank Churchill: The Exception

Frank Churchill is a naughty boy who gets lucky. He flirts shame-lessly with Emma, partly to make Jane Fairfax jealous, and partly out of pure enjoyment. Hard to say which motive is worse! He is thoughtless—he gives Jane Fairfax a piano anonymously, which puts Jane in a very difficult position, as everyone is speculating on the identity of the donor, and it causes her a great deal of embar-rassment. It's a gift Frank makes selfishly—to please himself—rather than thinking of the impact it will have upon the recipient. And yet Frank ends up with a fortune and the woman he wants, who is too good for him. We can only hope that Jane will have a beneficial influence upon him. Frank has got his cake and eaten it without ever having to earn it. With luck, his love for Jane will make him mend his ways.

Darcy: Pride Before a Fall

What a transformation Darcy goes through! Unlike Frank Churchill, Darcy learns, through falling in love with the right woman, how bad his previous behavior has been, and how much he needs to change. Darcy, however, has the advantage, underneath his snobbery and boorish behavior, of having strong principles and being essentially thoughtful. And Darcy isn't a charming flirt on the Frank Churchill model. He's a quiet, reserved man who comes out of his shell through contact with the vivacious and outspoken Eliza-beth. Darcy learns to look behind façades and see people clearly—a vital lesson in Jane Austen's world. His first lesson is, of course, Elizabeth. And then he reassesses Jane's attachment to Bingley and takes a good hard look at his own arrogant behavior, and by the time Elizabeth turns up at Pemberley he can see that her uncle and aunt, the Gardiners, are solid, intelligent people, rather than dismissing them because their class isn't quite on a level with his. Through the course of the book Darcy finds out that his own judgment is actually much better than he ever realized, once he's stripped it of the snobbish social veneer that he's picked up from people like Miss Bingley and her sister, Mrs. Hurst . . . and he finally becomes worthy of Elizabeth.

Anne: Strength Through Adversity

Anne, too, has to learn to trust her own judgment. Maybe all those years ago when she met Wentworth it was too early for them to get married . . . and maybe it wasn't. But she was never in the right position to decide, because she was influenced too much by other people. Anne needs to come out from under the shadow of others and get in touch with her own feelings and judgment, and it's lovely to watch her growing up. She regains her looks, which she's lost moping away passively and burying herself alive in the country without standing up for herself. She's already refused one match—Charles Musgrove—although he's eligible, because she's not in love with him. And now we watch her making a much more difficult decision: that Mr. Elliot, much though she likes him, doesn't share her most essential values, and therefore won't make her a good husband. Negative choices are all very well, but after that, Anne has to learn to be positive, to go after what she wants, to show Wentworth that she still loves him. And she manages it. What a happy ending!

Colonel Brandon: Patience

Poor Colonel Brandon, losing the first woman he loved and then having to wait for Marianne through all of her drama with Willoughby! Finally, his constancy is rewarded. And his tact. Colonel Brandon is clever and sensitive enough not to push at Marianne when she's delicate, or still in love with another man; he waits until she's as over Willoughby as she'll ever be. It's a very good lesson for all of us. Pick your moment and don't be in a hurry. Patience, as the Chinese fortune cookie says, is the key to joy.

Mary and Henry Crawford: The Lost Souls

Brought up very badly in the licentious atmosphere created by their libertine uncle, Mary and Henry didn't have much of a chance. They learned all the wrong lessons. Frivolity, immorality, overreliance on money, cruel wit at the expense of sensitivity, carelessness of other people's feelings. Their natural gifts—intelligence, charm, humor, good looks—are all squandered. Mary loses Edmund and Henry loses Fanny. He would have done well to take a lesson in patience from Colonel Brandon; if he'd cleaned up his act he might well have got Fanny in the end, and she would have been the making of him. Mary and Henry's instincts are very good— they go for the right people—but their bad training lets them down and they go for the easy path rather than the right one.

Fanny: Always Right (but Repulsive)

When Jane Austen said she was creating Emma, a heroine she liked but didn't think anyone else would, she would have done much better to apply the latter part of her description to Fanny Price. Fanny is always right. She always follows her own moral course. But that continual rightness is incredibly irritating. Like Anne, she knows how to love longest, even when hope is gone, and like Anne she is rewarded for it, getting her Edmund in the end. Fanny is a good lesson to us; she won't be bullied into making a good match, even though someone is very eligible. She sees people clearly, but from the sidelines of life; she's never in the middle of it, having fun. It's not appealing. We can learn from Fanny without ever wanting to be her, or even wanting to have her as a friend.

Emma: Always Wrong (but Wromantic)

If Fanny Price, like Sellar and Yeatman's descriptions of the Roundheads, is always right (but Repulsive), Emma Woodhouse, like the Cavaliers, is always wrong (but Wromantic). And it's much more endearing. Emma is incapable of seeing what's directly under her nose. She doesn't know that Mr. Elton fancies her; her social snobbery prevents her from seeing that Harriet and Robert Martin are a perfect couple; she misjudges Jane Fairfax, out of jealousy of Jane's beauty and attainments; and it takes Harriet's crush on Mr. Knightley to make Emma finally understand that she herself is in love with him. And yet we warm to Emma much more than we do to Fanny. Emma's fallibility is endearing, and we can identify with it. We've all got things wrong because of false assumptions and our own dodgy judgment. And we've all wanted to matchmake and see ourselves as omnipotent. And we also like her because Emma, for all her blindness, isn't a fool. She can sum up people pretty well when she has to, or when their lives have a direct impact on hers. She knows by instinct that Frank Churchill isn't seriously interested in her, after she's observed his behavior for a while; she can protect herself from serious emotional hurt. Emma's hard road to self-understanding is the one we all took in adolescence. The mistakes she makes are the ones we made ourselves. It's impossible not to warm to her and wish her well.

Marianne: The Wild Romantic

We've all made Emma's mistakes, and we've all been Marianne, too, in adolescence, caught up in the ecstasies of having our first crush returned. Marianne throws herself into love with the handsome and charming Willoughby the second she meets him, and her passion, combined with her own beauty and charm, is enough to make him love her back. And Marianne wants the world to know about it. She hasn't yet learned the hard lessons of discretion and cautiousness. To be fair to her, Willoughby gives her every encouragement at first to make her throw caution to the wind; but once he's shot off abruptly to London, without making the proposal of marriage she had a right to expect, Marianne should have pulled back, guarded her emotions, and protected herself. Instead, she plows ahead recklessly, riding for a fall, wearing her heart on her sleeve, and gets an awful rejection that nearly ends up being the death of her. Marianne's behavior teaches us the importance of balance, and being careful with our feelings, rather than, as she does, feeding our love by reading overromantic novels and music. Staying at home weeping endlessly and playing Whitney Houston's "I Will Always Love You" over and over again—as one woman in England recently did, until her neighbors called the police in desperation because they'd been hearing the song nonstop for three days—is classic Marianne behavior.

Elinor: Self-Control

We don't identify with Elinor the way we do with Marianne. In fact, we understand Marianne only too well when she reproaches Elinor for keeping her feelings too close to her chest and not sharing them with the people who love her best. And yet Elinor does exactly the right thing. Only too aware of the economics of the situation—Elinor has no money, while the man she loves, Edward Ferrars, has no profession and is completely dependent for his income on the whims of his controlling mother—she realizes how unlikely it is that they will ever be able to marry. So she keeps quiet about her love. The teasing about Edward is kept to a minimum; she will never be humiliated in front of half of London, like poor Marianne. And her judgment is unimpaired by events. She knows, despite the revelation of Edward's engagement to Lucy Steele, that Edward is in love with her, because she has assessed him and his behavior correctly. And in the end, circumstances mercifully alter, and she gets Edward—with only a small income, but Elinor is far too sensible to expect to have the world given to her on a plate. With the man she loves, just enough money to get by, and a nice little country rectory, Elinor is perfectly happy.

Catherine: The Lucky Little Girl

Catherine Morland is the classic example of a pretty, not-too-bright, but very nice young thing who finds happiness through . . . being a pretty, not-too-bright, but very nice young thing. She has the very good luck to fall in love for the first time with a young man who is charmed by all her flaws—her naïveté, her excess of romanticism, her simplicity and prettiness. Catherine has a great deal of luck. And being lucky in love is something we can all envy. It's not the lesson that we have to learn from Catherine, though. Catherine originally attracts Henry's interest precisely because she is interested in him, and shows it very clearly. Without that, Henry would probably never have given her a second glance. Catherine reminds us that acting aloof will either leave you alone in all your glorious standoffishness, or attract only people who are piqued by your remoteness and want to collect you as a trophy. Neither fate is much fun. Much healthier to find someone who likes himself, and thus likes you for liking him!

Henry Tilney: The Marrying Man

Henry wants to get married, bless him. Like Captain Wentworth in *Persuasion,* Henry would say that the first pretty girl to smile his way and say nice things can have him for the taking. Only, unlike Wentworth, who's never got over Anne and whose heart isn't as free as he asserts, Henry really means it—he's fancy-free and free for anything fancy. A rare breed, Henry just wants to fall in love and settle down. And he's got a decent backbone, too—once he's sure Catherine is the one he wants, he's able to stand up to his domineering father and fight to be able to marry her. Henry is a nice, solid, funny bloke with a good heart. The kind we would all do very well meeting—if we have enough confidence to show him that we like him!

Willoughby: Too Good to Be True

Willoughby is exactly the kind of man you should run a mile from, if you're smart enough to spot who he is. And you need to be pretty smart. He's charming, gorgeous, well off, well connected, he makes friends with your family so that they fall in love with him as well. He says and does all the right things (he even takes Marianne round his aunt's house, the one she assumes they'll live in when they get married). And then . . . he disappears. Of course there's a reason. But by the time you find it out, your heart is broken. The only consolation is that Willoughby suffers, too. He gets in over his head and what he intended to be a light, amusing flirtation turns into his falling in love as well as his victim. It would be nice to think that life always worked like that! Willoughby is so good at what he does that everyone is taken in by him. Including, in the end, himself. But it's a terrible object lesson. If someone seems too good to be true . . . well, he probably is.

Mr. Bennet: An Awful Warning

When you fall for someone just because he's pretty—and you probably will, almost all of us do— take the time to work out whether you are compatible in other ways before you accept his proposal and saddle yourself with him for the rest of your life. If not, you'll end up like Mr. Bennet, married to somebody you don't respect and with whom you have nothing in common. Mr. Bennet, for all his intelligence, never used his considerable skills to decide whether Mrs. Bennet had a brain behind her pretty face. And now he's paying for it. Not only that, but his intelligence has been degraded into sarcasm and cynicism because he doesn't have a mate worthy of him. Marrying Mrs. Bennet has not only made him unhappy, but compromised his own considerable gifts. If he'd picked a woman as smart as himself, he would have made a much better father and husband.

Edward Ferrars: Shy and Retiring

Taken advantage of by the scheming Lucy Steele when he was still at school and too young to know any better, Edward Ferrars got trapped into a very imprudent engagement. Now that he's in love with Elinor Dashwood, he knows the difference between a woman like Lucy, who's only looking to snare a rich husband, and one like Elinor, who truly loves him for himself. Quiet, self-controlled Elinor knows that Edward has a good heart but needs encouragement and help to find his way in life, and she is fully prepared to provide that for him. Being a country vicar is a perfect profession for Edward, who has no desire to shine in life—all he wants is a quiet home with the woman he loves. Edward's sense of honor won't permit him to break his engagement to Lucy, much as he wants to, and in this he's behaving correctly according to the morals of the time. But when Lucy runs off with Edward's richer brother, the path is clear for Edward and Elinor. As soon as Edward is free of his engagement, he steps up to the plate and proposes to Elinor. Shy as he is, he's capable of going after what he wants, and Elinor is very happy to accept.

Charlotte: The Settler

Marrying Mr. Collins, according to Charlotte, is better than marrying nobody at all. She decides to settle for him. For all his innumerable faults, he has a profession, a stable income, and good prospects—he is the heir to the Bennet property, which is entailed to the closest male relative. Charlotte does make the best of it. She tries to close her eyes to his annoying traits and enjoy her life as best she can. But none of us would want to be in her position. Charlotte has made her decision based on the little she feels she has to offer in the marriage mart. She isn't attractive, she isn't charming, and Mr. Collins is her best prospect. All true. But still . . . she has to endure a lifetime with the most annoying man Jane Austen ever created, and she may end up like Mr. Bennet, with her good qualities perverted by association with him. It's a fate you would only wish on your worst enemy, and it's very hard for Elizabeth to watch it happening to her best friend.

Miss Bingley: The Bitch

No redeeming characteristics for the awful Miss Bingley. She's bitchy, snobbish, cold, scheming, and a false friend. How satisfying it is that she gets exactly what's coming to her. She loses Darcy and has to see her brother marry the girl she pretended to befriend and then dropped like a stone when it suited her. Now Bingley is married to Jane, and Darcy to Jane's sister, Elizabeth, Miss Bingley's rival. And we know perfectly well that Miss Bingley won't learn a thing from this experience; she won't take a good hard look at her own behavior and modify her bad qualities. She'll just cruise along with her nose in the air, as nasty a bitch as always. The best-case scenario for Miss Bingley, and it's not much of one, is that she'll end up getting married—her goal. But it will be to someone like her sister's husband, Mr. Hurst, a snobbish block of wood who, unlike Darcy, has no possibility of being redeemed by a woman who's more open and affectionate than he is.

Lydia: The Flighty, Silly Flirt

All Lydia Bennet wants is male attention—a lot of it. She's a wild flirt who in this day and age would be in the tabloid papers, wearing the minimum amount of clothes and loads of makeup, falling out of limousines blind drunk, with a new man on her arm every night. Lydia doesn't care whether she gets married; she's quite happy to run off with Wickham even though he hasn't proposed to her. The modern Lydia is just looking for a good-for-now guy she can have fun with. The future is completely irrelevant to her—she's got no intention of settling down.

Jane Bennet: Pollyanna

Pretty, sweet Jane always sees the good in everyone. Even when she's confronted with egregiously bad behavior, it's very hard for her to criticize the person who's behaving appallingly. Jane is the kind of person who (as I wrote in one of my novels) wouldn't believe the worst of someone unless she saw them strangling a kitten in front of her—and even then, she'd try to make excuses for them. Jane is so nice to everyone that she nearly loses Mr. Bingley, the man she loves, because he can't distinguish her strong attraction to him from the sweet friendliness she shows everyone. Luckily for Jane, her smarter, more socially adept sister Elizabeth gets a message to Bingley through Mr. Darcy, Elizabeth's inamorato, that Jane is serious about Bingley—and as soon as he knows that, he's back in the village where she lives, ready to propose.

Mr. Bingley: Too Nice for His Own Good

Mr. Bingley, just like Jane, sees the good in everyone. He can't tell that his sisters, Miss Bingley and Mrs. Hurst, are nasty bitches, or that his best friend, Mr. Darcy, is haughty, snobbish, and often gives bad advice. Fortunately, Mr. Darcy's heart and prejudices are softened by his love for Elizabeth, and he acts as a matchmaker for Jane and Bingley. Jane and Bingley make a lovely couple, but, as Austen points out, they will be easy targets for anyone trying to take advantage of them, because their sweet, trusting natures mean that they always assume that other people are just as nice and well meaning as they are themselves.

Captain Wentworth: Once Bitten, Twice Shy

Straightforward and direct, as befits his profession, Captain Wentworth is open, happy, and actively looking for a wife. Rejected eight years ago by Anne Elliot, he has no intention of looking her up and proposing to her again. Still, he wants to get married, having made his fortune and established his career. He flirts with two other girls, Louisa and Henrietta Musgrove, and ends up preferring Louisa simply because she makes a more determined play for him (Henrietta already has an understanding with her cousin Charles

Hayter, and doesn't go after Captain Wentworth as wholeheartedly as Louisa does). He is close to proposing to Louisa when a reckless act of hers makes her very ill and causes Wentworth to change his mind about her—having been prejudiced against Anne for being too persuadable, he now realizes that he has gone too far in the other direction with Louisa, a girl who is too impulsive to make a good match for him. Wentworth finds his balance and gradually begins to remember how much he loved Anne, and how much he appreciates her good qualities—particularly her strength and competence in the crisis when Louisa injures herself. Wentworth recognizes that it has been Anne he has loved all along, and when she encourages him, showing him that she is not romantically interested in her cousin Mr. Elliot—of whom Wentworth has been jealous—he gets his courage up and proposes once more to Anne, this time with success. It's a real happy ending.

Edmund Bertram: Learning to Resist Temptation

Though Edmund Bertram seems stable and sensible, he's actually less mature than he appears. Under the influence of the seductive, flirtatious Mary Crawford, he is led into behavior that he knows to be wrong. He initially refuses to take part in a play his brother Tom is organizing at Mansfield Park, their family home, feeling that their absent father would not approve—and he's quite right. But when Mary deliberately makes him jealous, he yields to the temptation of playing a love scene opposite her—a love scene in which his character is a clergyman behaving rather scandalously. All the more reason for Edmund, who is about to be ordained as a vicar, to refuse the part! But, led on very cleverly by Mary, he agrees against his better instincts and is mortified when his father returns unexpectedly and, as Edmund knew he would, disapproves entirely of the amateur theatricals. Mary is capable of making Edmund do things he knows he shouldn't—up to a point. When she finally goes too far, Edmund comes to his senses, rejects her, and eventually finds love with his quiet cousin Fanny, who will be a much better influence on him. Edmund's life with Fanny won't exactly be exciting—but it's the kind of life he needs in order for his conscience to rest easy, and she's the perfect wife for the country vicar he becomes.

Mr. Wickham: Bad to the Bone

A liar and a gambler, with plenty of bad debts to his name and a propensity for running off with young girls, Mr. Wickham is the most charming scoundrel in Jane Austen's novels. He enchants everyone, even Elizabeth, who ought to know better. Wickham can have any woman he wants—and he does. A Wickham will run through your money, seduce your best friends behind your back, and dump you in a heartbeat for someone who's a better prospect. He has no scruples and no morals, and hopefully one day he'll get his just deserts. At least the Wickham of *Pride and Prejudice* ends up married to Lydia Bennet, who will spend his money, cheat on him, and be just as prepared to run away with a rich man as he would be to run off with a rich woman!

ACKNOWLEDGMENTS

With many thanks to:

My fantastic agent Deborah, who has always had boundless faith in this book. I am so grateful for all your support and encouragement.

My editor at Hyperion, Peternelle; her assistant, Kiera; and all the team at Hyperion, who, like Deborah, have been fantastically supportive from the very first moment. Thanks so much for your enthusiasm, energy, and creative suggestions.

Chris Manby, Maddy Wickham, Stella Duffy, Serena Mackesy, Victoria Routledge, Jolene McGregor, Chris Niles, Rod Huntress, my sister Lisa (aka Lydia Bennet), and everyone else who helped me road-test the quizzes.